The Jacobite Rebellions
of the British Isles

The Jacobite Rebellions of the British Isles

Andrew Jackson

First published in Great Britain in 2024 by
Pen & Sword History
An imprint of Pen & Sword Books Limited
Yorkshire – Philadelphia

Copyright © Andrew Jackson 2024

ISBN 978 1 39908 907 4

The right of Andrew Jackson to be identified as
Author of this Work has been asserted by him in accordance
with the Copyright, Designs and Patents Act 1988.

A CIP catalogue record for this book is
available from the British Library

All rights reserved. No part of this book may be reproduced or
transmitted in any form or by any means, electronic or mechanical
including photocopying, recording or by any information storage and
retrieval system, without permission from the Publisher in writing.

Typeset by Mac Style
Printed in the UK by CPI Group (UK) Ltd, Croydon, CR0 4YY.

Pen & Sword Books Limited incorporates the imprints of After the
Battle, Atlas, Archaeology, Aviation, Discovery, Family History,
Fiction, History, Maritime, Military, Military Classics, Politics,
Select, Transport, True Crime, Air World, Frontline Publishing,
Leo Cooper, Remember When, Seaforth Publishing, The Praetorian
Press, Wharncliffe Local History, Wharncliffe Transport,
Wharncliffe True Crime and White Owl.

For a complete list of Pen & Sword titles please contact

PEN & SWORD BOOKS LIMITED
47 Church Street, Barnsley, South Yorkshire, S70 2AS, England
E-mail: enquiries@pen-and-sword.co.uk
Website: www.pen-and-sword.co.uk
or
PEN AND SWORD BOOKS
1950 Lawrence Rd, Havertown, PA 19083, USA
E-mail: Uspen-and-sword@casematepublishers.com
Website: www.penandswordbooks.com

Contents

Introduction		vii
Chapter 1	A Background to the Religious Tensions that Existed in the British Isles Prior to the Ascendancy of James II in 1685	1
Chapter 2	The Coronation of the Catholic King James II (R. 1685–1688) Leading to Protestant Rebellion and Ascendancy	18
Chapter 3	The Williamite Wars in Ireland (1689–1691)	45
Chapter 4	The 1689 Jacobite Rebellion and the Subsequent Events that Led to a Further Jacobite Rebellion in 1715	60
Chapter 5	The 1715 and 1719 Scottish Jacobite Rebellions and Further Jacobite Activity until 1737	88
Chapter 6	The Build Up to the 1745 Jacobite Rebellion Against the Backdrop of the War of the Austrian Succession (1740–1748)	102
Chapter 7	The 1745 Jacobite Invasion Force Sets Sail	107
Chapter 8	The Early Exchanges of 'The 45' and the Battle of Prestonpans	112
Chapter 9	The Jacobite Foray into England and the Subsequent Retreat back into the Highlands	117
Chapter 10	Culloden	129
Chapter 11	The Prince on the Run	141

Chapter 12	Women of the Jacobite Rebellions	147
Chapter 13	The Pacification of the Highlands	179
Chapter 14	Further Nails in the Jacobite Coffin	182
Chapter 15	The Highland Clearances 1750–1880	186
Chapter 16	The Last Vestiges of Jacobitism	189
Chapter 17	The Legacy of the Jacobite Williamite War of 1689–1691 as a Major Factor in the Sectarian Division of Northern Ireland and the Troubles of 1968–1998	191
Chapter 18	Current Issues	199
Notes		201
Bibliography		204

Introduction

An insight into the Jacobite rebellions can only be fully appreciated by looking at the background of the earliest sectarian seeds of discontent, as well as the whole story of the various risings and their aftermath and ramifications.

Without doubt, the single most important manifestation of religious discord was the Reformation, during which Henry VIII changed the official religion of England from Catholic to Protestant and simultaneously declared himself the head of the English Church instead of the Pope. This facilitated his divorce from his first wife, Catherine of Aragon, and enabled him to marry Catherine's lady in waiting, Anne Boleyn.

Henry's two daughters, Mary I and Elizabeth I, also merit inclusion in the overall story, as they, along with their relative, Mary Queen of Scots, were instrumental in continuing to propagate the religious strife that existed in the British Isles during this period, and which subsequently led to the organised plantation of Ulster with Scottish Protestants by James I in 1609.

Further turbulent times and civil war followed, leading to religious tension and discontent boiling over when the Catholic King James II came to the throne in 1685. He was immediately beset by a Protestant rebellion led by the Duke of Monmouth, which set a chain of events in motion with far reaching implications. The rebellion was crushed at the Battle of Sedgemoor, the last pitched battle to occur on English soil, but the bitter recriminations in the form of the Bloody Assizes caused such widespread revulsion and disgust that further measures were taken to depose the Catholic king.

Subsequently, the Protestant William of Orange of the Netherlands and his wife, Mary II, came to England by invitation in 1688, along with a large army of English and Dutch soldiers, in what was the last invasion of England. The bloodless coup resulted in William and Mary being crowned as joint monarchs. Meanwhile, King James II fled the country to exile in France and it was his removal from the throne that created the spark for his supporters to orchestrate a series of revolts, known as the Jacobite Rebellions (the name coming from *Jacobus*, the Latin for James).

* * *

These uprisings, which included the rebellions from the Highlands of Scotland, and the Williamite Wars in Ireland, also formed part of the wider picture of a European war – known as the Nine Years War, the War of the Grand Alliance, or the War of the League of Augsberg (1688–1697) – during which King Louis XIV of France strived to realise his expansionist plans whilst enforcing the Catholic religion and continuing to promote the Jacobite cause for his own ends.

Later, King Louis XIV was instrumental in initiating another conflict in Europe, the Spanish War of Succession (1701–1714), which led the French to continue to support Jacobite risings in Scotland during the same period and beyond, ultimately leading to Bonnie Prince Charlie's audacious bid for the British throne in 1745.

The '45' rebellion was eventually put down in the crushing military defeat at Culloden in 1746, the last pitched battle on British soil, which finally sounded the death knell for the Catholic and Stuart monarchy. However, the legend of the dashing prince, who came so near but yet so far in his bid to win the throne back for the Stuarts, is still very much alive in Scotland, especially as he continued to frustrate the extensive government manhunt to capture him amidst a savage backdrop of reprisals being wreaked on the Highland Jacobites by the 'Butcher', Duke of Cumberland. The legend is all the more romantic because of the prince's dramatic involvement with Flora MacDonald as they went 'Over the Sea to Skye' in an escape that has become immortalised in song, and during which the pair were reputed to have fallen in love.

However, the sectarian divisions that caused the Jacobite Rebellions never disappeared completely, particularly in Ulster, where the Protestant victories in the bitter conflict of the Jacobite Williamite Wars of Ireland (1689–1691) continued to be celebrated, and still are, as part of the 'Marching Season' of Northern Ireland. Most marches pass off without incident, but unresolved issues and the consequent deeply entrenched beliefs on both sides of the divide mean that marches that pass near or through Catholic neighbourhoods are seen by their inhabitants as confrontational, supremacist and triumphalist, whilst Protestant Loyalists insist it is their right to march their traditional routes. These tensions really came to a head on 12 August 1969, when the annual Apprentice Boys Parade in Londonderry/Derry erupted into violence in the 'Battle of the Bogside', which in turn provided the catalyst for the Northern Ireland Troubles.

The signing of the Good Friday Peace Agreement of 1998 has led to more neighbourly behaviour between the two Northern Irish communities, and has, hopefully, finally put the whole Jacobite conundrum to bed, or at least allowed it only to simmer quietly in the background.

Chapter 1

A Background to the Religious Tensions that Existed in the British Isles Prior to the Ascendancy of James II in 1685

The Protestant Church of England came into being in 1533, when Henry VIII declared himself the head of the English Church instead of the Pope. He did this to enable him to divorce his first wife, Catherine of Aragon, and marry Catherine's lady in waiting, Anne Boleyn. This period was known as the Reformation, as the official religion of England changed from Catholic to Protestant.

The next monarch was King Edward VI. He was King Henry VIII's and Jane Seymour's son. He was only nine when he came to the throne, so was 'guided' by the King's Protectors, initially by his uncle, Edward Seymour, the Duke of Somerset, and then by the ruthless Duke of Northumberland, who overthrew Somerset. Edward became dangerously ill in 1552, meaning that Catherine of Aragon's daughter, Mary, a devout Catholic, was next in line to the throne. Northumberland tried to prevent this by arranging a marriage between his own son and King Edward's second cousin, Lady Jane Grey. He then forced the dying young king to disinherit Mary and name Lady Jane Grey as his successor. However, Lady Jane Grey was queen for only nine days as the Privy Council of England, realising that there was a refusal among the public to accept Lady Jane Grey as queen, changed their allegiance to Mary, who subsequently became Queen Mary I of England (r. 1553–1558) and Northumberland was subsequently executed for his role in this debacle.

On her ascension, Mary was thirty-eight years of age and wanted to marry quickly in order to produce an heir. She chose her cousin Philip of Spain, the Catholic son of the powerful Holy Roman Emperor Charles V. Her mother was Spanish, and due to the influence of her husband, she allowed Spaniards to virtually control the government. She also immediately sought to make the English Church loyal to the Pope again. She reintroduced laws against heresy and wrought terrible revenge on those who practised the Protestant faith, hence her nickname, Bloody Mary (from which the drink is named). However, Mary found that she was unable to restore the monasteries that her father had destroyed as they were now divided among thousands of small land owners.

Mary continued her vendetta against Protestants and the populace were appalled when she ordered the burning at the stake of Protestant bishops and some 300 Protestant heretics, who actually turned out to be ordinary men and women. Accordingly, there was a national mood of discontent when, in 1554, Thomas Wyatt led a failed insurgency which resulted in Mary ordering Lady Jane Grey and her husband, Guildford Dudley, to be executed. Mary's Protestant half-sister, Princess Elizabeth, was also suspected by Mary of being involved and was imprisoned in the Tower of London for over a year as a result.

Religious tensions were also prevalent in Scotland, and in December 1557 the first Covenant, which referred to a bond or agreement with God, was signed by the Lords of the Congregation. Its members sought to maintain the Kirk (the Church of Scotland) as the sole form of worship in Scotland. It was Presbyterian in structure – and was a branch of the Protestant Church. It was governed by a body of elected elders, and was Calvinist in doctrine – in that it emphasised God's power and the weakness of humans.

* * *

Mary died in 1558, loathed and detested; her marriage to Philip had failed and she had also failed to produce a Catholic heir. She was succeeded by Elizabeth I (r. 1558–1603), who was the daughter of Henry VIII and Anne Boleyn.

As a child, Elizabeth had to witness the trauma of her father Henry VIII ordering the beheading of her mother, Anne Boleyn. To add insult to injury, he then declared Elizabeth illegitimate, making her ineligible to be queen. However, Henry later relented, and upon her accession the Protestant Elizabeth I was welcomed (especially after the recent experiences of Bloody Mary) and soon made herself very popular when she wasted no time in re-establishing the Church of England. However, in her private life, although Elizabeth attracted many suitors, including Mary's former husband, Philip of Spain, she never married.

In 1560 the Parliament of Scotland adopted the 'Reformed Confession of Faith' largely written by John Knox, in the 'First Book of Discipline'. It proposed a social programme for the church that would provide education and relief for the poor, as well as rejecting many teachings and practices of the Catholic Church.

Queen Elizabeth presided majestically over this age and seemed to personify the spirit of the time, resulting in her being given names such as the 'Sun Queen' or 'Glorianna'. However, Elizabeth did have to face one intractable problem in the form of her Catholic cousin, Mary Queen of Scots.

Mary Queen of Scots became Queen of Scotland at six days of age, but in 1547 was sent into exile in France to avoid Henry VIII's English forces, who were trying to force a marriage between the infant Mary and his son, the future Edward VI, in a blatant attempt to secure his Northern borders and at the same time force Protestant reformation on the Scots. This idea was rejected by the Scots, who were on the point of triggering the Auld Alliance with France when Henry launched an invasion force led by Edward Seymour, the Duke of Somerset, who defeated the Scots at the Battle of Pinkie, on 10 September 1547, at Mussleburgh, near Edinburgh (also known as the Rough Wooing).

In 1561 Mary returned to a hornet's nest in Scotland. The Scottish Reformation had resulted in Scotland breaking free from the Catholic Church and prominent Protestant Scots such as John Knox openly questioned her authority.

In 1565 Henry Stuart, Lord Darnley, came to the Scottish court with the intention of making his cousin Mary his bride. He achieved his aim, and in the process enraged Elizabeth and her Privy Councillors in England as it strengthened Scottish claims to the English throne. Meanwhile, Protestants in Scotland were not greatly enamoured with the all-Catholic liaison either, and hoped to count on English support when they mounted a rebellion against Mary. However, English support was not forthcoming due to a reluctance to be drawn into a full-scale war with their Scottish neighbours.

The rebels were easily crushed, and Mary's marriage was safe. However, the relationship turned sour and Darnley and some co-conspirators stabbed Mary's extramarital lover, Riccio, to death in front of her. Mary was mortified, but feigned reconciliation with Darnley in order to gain revenge, which eventually led to plotters burning his house down and murdering him at her behest.

Mary then lost her crown in Scotland and had to seek sanctuary in England under the protection of her cousin, Elizabeth. However, Mary's arrival in England posed an embarrassment and a threat to her Protestant cousin as she was next in line to the throne. A decision was made to keep Mary captive in the Tower of London for the next nineteen years. An action, which in 1580, resulted in the Pope excommunicating Elizabeth and calling on all Catholics to overthrow her. Consequently, a plot was hatched by the Catholic nobleman Anthony Babington to kill Elizabeth and put Mary Queen of Scots on the throne instead. The plot was discovered, and with a heavy heart, Elizabeth ordered the execution of her cousin in 1587.

This was the time of the Renaissance, the age of Shakespeare and other great English writers. Accordingly, Elizabeth's court became a centre for the arts and culture for musicians, poets, scholars and artists, including the poet and adventurer Sir Walter Raleigh. In 1588 Elizabeth visited Tilbury to meet the crews about to set sail to defeat the Spanish Armada and inspired them with her words: 'I know I am a weak and feeble woman but I have the heart and stomach of a king and a King of England too.' This was also the age when English sea adventurers such as Francis Drake, John Hawkins and Martin Frobisher started to challenge Spanish and Portuguese dominance. Drake became the first Englishman to sail round the world, while John Hawkins was renowned for building ships that were the fastest in the world.

On the death of Elizabeth, Mary Queen of Scots son, who was already James VI of Scotland, inherited the English, Welsh and Irish throne as James I (1603–1625). He was descended from Margaret, the older daughter of Henry VII and since the days of Henry VIII, the English monarch also ruled Wales and Ireland.

James I and VI hoped to bring about a union of the nations of the British Isles and introduced the Union Jack flag in 1606 in an attempt to achieve this (Wales were united with England at the time and not a separate principality, hence their non representation in the flag). However, his aims of unity were thwarted by the English Parliament.

He was a Protestant himself, but sought to keep a fragile peace between Protestants and Catholics by steering a course of toleration towards both religions. James' wife, Anne of Denmark, converted to Catholicism, which could have caused issues, but James skilfully used the situation to gain greater acceptance from Catholics.

James also advocated a unified Church of England and Scotland as the first step in the unification of England and Scotland, and had previously endorsed this arrangement in 1590 and 1596 as King of Scotland, and then again in 1603 when he also became King of England. However, the leaders of the Church of Scotland (Kirk) differed with James on the governance of the church, as they objected to many of the Church of England practices. He also introduced a new version of the Bible, the King James Bible, which was intended to remove some of the more extreme Puritan doctrines. This version of the Bible was a lasting legacy that endured for centuries.

James's middle of the road religious policy caused discontent and unrest among those at the more extreme ranges of the Catholic and Protestant religious spectrum, which led him to persecute extremists of both denominations. The Catholics responded with many plots against him, one of which was the Gunpowder Plot to blow up Parliament in 1605. Meanwhile, Protestant Puritans were leaving the country as pilgrims. The first group to do so were the Pilgrim Fathers, who left from Plymouth in 1620, bound for America. They were followed by many other Protestant Non-Conformist Puritan settlers from south-west England and elsewhere.

In 1607 the Earls of Tyrone and Tyrconnell, fearing arrest for their part in the Nine Years War (1593–1603) against English rule in Ireland, fled Ireland to Continental Europe, with the intention of returning with a Spanish-backed army. However, the Spanish fleet was defeated by the Dutch at the Battle of Gibraltar on 25 April 1607, putting paid to those plans.

In order to strengthen his rule in Ireland, James took the opportunity left by the earls' departure to fill the power gap in the rebellious north of Ireland with Protestant settlers, who he considered would be likely to be more kindly disposed towards the monarchy. Accordingly, in 1609 land was confiscated by the Crown from Irish native Gaelic chiefs in Armagh, Cavan, Fermanagh, Tyrone, Donegal and Londonderry/Derry, while land in Antrim, Down and Monaghan was also privately colonised with the king's agreement. It was seen as a means of colonising and civilising Ireland. The colonists, who had to be English-speaking Protestants and loyal to the king, were mostly Protestant Scots. It created a lasting Ulster Protestant community and precipitated centuries of sectarian bitterness.

In 1624, much to the delight of a large section of the public and the Protestant House of Commons, James I failed, despite protracted negotiations, in his bid to marry his son, Charles, to a Catholic princess, the Infanta Anna, daughter of Phillip III of Spain. Then, in 1625, James I died and Charles I (1625–1649), the second son of James I, ascended the throne, his older brother, Henry, having died in 1612.

By the 1620s Catholicism in Scotland was mainly found amongst the clansmen of the Highlands and members of the aristocracy. Generally, the Catholic religion was feared in Scotland as many had the impression that Protestant Europe was under attack from France's King Louis XIV. Consequently, the reign of Charles I was a time of great turmoil and conflict. This worsened in 1637 when John Knox's Book of Discipline was replaced in Scotland by a new Common Prayer Book, by order of King Charles I of England, without any consultation with Scottish ministers. The orders also stated that anyone who denied the king's supremacy in church matters would be excommunicated.

The resultant religious tensions eventually erupted into a series of conflicts known as the Wars of the Three Kingdoms, which took place in Scotland, England and Ireland from 1639 to 1653. These wars consisted of: the Bishops' Wars (1639 and 1640); the Irish Confederate Wars (1641–1652); the First English Civil War (1642–1646); the Second English Civil War (1648); the Third English Civil War (1649–1651); the Cromwellian Conquest of Ireland (1649–1653).

The Bishops' Wars were two separate conflicts that took place in Scotland in 1639 and 1640 and were the first of the Wars of the Three Kingdoms.

In February 1638 representatives from all sections of Scottish society agreed a National Covenant, which pledged to resist the imposition by Charles I of the Church of England's religious practices, including the role of bishops in the church and the introduction of the Common Prayer Book in 1637. The covenant was brokered by the Marquess of Argyll and six other members of the Scottish Privy Council.

Most Scots supported a Presbyterian Kirk, but they preferred one that was ruled by elected Presbyters, rather than one that was ruled by bishops appointed by the king. Consequently, the Covenant was supported by the majority of people in Scotland, but was met with resistance in Aberdeenshire, which was a stronghold of the bishop-led Episcopalian worship.

The Covenanters pledged to oppose Charles's innovations and expelled bishops from the Kirk, which resulted in an attempt by Charles I to impose the measures by military force in the 1639 and 1640 Bishops' Wars.

The outcome of the Bishops' Wars was that Charles was defeated in his attempts to impose his authority, and the resulting settlement left the Covenanters in control of Scotland's government. It then became a requirement of holders of civic office to sign the National Covenant, which in effect gave the Scottish Parliament the power to approve all of the king's officials in Scotland.

The Irish Confederate Wars (1641–1652), which are sometimes referred to as the Eleven Years War, were a result of various English involvements in Ireland, including the Ulster Plantation of 1609. The simmering tensions sparked an uprising by Irish Catholics against discrimination and the issue of whether Irish Catholics or English and Scottish Protestants should have the most political power and own the majority of the land. Another factor in the conflict was whether Ireland should be a self-governing kingdom under Charles I or subordinate to the English Parliament.

The Irish Confederate Wars overlapped with the English Civil War and developed along similar religious lines with Irish, Scottish and English Catholics supporting the Cavalier Stuarts, while English and Irish Protestants and Scottish Presbyterian planters supported Cromwell's Roundheads. It was mostly Protestant and Catholic volunteers from Scotland that fought in Ulster to support their particular affiliates, and the acrimony of this conflict further polarised views in both Scotland and Ireland. The Irish Confederate Wars are thought to have been responsible for around 200,000–600,000 deaths and are considered to be the most destructive in the history of Ireland.

Charles I believed in the 'Divine Right of the Monarchy', and didn't take kindly to advice from a Parliament now dominated by Protestant Puritans. He had also further antagonised his Protestant Puritan detractors by marrying a French Catholic princess, Henrietta Maria (1609–1669), who was the youngest daughter of King Henry IV of France and Marie de Medici. She was born at the Hotel du Louvre in Paris and became the mother of Charles II and James II. However, when Charles was coronated at Westminster Abbey on 2 February 1626 she was not crowned queen at this ceremony due to her Catholicism.

Charles is said to have approved of the marriage, but that didn't stop a number of infidelities with various mistresses, making the early years of their marriage difficult. However, the couple did go on to develop a close relationship. She involved herself in her husband's attempts to overthrow Parliament, and further antagonised many by seeking to enlist support for the king from the Pope, as well as overtly practising the Catholic religion herself.

King and Parliament were at loggerheads and Charles I decided to have five of the leading parliamentary Puritans arrested. This precipitated the First English Civil War (1642–1646), which pitched the Protestant, Puritan and Parliamentarian Roundheads against the predominantly Catholic Royalist Cavaliers.

At the outbreak of the First English Civil War in 1642, the majority of English people supported the institution of the monarchy, but the issue was whether the monarchy or Parliament had ultimate power. Those who supported Charles I in his claim of 'The Divine Right of Kings' and the monarch's superiority over Parliament were known as Royalists, while their Parliamentarian opponents were in favour of a constitutional monarchy.

Initially, the Royalist enjoyed great success, securing victory at Edgehill on 23 October 1642, which put the Parliamentarians on the back foot. However, in 1643 the Covenanter Scots, led by Argyll, advocated civil and religious union with England as the best way to preserve a Presbyterian Kirk. They made an agreement called the Solemn League and Covenant, in which the Scottish Covenanters agreed to offer military support to the English Parliamentarians. The combined force of English Parliamentarians and Scottish Covenanters then won a series of battles in 1644, and, most significantly, the Battle of Marston Moor on 2 July 1644.

Another factor in the Parliamentarians' success was the founding of the first professional army in England, known as the New Model Army, which led to further success, at the Battle of Naseby in June 1645.

Following defeat in the First English Civil War, Charles initially escaped but then decided to surrender to the Scots instead of the English. His intention was to exploit the ideological differences between the Scots Presbyterians and the English Independents. Consequently, he travelled to the nearest Scottish army base, which was at Southwell, Nottinghamshire, where the Scots Covenanters were besieging the nearby town of Newark. He arrived at Southwell on 5 May 1646, from where he was taken to Newcastle. Whilst he was held there, discussions took place between the Scottish and English Parliaments. These became known as the Newcastle Propositions and involved Charles negotiating separately with different factions.

Presbyterian English Parliamentarians and the Scots Covenanters wanted him to accept a modified version of the Newcastle Propositions, which crucially did not require a Presbyterian reformation of the church but would have required every subject in Scotland, England, Wales and Ireland to sign the Solemn League and Covenant, making in effect, the church in each country Presbyterian.

The Scots spent several months trying to convince Charles to agree to these terms, but he refused to do so and instead signed an agreement known as the Engagement, in which he agreed to respect the Solemn League and Covenant by Act of Parliament in both kingdoms and to accept Presbyterianism in England, but only for a trial period of three years.

The Scots were divided on whether to accept the Engagement. Supporters of the Engagement tended to be Presbyterians and Covenanters and were known as Engagers, whereas those against the agreement were known as Kirk Party Fundamentalists or Whiggamores. Royalists and moderates in both Scotland and England also tended to oppose the Engagement, while religious independents such as Oliver Cromwell pledged to resist it.

After a bitter political struggle, the Engagers gained a majority in the Scottish Parliament, by which time war had broken out again in England between Royalists and Parliamentarians. Accordingly, when Oliver Cromwell gained control of England he had little consideration for the Presbyterians and Covenanters and disregarded the Engagement.

Over time, the Scottish Covenanters and their English Presbyterian partners gradually came to see the independents who dominated the

New Model Army as a greater threat to them than the Royalists, so, in December 1647, the Scottish Engager Covenanters agreed to supply military support to help Charles regain the English throne in return for Charles committing to the imposition of Presbyterianism in England and curbing the Independents. They were also supported by Royalist risings in South Wales, Kent, Essex and Lancashire. However, the uncoordinated risings were defeated individually by Cromwell's forces and the Second English Civil War (1648) was concluded with Charles I's defeat at the Battle of Preston on 17–19 August 1648. The rout of the Engager army led to a further political upheaval in Scotland, and the faction that had been opposed to the Engagement were able to reclaim control of the government.

Meanwhile in England, Cromwell evicted the existing Parliament and formed the Rump Parliament, which had Charles I tried for treason against the English people. He was subsequently executed on 30 January 1649 and the Republican Commonwealth was created, and controlled by Oliver Cromwell.

Charles I's son, also Charles, sought an alliance against Cromwell with the Scots Presbyterians. However, the Scots insisted that he first sign the Covenant, which recognised the ascendancy of the Kirk in religious matters and that of Parliament in civil affairs. Charles initially refused to agree to these conditions, but had to acquiesce when Royalist support from Ireland dried up after Cromwell's campaign.

The future Charles II then raised an army in Scotland of 10,000 men and a plaque exists in the wall of Brae House in Garmouth, Moray, which commemorates the signing by Charles of the Solemn League and Covenant in 1650. This was the catalyst for the Third English Civil War, which was also known as the Anglo-Scottish War (1649–1651).

Cromwell was becoming increasingly alarmed by Scottish sabre rattling and Thomas Fairfax, Lord General of the New Model Army, was ordered to invade Scotland in a pre-emptive military action. However, Fairfax resigned his commission rather than break the Solemn League and Covenant, which he believed still bound England and Scotland, so Cromwell went to Scotland in his place.

Once in Scotland, supply chain issues and hostility from the locals forced Cromwell to resupply from the sea. But this was also difficult, as the Scottish commander, David Leslie, had blocked the port of Leith by preparing a defensive line between Edinburgh and Leith. So instead, Cromwell captured the port of Musselburgh.

Due to the difficulties of obtaining supplies, Cromwell's army had to leave Musselburgh on 31 August 1650 and make a tactical withdrawal to Dunbar, which they achieved, despite being pursued and harassed all the way. As a result, the Cromwellian army arrived at Dunbar, tired and hungry and in a poor state, to find that the Scots had blocked the escape route via Berwick to England at the easily defended narrow gorge at Cockburnspath. Meanwhile, the main Scottish force was camped at Doon Hill, to the south of Dunbar, where they were fully exposed to the horrendous weather.

The Scots held a council of war and came to the conclusion that their position was untenable due to the terrible weather, and instead elected to attack the English, who were in a disadvantageous position themselves. However, Cromwell also had the intention of launching a dawn assault, and, unbeknown to the Scots, had moved his troops into a position to achieve this.

At approximately 4am on 3 September 1650, the English cavalry advanced and took the Scots by surprise. Once they had recovered from the initial shock, the Scots second line of cavalry mounted a counter charge and the battle was on a knife edge. The English cavalry gradually gained the ascendancy and finally broke the Scottish lines, allowing Cromwell's men to break out of the stranglehold and inflict a heavy defeat on the Scots.

The Scottish survivors from the Battle of Dunbar withdrew to the important strategic position of Stirling and prevented the English army advancing beyond there. However, on 17 July 1651 the English managed to cross the Firth of Forth and defeat the Scots at the Battle of Inverkeithing on 20 July 1651.

The rest of of the Scottish army were now isolated at Stirling, and Charles II, after being crowned King of Scotland at Scone on 1 January 1651, advanced into England in August that same year, believing that the only other alternative was surrender. However, his predominantly Scottish Royalist army was viewed with suspicion across the border and consequently failed to attract much English support. The Scottish army advanced southwards as far as Worcester, arriving on 3 September 1651, a year to the day after the Battle of Dunbar. Cromwell and his forces had also arrived on the scene and proceeded to destroy the severely outnumbered Scottish Royalist army. In the aftermath of the battle, Leslie was imprisoned in the Tower of London, where he remained until the restoration of the monarchy in 1660.

Charles escaped and was on the run for six weeks before escaping to France. One of his many hiding places whilst a fugitive in England was an oak tree at Boscobel House on the Staffordshire/Shropshire border, an escapade, which is remembered for posterity by the numerous English pubs called the Royal Oak.[1]

The Scottish defeat in the Third English Civil War (Anglo-Scottish War), resulted in Scotland being integrated into the Commonwealth of England, Scotland, Ireland and Wales under the rule of Cromwell as Lord Protector.

Following these events, Cromwell decided his best course of action was to abolish the power of the Scottish gentry and the Kirk. He achieved this by enforcing military rule and abolishing the Scottish Covenanter government. Then on 12 February 1652, Cromwell declared The Terms of Incorporation, which founded a new Council of Scotland, responsible for regulating church affairs and allowing freedom of worship for all Protestant sects.

This led to the Covenanters splitting into two factions: The Resolutioners – who supported re-admitting Royalists and Engagers; and The Protestors – who were largely former Kirk party fundamentalists, also known as Whiggamores, who were against readmitting Royalists and Engagers.

Meanwhile, trouble was also brewing in Ireland. Following the Irish Rebellion in 1641, the majority of Ireland now came under the auspices of the Irish Catholic Confederation, and in early 1649 the Catholic Confederates sought an alliance with the English Royalists who had suffered defeat at the hands of the Parliamentarians in the Third English Civil War. This prompted Cromwell to reconquer Ireland with his New Model Army on behalf of the English Parliament in what became known as the Cromwellian Conquest of Ireland (1649–1653). He put down the insurgence and brought Ireland under his control. He then returned to England in 1650 and passed command in Ireland to Henry Ireton, who in turn defeated the Irish Confederate and English Royalist coalition.

The brutality of the Cromwellian conquest of Ireland means that Cromwell is still a hate figure in the country. He prevented Catholics from carrying out their religion and also denied them the right to hold public office. His reputation was further tarnished as the war also led to severe famine and bubonic plague.

Cromwell died on 3 September 1658 and was succeeded by his son, Richard, who soon found himself unsuited for government. A chaotic period ensued during which he was unable to control the warring factions of the army and Parliament. In May 1659 he was ordered to resign by the army and Prince Charles I's exiled son was then invited by Parliament to ascend the throne as Charles II in 1660.

The restoration of the monarchy also involved the restoration of the Church of England, as opposed to Cromwell's more puritanical version of the Protestant religion. Many in England preferred the more puritanical strain, and these people were known as Non-Conformists.

The 'Cavalier Parliament' of Charles II, which was elected in 1661, wanted to punish the Puritans in revenge for the Civil War, and for imposing their way of life on the nation. As a result, the 1664 Conventicle Act was passed, and all Puritan Non-Conformist preachers were banned from large centres of population. Also non-attendance at the parish church and attendance at non-Anglican meetings was punished with varying degrees of severity depending on the local magistrates.

The backlash against Non-Conformist Puritans by Charles II left a simmering anti-Royalist, anti-establishment and anti-Church of England resentment in many areas of England. The fear of a return to a Catholic monarchy, which was even more of an anathema to the Puritans, was also prevalent, particularly as King Charles II and his wife had failed to produce any children.

Despite being a closet Catholic himself, King Charles II opposed his brother James's conversion to Catholicism, and insisted that James's daughters, one of whom was Mary, who later ruled Britain jointly with her husband, William of Orange, and another the future Queen Anne, be raised in the Church of England. In this way King Charles II cunningly managed to keep a lid on the simmering religious tensions. However, anti-Catholicism was widespread, and later in 1673 the Test Act went so far as to exclude Roman Catholics from both Houses of Parliament.

In Scotland it was the Covenanters who were suffering cruel oppression, and a spontaneous rising took place on 28 November 1666, when Covenanters marched on Edinburgh in protest at government attempts to restore Episcopacy to Scotland. They were stopped and defeated by the king's troops at the Battle of Rullion Green, eight miles south of Edinburgh in the Pentland Hills. Around fifty prisoners were taken and were either transported or executed.

After the rising, a more conciliatory policy was adopted, which allowed the Covenanters to retain their churches without having to accept Episcopacy. Ministers who had previously been evicted were permitted to return as long as they agreed to steer clear of politics.

A number returned, but the more hardline elements refused the offer and continued to hold illegal outdoor meetings or Convecticles. This meant a return to persecution as attending a Convectile was made illegal and preaching at one was punishable by death. To enforce these rules and impose sanctions in 1678, 3,000 Lowland militia and a Highland militia of 6,000, known as the Highland Host, were billeted in the Covenanting Shires to detect attendance at Convecticles. The meetings were often broken up by squads of government dragoons, including those led by John Graham of Claverhouse, the 1st Viscount Dundee.

The murder of Archbishop Sharp by Covenanter rebels in May 1679 on Magnus Muir was the catalyst for further Covenanter revolts in Scotland. The first of which occurred when a large group of Covenanters, on Sunday, 1 June 1679, went ahead with a large Convectile at Loudoun Hill on the borders of Ayrshire and Lanarkshire, in open defiance of government rules. The Covenanters were aware that John Graham of Claverhouse's dragoons were advancing on the area to break it up, prompting the Rev Thomas Douglas to allegedly break off his sermon with the words, 'Ye have got the theory. Now get the practice.' The 200-strong Covenanter force then moved to confront Claverhouse at the boggy moor of Drumclog, and though only armed with rudimentary weapons such as muskets and pitchforks, the Covenanters were a force to be reckoned with under the capable command of Robert Hamilton and William Cleland, especially as they took up a strong position that meant the enemy would have to cross a bog to attack them.

As the battle progressed, Claverhouse's forces appeared to be gaining the ascendancy, but were unable to negotiate the bog and confront the enemy and instead were reduced to firing across it. Meanwhile, William Cleland successfully skirted around the bog with a group of Covenanters and was able to cause Claverhouse's line to break, leading to a rout.

The victory was a huge triumph for the Covenanter rebels, and it forced Claverhouse to flee to Glasgow. The battle of Drumclog is still recognised by some in Scotland as a victory for freedom of worship and a memorial was created at the site of the battle in 1839.

The Covenanters built on this battle and became stronger, but to quell their mutinous aims a certain Duke of Monmouth, Charles II's illegitimate son, was sent northwards. He, along with John Graham of Claverhouse, led the government forces to confront the Covenanter rebels, who were led again by Robert Hamilton and the hero of Drumclog, William Cleland. The opposing factions clashed on 22 June 1679 at the Battle of Bothwell Bridge, on the River Clyde in Hamilton, South Lanarkshire, near Bothwell.

The Covenanters positioned themselves on the south bank of the river, to the north of Hamilton, while the government troops took up position on the northern or Bothwell bank, on sloping ground that has now become known as the Covenanters Field, and which was, for many years, the venue for a Covenanters Convectile organised by the Scottish Covenanters Memorial Association. The battle became focused on the narrow bridge because Monmouth and his troops were required to cross it to get to the Covenanters.

Hamilton was defending the bridge and met with some success initially. However, his men had insufficient artillery and ammunition and were forced to withdraw. This allowed Monmouth's men an opportunity to get across and rout the Covenanters.

Many escaped to the adjacent Hamilton Palace, which was the seat of Duchess Anne, a staunch Presbyterian. That did not save them, however, as they were pursued there and killed by government troops. Those that escaped with their lives were taken to Greyfriars Kirkyard in Edinburgh and kept in an area still known as the Covenanters Prison, where they were held whilst awaiting transportation to the colonies.[2]

* * *

All those who had fought for the Covenanters were denounced as traitors. They were oppressed by royal troops who carried out numerous extrajudicial executions as they enforced the king's authority. This period (1679–1688) became known by the Protestant community as 'The Killing Time', and the Covenanter defeat at Bothwell Bridge subsequently split the movement into Moderates and Cameronian Covenanters.

The more extreme Cameronian faction was led by Richard Cameron and Donald Cargill. They both had government bounties on their heads and were wanted dead or alive. Consequently, Cameron, who became known as the 'Lion of the Covenant', and his followers kept on the move, finding shelter and sleeping rough where they could.

The Cameronian Convenanters arrived in the town of Sanquhar in Dumfries and Galloway on 22 June 1680, the first anniversary of the defeat of Bothwell Bridge. They immediately poured fuel on to the fire by nailing their inflammatory Sanquhar Declaration to the market cross. The declaration pledged that the Cameronian Covenaters disavowed allegiance to King Charles II and his Catholic brother, James, and the government of Scotland in the cause of the true Protestant and Presbyterian religion.

The Cameronian Covenanters continued to move around the Lowlands of Scotland, but were taken by surprise at Airds Moss on 22 July 1680 by a troop of government horse under the command of Bruce of Earlshall. A brief skirmish ensued in which, among others, Richard Cameron was killed. Those who were taken prisoner were taken to Edinburgh where they were later hanged.

The brutality of the recriminations gained the Covenanters a great deal of sympathy. This was recognised in the 1681 Scottish Succession and Test Acts, which upheld the primacy of the Kirk but still made allegiance to the monarch compulsory regardless of religious faith. However, the Covenanters continued to resist King Charles II's efforts to impose Episcopalian rule and instead wanted to restore the constitution that was in place in 1640.

A number of high-profile individuals such as James Dalyrymple, Chief Legal Officer, and Archibald Campbell, 9th Earl of Argyll, refused to pledge allegiance to the monarch. As a result, Argyll was convicted of treason and sentenced to death, though he and Dalyrimple managed to escape to the Netherlands. Meanwhile, in 1684 the Cameronians had a new leader after the loss of Richard Cameron; he was James Renwick, a Presbyterian minister who had been branded an outlaw in 1680 for declaring that King Charles II was a tyrant and a usurper.

Both Covenanter factions distributed copies of a document called the Apologetical Declaration in various locations, which effectively declared war on government officers. Consequently, the Scottish Privy Council sanctioned the summary execution of any Covenanter caught with weapons. This decree was enthusiastically followed by Claverhouse and his soldiers, who enforced this policy concurrently with a same-day trial and execution procedure for those who refused to swear allegiance to the king.

To add to the general anti-Catholic sentiment that existed in both England and Scotland, Titus Oates falsely alleged that there was a Catholic conspiracy to assassinate Charles II and implicated Catherine of Braganza (1638–1705), Charles' wife, among others of being part of a plot to poison him.

For his part, Charles never doubted his wife and he stood by her until the allegations were proved to be false. However, by then, Oates' pack of lies had resulted in the execution of twenty-two innocent men and was a major factor in the Exclusion Bill Crisis of 1679–1681, which – when it became apparent after several miscarriages that Catherine would remain childless – sought to exclude the king's brother, the Catholic James, Duke of York, from ascending the throne and encouraged Charles to divorce Catherine and marry a Protestant instead.

Catherine's faith no doubt helped her through these times, and she helped convert Charles to the Roman Catholic Church shortly before he died in 1685.

Chapter 2

The Coronation of the Catholic King James II (R. 1685–1688) Leading to Protestant Rebellion and Ascendancy

James II was born in 1633; his parents were Charles I and Henrietta Maria. He came to the throne on the death of his brother, King Charles II, on 23 April 1685, and was crowned at Westminster Abbey as King James II of England, Wales and Ireland, and James VII of Scotland. He believed in the 'Divine Right of Kings', and had the intention of making the nation Catholic again.

Before James II came to the throne, he had married Anne Hyde (1637–1671), whose father Edward was an advisor to Charles I whilst he was in exile in the Netherlands. She was brought up as an Anglican, but had become interested in the Catholic religion and was instrumental in James' conversion. After the wedding, on 24 November 1660, she was given the titles of the Duchess of York and Albany. James and Anne had four sons and four daughters. Only two survived infancy, and eventually became the future monarchs Mary II and Anne.

By the time James II ascended to the throne his first wife, Anne, had died, and shortly after her death James married Mary of Modena of Italy in 1673. Mary of Modena (1658–1718) was born at the Palazzo Ducale di Modena, Italy, on 5 October 1658, and as the daughter of Alfonso IV, Duke of Modena, had been brought up a committed Catholic.

James' deceased younger sister, Hentrietta Anne, had been married to Louis XIV's younger brother, Philippe, and King Louis liked the idea of continuing to exert influence in the English court. Thus, the marriage of the fifteen-year-old Mary of Modena to the forty-year-old widower James was arranged through French diplomatic channels and they were married by proxy on 30 September 1673. Parliament was furious at this arrangement and there were various attempts to get the marriage annulled, all of which failed as King Charles II had decided to allow it to go ahead.

A large proportion of the public were initially prepared to tolerate a Catholic king as it seemed that due to James' health, the situation would only be temporary and then Mary, his Protestant daughter, would succeed him soon enough. So, despite his Catholicism, James II, became king with little disruption in either Scotland or England, mainly because the war-weary citizens of both nations feared the massive disruption of civil war.

However, there were certain factions that vigorously opposed the new monarch, in what became known as the 'Exclusion Crisis'. For instance, in Scotland, the Covenanters under Renwick disputed James' right to be king. As a result, James actively persecuted them, and particularly made an example of Renwick, who refused to swear an oath of allegiance. He was hanged on 17 February 1688 at the Grassmarket, Edinburgh, and his hands were then cut off and fixed to the city gates.

In England, before his death, Charles II had been urged by influential Protestants to legitimise his illegitimate son, the staunchly Protestant Duke of Monmouth, but Charles refused. Historians speculate that this was because Monmouth's mother, Lucy Walter (1630–1658), was a commoner. She was born at Roch Castle, near Haverfordwest, Pembrokeshire. In 1644 Roch Castle was destroyed by Parliamentary forces and she sought refuge in the Netherlands, where she became the mistress of the future King Charles II while he was in exile and with whom she had a child, on 9 April 1649.

The child in question, the future Duke of Monmouth, spent his early years under the care of Lord Crofts. He always claimed that his mother was the legal wife of King Charles II, and, therefore, his birth was not illegitimate. He claimed they were married in a private ceremony in the Netherlands and that his mother had a black box containing the wedding certificate. King Charles II, on the other hand, acknowledged that he was the father, but said that he only ever had one wife, Catherine of Braganza, and insisted that his brother, James, should ascend the throne.

Although he treated his son very well and was fond of him, King Charles II did not acknowledge his son publicly, until Monmouth married Anne Scott, Countess of Buccleuch (1651–1732), in 1663. She was the daughter of Francis Scott, 2nd Earl of Buccleuch, and Margaret

Leslie, daughter of John Leslie, 6th Earl of Rothes. Anne was twelve years old at the time of her marriage and her husband, James Croft, the Duke of Monmouth, was fourteen. Upon their marriage, Monmouth took the surname of Scott as his own. They had six children, but only two survived infancy.

* * *

Charles awarded various titles to his son: the Duke of Monmouth, the Duke of Orkney, the Knight of the Garter, and then, in 1670, he made Monmouth Commander in Chief of the army, before promoting him to Captain General in 1678. He went on to prove himself as a charismatic, courageous and capable soldier in the defeat of the Scottish Covenanters at Bothwell Bridge in 1679. He also led a successful campaign in the Netherlands during the Third Anglo-Dutch War (1672–1674), where he defeated the Dutch at the Siege of Maastricht (1673).

However, the Protestant Duke of Monmouth continued to be a figurehead for those working to prevent the Catholic Duke of York (later to become James II) succeeding to the throne. One of the most influential of these was the Earl of Shaftsbury, who, as a result, was accused of treason. He fled to the Netherlands before he could be tried and later died of natural causes while still in exile, so wasn't involved in either the Rye House Plot or the Monmouth Rebellion.

The Rye House Plot in 1683 was a plot to assassinate both Charles II and his brother, the Duke of York, which was concocted at Rye House, the home of Richard Rumbold. The intention was to assassinate the royals as they returned from the Newmarket Races. Monmouth refused to sanction the plan, resulting in its abandonment. However, the plotters were betrayed to the government, and the ringleaders were either executed or managed to escape to the Netherlands. Monmouth was also exiled to the Netherlands by King Charles II as an act of political necessity. In reality, the king appreciated that Monmouth had put a stop to the plot.

Two of Monmouth's friends, Lord Essex and Lord Arlington, both fellow Protestant sympathisers, later died in mysterious circumstances. They were rumoured to have been poisoned at the behest of the Duke of York. Charles II also died two days after the death of Lord Arlington, causing Monmouth to believe that York was behind all three deaths.

The Coronation of the Catholic King James II

Monmouth accused York of poisoning his father, and also accused him of collecting taxes without authority, and placing scandalous men on the bench, a thinly veiled reference to Judge Jeffreys. These factors motivated an enraged Monmouth to fight for what he believed was his rightful place on the throne on the accession of the Duke of York to become James II on 23 April 1685.

Meanwhile, Archibald Campbell, 9th Earl of Argyll (1629–1685), Chief of the powerful Clan Campbell, was also planning rebellion. He had already been convicted of treason and been sentenced to death after raising objections to the 1681 Scottish Trust Act, and his subsequent refusal to pledge allegiance to King Charles. He was then issued a further death sentence for his involvement in the 1683 Rye House Plot, a charge widely regarded as another example of the vindictive nature of James II. He had managed to escape from prison and went into hiding in England, before eventually fleeing to the Netherlands, where he joined a burgeoning group of English and Scottish political exiles, which included the Duke of Monmouth. They were united in their opposition to the Catholic King James II and were planning rebellion. The plot had the backing of William of Orange, who was a great Protestant champion, as well as being the nephew and son-in-law of James II. He provided money, a thirty-two-gun frigate and two smaller vessels, as well as just eighty-three soldiers. The plan was to coordinate a landing in the south-west of England with a simultaneous landing in Scotland led by Argyll; the intention being to occupy James II's Royalist army on two fronts and stretch their resources.

The south-west of England was chosen as the spot to launch the main invasion force over other disenfranchised areas of England, mainly because the Duke of Monmouth and his promoter-in-chief the Earl of Shaftsbury, had visited the area in 1680 and had been enthusiastically received by commoner and wealthy landowner alike. It had also been an area of great support for the Parliamentarian cause during the Civil War, and there was also great resentment against King James II's Catholicism in this part of England. Monmouth's intention was to raise support in the West Country and dominate this area by taking the city of Bristol, which was then England's second city[1], before moving on to London to wrest the throne from King James II.

The Lowlands of Scotland were also seen as an area with a large Protestant Presbyterian population, from which an invasion would gain a lot of support, and the plan was for Argyll to recruit his Campbell clansmen.

Argyll controlled an area of south-west Scotland where many of the inhabitants were opposed to Catholicism and were Covenanters. His power as clan chief meant that he would be able to raise several thousand tenant clansmen who were obligated to serve their chief due to the feudal clan system. It was also anticipated that many other Presbyterians and Covenanters in southern Scotland would join the cause and that he would gather support as he made his way south through the north of England and the Midlands to London.

Monmouth was keen to coordinate an invasion with the Scottish conspirator, but Argyll was profoundly distrustful of Monmouth, not least because of his role at the Battle of Bothwell, and Argyll had to be convinced of the logic of cooperating with his fellow exile. However, in early March 1685 they agreed that Monmouth would be responsible for England, the south of Ireland, and foreign relations, while Argyll would deal with Scotland and the north of Ireland. Monmouth promised that if he were to secure victory, he would not declare himself king unless proposed by Parliament, and to depart no more than six days after Argyll. In the event, Monmouth did not sail until nearly a month later.

Argyll's Rising 1685

Argyll's Rising of 1685 got underway when three ships – the *Anna*, the *Daniel* and the *Sophia* – were loaded with weapons and a contingent of 300 Scottish soldiers serving in the Dutch army. They eventually left Amsterdam on the evening of 2 May 1685, having waited several days for a favourable wind. The difficult crossing was hindered by bad weather and they were blown off their intended course between the Shetlands and the Orkneys and instead had to anchor in Swanbister Bay on the south coast of the Orkneys.

A crew member by the name of Spence had an uncle living in the Orkney town of Kirkwall and sought permission from Argyll to go ashore to find a pilot. But when attempting to affect this, Spence and his companion were arrested and the authorities alerted of the rebel's presence. In response, a landing party from one of the rebel ships was dispatched and took seven local gentry as hostages to be used as bargaining tools. However, when

Argyll sent a message to the Bishop of Orkney to exchange the prisoners, he received no response.

The rebels and their hostages continued westwards and reached the Sound of Mull by the evening of 11 May 1685. Argyll's son, Charles Campbell, was then sent ashore to raise Campbell clansmen, whilst the main invasion force sailed southwards to Islay.

They disembarked at Kilarrow on the island of Islay in the early hours of 17 May 1685, hoping to make a surprise night attack on the local militia. However, they landed unopposed, as the local militia had got wind of their arrival and had escaped to Kintyre. It was a slightly disappointing start in terms of recruitment; they only managed to gain eighty local recruits, whereas they were expecting more like 600.

On 20 May 1685 the ships crossed over to Kintyre and landed at Campbelltown, the epicentre of the Campbell Clan and the centre of Argyll's regional influence. Here, he read out two manifestos, the first of which claimed that he only wanted to recover his estates; the second was more like a long-winded list of grievances. The contents of both manifestos failed to convince their most likely recruits of Presbyterian dissidents and disenchanted Cameronian Covenanters. Both groups withdrew their support because no mention was made about overthrowing the Kirk establishment, which was the main reason for either group to get involved.

Argyll then ordered his forces to Tarbert, where they arrived on 27 May 1685 and joined up with the 1,200 Campbell Clan levies, raised by his son, Charles, and Sir Duncan Campbell of Auchinbreck, bringing the total strength to around 2,500. The recruits were then organised into three regiments of horse and foot.

One difficulty that Argyll had was that many of his estates had been confiscated and occupied by John Murray, 1st Marquess of Atholl, a Royalist supporter of King James II who held the prominent government office of the Keeper of the Privy Seal of Scotland. This meant that Argyll was unable to recruit any of his clansmen tenants from those estates. He was also acutely aware that his Highland clansmen would be wary of fighting in the Lowlands while Atholl's men roamed the Highlands and threatened their homes.

Argyll also saw the rising as an opportunity to reassert his authority on the whole of Argyllshire, but other members of the council vetoed the idea, believing he was only interested in this course of action for the self-serving reason of regaining his estates.

The council also realised that there would be difficulties with that plan as Monmouth had still not yet set sail, despite it being nearly a month after he had promised to do so. This meant that James II's forces were still concentrated in Scotland and occupying Argyll's prime recruiting area of Argyllshire, rather than being dissipated to the south-west of England. The council therefore persuaded Argyll to visit the Lowlands by sea, rather than risking making the journey by land and encountering Atholl's men. However, in the event, the plans were changed the following day and they crossed to the Isle of Bute instead, which proved to be a futile exercise and wasted three days.

Some of his officers, still thought they should head to the Lowlands, while Argyll was insistent that they deal with Atholl first, in order to make recruitment easier. A compromise was reached which involved Cochrane marching to Renfrewshire with 200 men. They routed a troop of militia near Greenock, but failed to raise much support, and upon his return, Cochrane concurred with Argyll's view of dealing with Atholl first.

Argyll then moved northwards to confront Atholl and utilised the old castle of Eilean Dearg at Loch Riddon as his base, which he strengthened by the addition of more earthworks. He also sent one of his commanders, Rumbold, with a detatchment of infantry and cavalry to hold Glendaruel, a town through which the River Ruel flows before it goes into Loch Riddon. He also brought Ardinglas Castle near Inverary under his control.

On 11 June 1685, the same day that Monmouth did finally land in Dorset, the council decided to begin a march to the Lowlands, leaving Elphinstone of Lapness in charge of the garrison at the old castle of Eilean Dearg. The castle promptly came under attack from a Royal Navy Squadron, which consisted of the frigates *Kingfisher*, *Falcon* and *Mermaid*, meaning that Elphinstone was forced to abandon the fort, along with the supplies and the hostages they had taken in Orkney, who subsequently took the opportunity to rejoin their comrades near Loch Long.

News of this calamity, allied to the fruitless recruitment mission to the Lowlands and combined with Argyll's inexperience as a commander, led to disagreements amongst the rebel leaders. This had a deleterious effect on morale and resulted in the desertion of many of the rebels, reducing them to less than 1,000 men. They also began to run low on supplies, and to add to their problems, Atholl was hot on their tails in pursuit. However, they knew that the Earl of Dumbarton was waiting with reinforcements near the strongly Whig city of Glasgow, so they headed there.

Before reaching Glasgow, the leaders held a council of war; Argyll still favoured forcing a single pitched battle, while Patrick Hume, one of the senior commanders, suggested that the rebels should split into three groups. He suggested that those from Argyllshire should return to the Highlands via Glencoe, while the Lowlanders and Dutch volunteers should make their way along the Gare Loch and Loch Long in two groups.

Those returning via Glencoe were involved in a catastrophic night march on 17 June 1685, which resulted in the scattering of the remaining forces through desertion, despite Rumbold and Argyll's efforts to keep them together. Argyll and Cochrane then had a discussion at an inn in the village of Kilpatrick, which ended in bitter recrimination and the two going their separate ways. Argyll set off with a group of companions, but was eventually captured and taken prisoner whilst fording a river with Major Fullerton. Meanwhile, Campbell of Auchinbreck continued to Argyllshire to attempt to raise further men, while rebel leaders John Cochrane, Patrick Hume and Major James Henderson crossed the River Clyde near Old Kilpatrick with about 150 men. Presently, their numbers were further reduced after a skirmish with local militia and further desertions. Consequently, a much-diminished group of less than a hundred reached Muirdykes, near Lochwinnoch, on the afternoon of 18 June 1685, where they were confronted by a group of Royalist dragoons led by Cochrane's relative William Lord Ross at the Battle of Muirdykes.

Cochrane refused the quarter that was offered by Ross and managed to hold the position until night-time when they established that the dragoons had moved on. However, on 20 June 1685 Cochrane learned that Argyll had been captured, which prompted him to liberate his remaining clansmen, advising them to make good their escape as best they could. Cochrane and his fellow officers also tried to escape but were all captured within a week and taken prisoner.

Argyll was already a wanted man and had been sentenced for treason before the rising, so after his capture he was summarily beheaded, on 30 June 1685. Whilst awaiting execution, Argyll, showed great fortitude and bravery and petitioned on behalf of his clansmen, who he argued should not be punished for their involvement as they had no choice in the matter. Prior to Argyll's execution, Rumbold was also quickly tried, convicted and executed on 26 June 1685, in case he died of his wounds first. Argyll, who criticised both Hume and Cochrane in his final correspondence, wrote: 'poor Rumbold was a great support to me and a brave man who died Christianly'. Rumbold's speech, which was delivered whilst standing on the scaffold, was printed and became popular as it included the phrase, 'None comes into this world with a saddle on his back, neither any booted and spurred to ride him.'

Ayloffe's family connections secured him an interview with James, who reminded the prisoner that he had the power to pardon. Ayloffe was said to have responded, 'It is in your power, but not in your nature to pardon.' He was subsequently executed on 30 October 1685 at the Inner Temple in London, along with Richard Nelthorpe, a fellow Rye House conspirator.

Cochrane was also granted an interview with James and is said to have saved himself by agreeing to pay a fine of £5,000. Some other prominent rebels were pardoned, among them Argyll's nephew Archibald, who went on to become Bishop of Aberdeen, while many others, including Duncan Campbell of Auchinbreck, fled to the Netherlands, only to return during the Glorious Revolution of 1688, whereupon he found that Stewart Royalist Maclean clansmen had destroyed Carnasserie Castle, stolen 2,000 head of cattle, hanged his relative Dugold MacTavish of Dunardy, and murdered his uncle, Alexander Campbell of Strondour.

Most of the rebel rank and file were transported to the colonies, as were hundreds of Covenanters, who were already in prison from earlier Covenanter battles and who had not played any part in the Argyll Rising. However, the Argyll Rising was generally punished less savagely than the Monmouth Rebellion, as it was appreciated that many of Argyll's men were feudally obliged to follow their clan chief. Also, of course, Judge Jeffreys was not involved in those trials.

As with the Monmouth Rebellion, many of those involved in Argyll's Rising lived to fight another day when they became involved in the Glorious Revolution a few years later.

The Monmouth Rebellion and the Bloody Assizes

The task force detailed to land in the south-west of England, including Monmouth himself on the thirty-two-gun frigate named *Helderenburg*, landed at dusk on 11 June 1685 on a shingle beach to the west of Lyme Regis in Dorset.[2] Lyme Regis was considered a suitable spot to land, as it would allow the rebels a considerable head start before King James II's Royal army could be mobilised from London. It was also considered near enough to the Netherlands to reduce the risk of the Royal Navy intercepting the convoy, and was not too far from the initial target of Bristol.

Upon landing, Monmouth raised his standard, which consisted of a green banner with the words 'Fear nothing but God' emblazoned on it in gold. He announced that he had come to defend the Protestant religion and to deliver the country from Catholicism and the tyranny of James II. He also promised freedom of worship to Non-Conformists and Anglican Protestants. The entire party then sank to their knees in prayer. As this was happening, two Lyme Regis customs officials informed the mayor, Gregory Alford, who galloped to London to inform the MP for Lyme Regis, Sir Winston Churchill (an ancestor of the Second World War leader), who in turn informed King James II. On the king's command, John Churchill, the future Duke of Marlborough (the Lyme MP Winston's son), began to mobilise his troops. Meanwhile, Louis de Duras, 2nd Earl of Feversham, was put in overall charge of the royal campaign and his plan was to coordinate the various army units available and assemble them in Bristol, whilst Churchill and his troops shadowed Monmouth.

Monmouth found a fertile recruiting ground among the Non-Conformist populations of West Dorset, East Devon, and particularly Somerset. Within Somerset, Taunton was a great centre of Non-Conformist dissention, resulting in the streets being strewn with flowers as Monmouth and his rebels were accorded a hero's welcome. Monmouth had previously declared himself king at Lyme Regis, Axminster, Chard and Ilminster, but in Taunton the 'coronation' was a bit more ostentatious, as the rebels acted out a charade in which Monmouth was crowned in the Market Cross area. The ceremony had the desired effect as enough volunteers joined to form a whole new regiment.

Monmouth also received a welcome from the 'Maids of Taunton', as they became known. They were twenty-seven schoolgirls who presented the soldiers with flags in Monmouth's colours. Their teachers, Mary Blake and Mrs Musgrave also presented Monmouth with a sword and a Bible.[3]

Monmouth and his band of rebels were eventually cornered by Royalist forces in an area of Somerset known as the Levels or the Plain of Sedgemoor, a low-lying, marshy region stretching from the Mendips to Taunton and Ilminster. The precise location was north-west of the village of Westonzoyland, in an area known as Langmoor.

The Rebel army were camped at Bridgewater on 3 July 1685, when a farm worker by the name of Richard Godfrey came forward to tell King Monmouth that James II's forces were encamped at Westonzoyland, less than four miles away.[4]

Using Godfrey's local knowledge[5], Monmouth's rebels marched in complete silence out of Bridgewater, along what is now the Bath Road to Bradney, where they turned and made their way through numerous country lanes avoiding royal patrols, eventually arriving in the vicinity of Westonzoyland. As a decoy, Monmouth had also sent a baggage convoy north towards Bristol.

At 1am Monmouth did what his enemy would least expect and launched his attack across the boggy marshes. Godfrey again acted as a guide leading the rebels through the treacherous marshy terrain and rhines (large open drainage ditches). Unfortunately, he lost his bearings in the mist and darkness at Langmoor Rhine, meaning that he then led them to a part of the Great Bussex Rhine, which was too deep to ford, having missed the Upper Plungeon (crossing point).

After some time he did find the plungeon, but then further disaster struck as a pistol shot rang out, betraying their presence to King James' troops. Treachery may have been a factor here, and some pointed the finger at Rebel captain John Hucker, a sergemaker from Taunton. However, it seems more likely that the shot was from a Royalist sentry who had spotted them approaching in the dark. Hucker certainly didn't receive any special favours from the Royal army and was imprisoned and executed after the battle, along with many other rebels.

Once the pistol shot rang out, a royal trooper (possibly the one who fired the shot) rode up and down the Bussex Rhine shouting 'Beat your drums; the enemy has come. For the Lord's sake beat your drums.'

Lord Grey led his cavalry forward, realising that he now had to improvise in order to maintain some element of surprise. However, the untried Rebel cavalry, astride panicky, inexperienced horses, struggled to breach the Upper Plungeon. Another Rebel cavalry section had been detailed to get to the Lower Plungeon, but they were met with a hail of musket fire as they rode alongside the rhine. Meanwhile, a detatchment of Royal cavalry returned from a patrol and joined the battle. They were ordered to outflank the rebels, whilst the dragoons performed the same manoeuvre on the other side.

The Rebel cavalry fled the field in disarray, charging through their own oncoming infantry in the process. This caused the infantry to arrive at the rhine in chaotic disorder, meaning they had to wait and form up before they could mount an attack. This in turn allowed the Royal artillery time to get their big guns into position and bring them to bear on the rebels.

In five hours, the last major battle to occur on English soil was over; 1,384 rebels had died on the battlefield, whereas only ninety were killed from the Royal army. A thousand more rebels were killed as they fled; others were rounded up, and many were shot or hung indiscriminately in cold blood. Colonel Kirke of the Royal army, who had served with distinction at Tangiers, and the soldiers under his command, who were known as his 'lambs', were responsible for many of the atrocities and brought great disgrace upon themselves.

The Royalist dead were buried in the churchyard of St Mary the Virgin in Westonzoyland, and 500 Rebel prisoners were also temporarily held in the church; twenty-two of whom received summary executions the next day. One prisoner managed to escape, and five died of their wounds.

Monmouth showed great courage during the battle, but when defeat was inevitable he took flight as the last of the battle raged on. He fled on horseback into the Polden Hills, before changing direction at Shepton Mallet and heading south into Dorset in an attempt to get to Poole, where he planned to board a ship to the Continent. As he attempted to escape, notices were posted all over the countryside offering a sizeable reward for his capture, as the area quickly filled with troops.

Initially, Monmouth was with three companions, but the group had to leave their exhausted horses behind at Woodyates on Cranborne Chase,

Dorset, where they disguised themselves as shepherds, split into two groups and continued on foot.

Lord Grey and Richard Hollyday were caught near Holt, Dorset, in the early hours of 7 July 1685. Meanwhile, the Rebel leader, Monmouth, and his German companion named Buyse fled across Horton Heath.

On 8 July 1685 an old lady by the name of Amy Farrant spotted the fugitives climbing through a hedge and alerted the soldiers to their hiding place. Buyse was apprehended and then soon after another exhausted wretch was found hiding in the bracken underneath an ash tree in a pea field. He was dishevelled and hungry, and dressed in shepherd's clothing. On searching him, the Dorset militiaman Henry Parkin soon realised this was no shepherd, when he found a badge of the Knight of the Garter and several gold guineas. The spot in which the duke was captured is still known as Monmouth's Ash, although the actual tree has long since gone. It was near Slough Lane in Horton, Dorset. There is a farm nearby called Monmouth Ash Farm, as well as a pub in nearby Verwood called the Monmouth Ash.

As Monmouth was being led away, he reputedly spotted the old woman who had betrayed him and shouted to her, 'I hope you die a lousy death.' Legend has it that she did die shortly afterwards of louse, and the lane was named Louse Lane, later corrupted to Slough Lane.

Monmouth was taken to be identified by the nearest magistrate, Anthony Ettrick of Holt Lodge, who was the recorder of the Borough of Poole. Ettrick ordered him to be taken to the Tower of London. En route to London, Monmouth and the other captives were first taken to Ringwood, Hampshire, where Monmouth pleaded on his knees for clemency from his uncle, James II. Monmouth's pleading fell on death ears. No royal pardon was forthcoming, and James duly signed his nephew's death warrant. Monmouth was then escorted from Ringwood to the Tower of London to be executed.

By now resigned to his fate, Monmouth met his end on 15 July 1685, with the same bravery as his grandfather, Charles I, had shown thirty-six years earlier at the same venue of Tower Hill. As a nobleman, the duke was entitled to be executed by beheading, rather than the more barbaric hanging, drawing and quartering. However, he suffered terribly as a blunt axe was wielded by an unskilled executioner by the name of Jack Ketch.

As he approached the execution block, Monmouth reportedly said to Ketch, 'Here are six guineas for you not to hack me as you did my Lord Russell. I heard you struck him four times. If you strike me twice, I cannot promise not to stir.' Lord Russell was a Rye House plotter who unwisely didn't flee to the Netherlands as the others did when the plot was discovered, which meant he faced execution at home. However, Ketch's botched job on Lord Russell was nothing to what the poor, unfortunate Monmouth had in store.

The first blow bounced off leaving only a slight wound. This caused the duke to rise from the block and fix Ketch with an accusing stare. The watching throngs were mortified and growing agitated as several more strikes failed to finish the job. At one point Ketch is said to have flung the axe down in an anxious state, saying, 'I cannot do it, my heart fails me.' Several more strikes were required before poor Monmouth died, and even then his head had to be cut from his body with a knife.

This was only the beginning of the reprisals. The western counties were to suffer severe consequences for the failed rebellion, as James II set up a special commission to conduct the Assizes in the south-west of England. The commission was overseen by Judge Jeffreys, and also included Chief Baron Sir William Montague, Sir Robert Wright of the Exchequer, Sir Francis Wythens for the King's Bench and Sir Cresswell Levinz of the Common Pleas. Such a large commission was needed because of the sheer volume of prisoners awaiting trial.

At the age of forty, Jeffreys was the youngest and most brutal Lord Chief Justice of England, and his malicious conduct in dealing with the Rye House plotters had made him a firm favourite with King James II. He had gained a deserved reputation for cruelty, which, allied to his barbaric behavior at the Bloody Assizes, was soon to give him the nickname of the 'Hanging Judge'. He was a Protestant himself, and it was as though he felt he had to overcompensate in showing that he had no sympathy with the rebellion as he toadied up to the Catholic King James II.

Town and village officials were required to provide a list of all those who had been absent from their homes during the rebellion, and in most cases this was the only evidence on which the prosecutions were based. Those thought to be involved in the rebellion were sentenced for high treason, for which the penalty was death; and in the case of a commoner, the method of execution was to be hanged, drawn and quartered. This involved being fastened to a hurdle and dragged by a horse to the place of execution, where he was then hanged almost to the point of death. The victim then had his genitals cut off, before being slit from the breast bone to the groin, whereupon his entrails were pulled out, and then burnt in front of him. Next he was beheaded, and then quartered – chopped into four pieces. The pieces were then put on public display in prominent places.[6] For reasons of public decency, the punishment for high treason for women was to be burnt at the stake.

In some instances, transportation was granted as mitigation. This was usually to work as a slave on the sugar plantations of the West Indies, and was tantamount to a death sentence anyway. James soon realised that a considerable income for the treasury could be raised by selling the convicts to middle men, who then shipped them to the West Indies sugar plantations for profit. Some prisoners were kept by King James so that he could profit directly from their sale, while others were given as gifts to his favourites so they could profit. Many didn't survive the six-week voyage, as they were kept in cramped conditions under the deck of cargo ships not designed for this purpose. There was no room to lie down, and contagious diseases were rife.

In theory, once the slaves had served a ten-year sentence they were free to return to England, but very few were actually able to do so. However, when William and Mary came to the throne they issued a general pardon and those who did manage to return reported the horrors of slavery. It is no coincidence that Bridgewater in Somerset, from where many were transported, was the first English town to petition Parliament for the abolition of slavery in 1785.

The Assizes started at Winchester on 25 August 1685, where only one prisoner was on trial –Lady Alice Lisle, a frail, elderly woman. Alice was an heiress, who, in 1636, married staunch Civil War Parliamentarian John Lisle. He was a trusted aide of Cromwell and was heavily involved in the trial and execution of King Charles I.

After Cromwell's death, and the restoration of the monarchy in the form of King Charles II, Lisle was a marked man. He escaped to the Continent, but was tracked down by Royalist assassins and murdered in Lausanne, Switzerland, in 1664. Alice, meanwhile, lived comfortably at Moyles Court (now a private school), in the New Forest near Ringwood.

She was said to be a Royalist herself, and not easily reconciled to her husband's part in the execution of King Charles I.

In 1685 a man she knew called John Hicks arrived at the door of Moyles Court, along with a friend, Richard Nelthorpe. John Hicks was a firebrand Presbyterian minister and Nelthorpe was a wanted man for his involvement in the Rye House plot. Alice was arrested shortly afterwards and charged with high treason for harbouring fugitives. In court, she insisted that she didn't know of their involvement in the Monmouth Rebellion, or that they were on the run from Sedgemoor, and, despite the haranguing of Jeffreys, the jury found her not guilty.

However, Jeffreys had already decided she was guilty before proceedings had even begun. He was determined to make a shocking example of her and set the tone for the rest of the Assizes. He was incandescent with rage and sent them out to reconsider. The jury reconsidered and duly brought in a verdict of not guilty a second time. This sent Jeffreys into absolute apoplexy. He berated the jury, and then, in what must surely be one of the most disgraceful examples of gross misconduct ever seen in a British court, he forced them on the third occasion to find her guilty by threatening them with a charge of treason if they didn't comply. Sure enough, they did comply this time and Jeffreys sentenced her to be burned at the stake. She pleaded with the king for mercy, and the sentence was commuted to beheading, as befitted her social status.

Her execution took place on 2 September 1685 in the square at Winchester, between the Buttercross and the cathedral, where Alice spent her last night in an upper room before stepping out of the large window onto a specially constructed scaffold. The historic building has been the Eclipse Inn since the early 1800s, so called as it eclipsed a nearby inn at the time called the Sun. She duly became the last woman to be beheaded in England. She was dispatched by the executioner Jack Ketch, who fortunately managed to do a better job than he did on Monmouth.

Hicks was also later beheaded at Glastonbury on 6 October 1685, along with four others, while Richard Nelthorpe was executed at Inner Temple, London, along with John Ayloffe, who was involved in Argyll's Rising as a colonel of one of Argyll's four cavalry regiments.

It is said that the swooshing sound of Alice's silk dress and the tapping of her heels are still occasionally heard around the corridors of Moyles Court School, and it is also said that a spectral driverless coach, pulled by headless horses, can sometimes be seen passing through the adjacent Ellingham Drove. Some also say that her ghost, in the form of an apparition of an elegant lady in grey, haunts the Eclipse Inn, Winchester, where she was beheaded.

Similar travesties occurred throughout the trials, but the Assizes really became the Bloody Assizes at Dorchester and beyond, as they became even more savage and barbaric. There was no leniency, as adults of either sex, or children as young as ten were beheaded or transported.

Jeffreys set out his stall before the trials began when he ordered the erection of gallows in the most prominent position in the centre of Dorchester, thus creating a sinister symbol to deter people from treasonable thoughts of defying the king. He similarly ordered the Oak Room of the Dorchester Assize Court to be adorned with red, symbolising blood, to further set the tone and provide a grim reminder of what lay in store for the prisoners. The painful kidney stones he was suffering from at the time certainly didn't help his mood.

The rooms where Judge Jeffreys lodged during the Bloody Assizes, at 6 High West Street in Dorchester, are now the Judge Jeffreys Restaurant and Coffee House, which is one of the oldest buildings in the town, dating to at least 1398. Jeffreys is said to have used a secret underground passageway to travel between his lodgings and the courtroom. Apparently the tunnel was sufficiently large for three people to walk side by side.

Jeffreys stated, as he also did at other trials, 'that if any pleaded not guilty, and were subsequently found to be guilty, they would not have long to live; and that, if any expected favour they should plead guilty.' Many prisoners had seen enough of him not to trust him to honour his word, or show any leniency. Indeed, those that did plead guilty, expecting mercy, received none.

In Dorchester Judge Jeffreys sentenced 313 rebels to receive the death penalty, although in the end only sixty-five actually received that sentence. This was mainly because the executioners, Mr Ketch and his assistant, Pascha Rose, were struggling, as the hanging, drawing and quartering was a time-consuming process and they complained that they could only cope with thirteen a day.

As a result, Jeffreys agreed that thirteen should be dealt with in Dorchester and the rest should be farmed out in batches to other towns in Dorset, namely Bridport, Weymouth, Poole and Wareham.

He also reluctantly agreed that it would be more expedient to commute many of the sentences to lesser punishments. In the event, 166 were transported to the West Indies as slaves, fifty-five were pardoned and nine were publicly whipped.

Another issue was that the number of prisoners being dealt with and awaiting trial resulted in Dorchester gaol being full to capacity, so All Saints Church was used to take up the slack. As a result, the building was severely damaged and also had to be fumigated afterwards due to an outbreak of smallpox and fever among the prisoners.

Some shocking travesties of justice and dastardly foul play occurred, one of which involved William Bragg, who was a lawyer by profession. He wasn't a Monmouth rebel, but his horse was stolen by Monmouth's men and he had been seen entering their camp in order to reclaim it. Whilst trying to explain his case in court to Jeffreys, he was cut short by the enraged judge, who simply said, 'He is a lawyer, so hang him.'

Later that evening, after presiding over many further appalling miscarriages of justice, it is said that Jeffreys persuaded a young girl to share his bed on the promise that doing so would ensure her brother's freedom. The poor girl awoke the next morning to the sight of her brother swinging from the gallows.

Local Dorchester legend has it that the very same morning, a Sunday, Judge Jeffreys attended service at St Peter's Church opposite his lodgings, and when the vicar extolled the virtues of clemency, Jeffreys could barely contain his mirth. During and after the Bloody Assizes the same church's railings came to be adorned with many severed heads placed on the spikes. The same church also features in several of Thomas Hardy's novels.

Lord Grey, the officer in charge of the Rebel cavalry, was sentenced to be whipped through Dorchester on market day, and then to receive the same punishment on market day in Shaftsbury. Others were whipped through all the towns of Dorset.

A Dorset phenomenon that is believed to be associated with the Bloody Assizes is the Dorset Red Post – the red signifying blood. They are believed to be sites of gallows, and are also thought to have doubled up as gibbets, where Judge Jeffreys ordered body parts from those that were hanged drawn and quartered to be put on public display.

Many believe that these gallows had another use in speeding up the columns of prisoners being forced marched to ports for transportation. This was achieved by simply hanging those who lagged behind. Some believe that the red posts also acted as route markers for the illiterate guards to escort convicts to the transport ships in Poole, Weymouth and elsewhere.

The red post on the A31 close to Bloxworth and Anderson in Dorset, about fourteen miles from Dorchester, is near what was Botany Bay Farm. It possessed a barn complete with shackles on the walls and was used as an overnight holding bay for prisoners en route to Poole for transportation. The building has long since been destroyed and an agricultural machinery depot is now at the same site.

In many instances, those of higher social status received less severe punishment. In the case of Lord Grey, his wealth was in life estate, which meant if he died, his land went to his heir, whereas if he were pardoned he would be able to pay a large ransom. Jeffreys extorted £40,000 from him, in return for the more lenient sentence of a public whipping as opposed to the death penalty.

On 15 September 1685 the Bloody Assizes horror show moved onto the Great Hall of Taunton Castle, where the highly venerated judge may have been influenced by the fact that Taunton had been a thorn in the Royalist side during the First English Civil War. The town was a major centre for Puritanism, and was under siege on three occasions due to its pivotal position in the West Country. The final siege was a major factor in the Parliamentary victory as 10–15,000 Royalist troops that would otherwise have fought at the decisive Battle of Naseby in 1645 were tied up here.

At the Taunton Bloody Assizes 514 rebels were tried and 144 were sentenced to be hanged, drawn and quartered. This gruesome process was performed throughout Somerset, but mainly at Porlock, Minehead, Crewkerne, Yeovil, Chewton Mendip and Castle Cary. More would have received this punishment had the king not issued a directive to Jeffreys that he wanted 1,000 rebels for transportation, so the remaining 370 were transported instead.

The Taunton Maids and their teachers, whose crime was to present Monmouth with a sword and a Bible, were languishing in prison awaiting their fate when Colonel Kirke, of the Battle of Sedgemoor infamy, arrived on the scene and informed their parents that he was prepared to save the girls from transportation and grant the freedom of any maid whose family could pay the large ransom of £20. He explained that Jeffreys charged a great deal more and the king most of all. The Taunton Maids escaped transportation, but their teacher, Mary Blake, died from smallpox in Dorchester gaol.

After the Bloody Assizes, Jeffreys was heard to boast that he had 'banged' more than all of the judges of England since William the Conqueror. Indeed, by the time he had finished, just about every thoroughfare in the West Country was lined with body parts, ensuring that his terrible legacy remained for many years. James II was impressed and rewarded Jeffreys for his sterling work with a promotion to the office of Lord Chancellor.

History lays the blame of the Bloody Assizes at the door of Judge Jeffreys, although in truth, James II should also take a large portion of the blame. One could say that Jeffreys was merely enforcing the king's wishes, though he certainly seemed to take great delight in doing so, and knew on which side his bread was buttered.

The Glorious Revolution 1688

Having crushed the Argyll and Monmouth Rebellions, James II was in a position to consolidate his power, and restore Catholicism as the nation's premier religion. He did not receive support from Parliament for these measures, but went ahead regardless, and to ensure his policies were adopted, he installed a menacing army of 13,000 troops lying in wait on Hounslow Heath on the outskirts of London.

Judge Jeffreys became James's henchman once more, and was president of the notorious Ecclesiastical Commission of 1686, which had jurisdiction over the governance of the Church of England and was empowered to punish any offences under the act.

In 1686 James placed Catholic clergy in prominent positions, particularly in Ireland, and then in 1688 instigated the Declaration of Indulgence, which allowed greater religious tolerance, and also suppressed all laws against Catholic freedom of worship. This may have been an act of benevolence, but many believed that James's real objective was to promote Catholicism, and simultaneously crush dissenters to the Catholic religion in the same fashion that Louis XIV had done in France.

James faced opposition from seven influential bishops, including the Bishop of London. As a result, the Ecclesiastical Commission under Jeffreys ordered the bishops to be sent to the Tower of London, where they were locked up in a single room. One of the bishops was the influential Cornishman Trelawney, who was the Bishop of Bristol at the time. His arrest caused quite a stir in Cornwall, and was the subject of the folk song and Cornish anthem, *the Song of the Western Men*, penned a couple of centuries later by another influential Cornishman, the Rev Hawker. It includes the iconic words 'and shall Trelawney die? Here's twenty thousand Cornishmen will know the reason why'. Upon his acquittal, and that of the other bishops, there were great celebrations as church bells were rung throughout the county of Cornwall.

The brutality, severity and unfairness of the proceedings at the Bloody Assizes had shocked and antagonised the whole of the country. James II's rule was becoming increasingly tyrannical and this, allied to his attempts to turn the nation into a kind of Catholic military dictatorship, were beginning to cause widespread alarm. Monmouth and Argyll came to be seen as noble martyrs for the Protestant cause and James' Protestant opponents began planning once more to remove the king.

The situation came to a head when the public's resigned tolerance towards the monarch and his Catholicism changed dramatically in June 1688, when Mary of Modena gave birth to a baby boy, James Francis Edward Stuart, who would obviously be brought up in the Catholic faith and who would succeed James to the throne, meaning there would be a long line of Catholic monarchs. Rumours abounded that the baby was, in fact, a 'changeling'; i.e., a baby secreted into the bed to give the impression that Mary had just given birth to him.[7]

This situation led to a meeting at Charborough House, near Sturminster Marshall, Dorset, the result of which was that seven leading statesmen and Protestant campaigners, including the Bishop of London, approached Mary, James II's Protestant daughter, to see if she was willing to take the throne in the event of her father being forced to abdicate.

Mary was born at St James' Palace on 30 April 1662 and was the eldest daughter and second child of James II and his first wife, Anne Hyde. Her mother had eight children, but only Mary and her younger sister, Anne, survived. As her uncle, Charles II, had no legitimate children, that left Mary as second in line for the throne behind her father, James II, unless a male heir was produced by her father.

At King Charles II's behest, both Mary and Anne were brought up in the Anglican Protestant faith, despite their parent's conversion to Catholicism. Then, at the age of fifteen, on 4 November 1677, Mary was married to William of Orange, her cousin, in a private ceremony at St James' Palace. She was initially against the liaison and was not keen to leave England for the Netherlands, but the marriage turned out well.

Mary agreed to become queen, on condition that her husband and cousin, William, would rule alongside her as a joint monarch. This was considered to be a suitable option, as King William of Orange was the Stadtholder of the Netherlands, and the grandson of Charles I. He was also known as a champion of the Protestant faith, having prevented King Louis XIV taking over the Netherlands during the Franco-Dutch War of 1672–1678.

The next stage of the plan involved an influential group of parliamentary ministers drawing up a Declaration of Rights, which accused James II of unconstitutional behaviour. At the same time, both William and Mary were invited to come to England from the Netherlands. This was termed the Glorious Revolution – in effect a coup d'état.

William's fleet was aided by a 'Protestant wind' from the east, which hastened progress towards the Devon coast. The same wind also had the effect of preventing James' fleet from getting out of the Thames Estuary. The captain of the *Den Briel*, on which William was aboard, carefully made his way into Torbay, not knowing quite what to expect, especially as the bouys marking the navigational channels had been removed by order of James II. However, William landed safely at Brixham, Devon, on 5 November 1688, unopposed, with an army of Dutch and English soldiers.

Having learned from the Monmouth Rebellion that it was unwise to arrive with a small force and hope that the population would be able to rise up, William arrived with a substantial force of 30,000 disciplined, professional troops, and such a large supply of equipment and supplies that it took two days to unload. William had made far better preparation for the assault than Monmouth, and a key factor in his success was the timing. He had waited for an invitation, and for a time when powerful men were prepared to provide backing.

From Brixham, William and his army marched to Exeter, where he wowed the residents with a ceremonial parade that was greeted with great enthusiasm and had the desired effect of both encouraging his supporters and winning round his doubters. He then stayed in the deanery of Exeter Cathedral for twelve days and took stock of the situation, whilst waiting for the political situation to become clearer. Initially, the response from the West Country had been a little subdued, as the population were still cowed from the excesses of the Bloody Assizes. However, the slight delay in the proceedings allowed time for various influential figures and leading politicians to join the cause. This is what Monmouth had hoped for, but was unable to achieve.

When William of Orange moved on to Taunton the response was anything but subdued. Daniel Defoe of Robinson Crusoe fame, who was involved in the Monmouth Rebellion himself, wrote: 'They suffered deeply in the Duke of Monmouth Rebellion, but paid King James home for the cruelty exercised by Jeffreys; for when the Prince of Orange arrived, the whole town ran to him with universal joy that twas thought if he wanted it, he might have raised a little army there and in the adjacent part of the country.'

William's army then advanced to Sherborne Castle in Dorset, where he was entertained, and where he issued a proclamation insisting that he came as a liberator not a conqueror. He was anxious that the coup would be popular and bloodless. Again, this is what Monmouth wanted, but was unable to achieve.

William of Orange's army then advanced towards Salisbury, where he was on a collision course with James II, who was also on his way to Salisbury Plain at the head of his Royal army, blissfully unaware that most of his officers were intent on changing sides. Once at Salisbury, James, an experienced soldier of some repute, suffered a terrible nosebleed, which prevented him from riding to Warminster to rally the rest of the troops. In modern terms this would probably be termed as a nervous breakdown.

Later, on Salisbury Plain, James II's army, under the command of John Churchill, pulled the proverbial rug from under the monarch's feet by coming onto the side of William and Mary. This was the same John

Churchill who was James's most experienced general and had fought for him against the Duke of Monmouth only three years earlier.

William then advanced towards London as an unstoppable force, with the country behind him. Meanwhile, James and his supporters were in despair. He was also deeply saddened by the defection of two of his own children, Mary and Anne. He made arrangements for his infant son, James Francis Edward Stuart, to move to exile in France, and then decided he too must go. He made a failed attempt to escape on 11 December 1688, but finally fled to exile in France on 22 December 1688. As he fled by barge from London, he made an attempt to make government without him impossible by throwing the Royal Seal into the Thames, so that Parliament could no longer be summoned in his name.

William and Mary, and Mary's sister, Anne, who was constitutionally intended as the Protestant heir, were then formally offered the crown, and the subsequent coronation, on 11 April 1689, was a truly momentous occasion, and heralded a new dawn in the history of the English constitution. In return for the crown, William and Mary were invited by Parliament to sign a Declaration of Rights which set out the personal and political rights of their subjects – a kind of second Magna Carta. The main points of the declaration were:

1. The monarchy must be Protestant
2. A new parliament must be formed regularly
3. There can be no standing army without parliamentary permission
4. Parliament can regulate the monarch's expenditure.

These measures established England as a constitutional monarchy, in which the edict of the 'Divine Right of Kings' had been removed, although the monarch remained the leading power in the land and still had the power to veto new laws suggested by Parliament. However, William did establish that he would not be bound to ruling through Mary, and that if that wasn't acceptable then he would return to the Netherlands.

In the meantime, Judge Jeffreys was captured trying to flee to the Continent and saw the last of his days out ignominiously in the Tower of London. It was unfortunate, given his history, that his passing away should be a natural death. However, his last four months were racked with pain due to his kidney stones, so some sort of natural justice did prevail.

The memories of Monmouth's Rebellion, and the bitter retribution meted out to his followers, helped people to warm to the only couple in British history to reign as joint monarchs. However, William gave the impression that he was more interested in the Netherlands than England. He lived in the Netherlands for long periods of the year and plied his Dutch cronies with wealth. He also spent long periods of his reign in Ireland fighting the Williamite Wars. His main foreign policy was to wage war with Catholic France, which, many felt, benefited the Netherlands more than England, and as a result, the high taxation required to pursue the war was greatly resented. In fact, King William's opposition to the Catholic regime of King Louis XIV in France marked the beginning of a series of conflicts, which historians often refer to as the 'Second Hundred Years War' with France (though it should really have been called the 126 years war as it was between 1689 and 1815).

* * *

England had now become a major player on the European stage. William being King of England had given the Netherlands a big advantage in the pan-European struggle between the Netherlands and France, much to the chagrin of King Louis XIV (R 1638–1715), who refused to recognise him as King of England and still insisted that the Catholic, James II was the rightful king.

King Louis XIV provided a constant threat from across the Channel and was a constant thorn in William and Mary's – and, indeed, in most of Europe's – side. He was King James II's cousin and ruled France for seventy-two years as a despot. He was an enthusiastic adherent of the 'Divine right of Kings' and an avid advocate and enforcer of the Catholic Religion. He greatly expanded France's empire through military power and annexation, and in his own country, French Protestants had a stark choice of either converting to Catholicism or emigrating.

After the Franco-Dutch War, France emerged as the leading power in Europe and King Louis as the most powerful monarch. During his long reign, France was involved in four major wars: The War of Devolution, fought to lay claim to the Spanish Netherlands in 1667–1668; The Franco Dutch War – 1672–1678; The Nine Years War, also known as the War of the Grand Alliance or War of the League of Augsburg – 1688–1697; The War of the Spanish Succession – 1701–1714.

As we have already seen, there wasn't a lot of religious tolerance around in these times, but one beneficial aspect of William and Mary's reign was the passing of the Toleration Act of 1689, which allowed Non-Conformist religions to have licensed chapels, and also allowed freedom of worship for Catholics. Meanwhile, in Scotland during this period, the Kirk readopted a Presbyterian structure, which is generally taken as marking the end of the mainstream Covenanter movement.

During the joint monarchs' reign, Mary had frequently found herself ruling alone in England whilst William was away on military operations. However, in his absence she proved herself to be a confident and effective leader, and by the time of her death, at the age of thirty-two, from smallpox, on 28 December 1694, she had certainly won the hearts of the people with her pleasant personality.

By 1680, as far as the French were concerned, everything King Louis XIV touched turned to gold, and his great military victories and the resultant expansion of the French Empire saw him revered as the 'Sun King' or 'Louis the Great'. However, the threat posed by the French superpower resulted in the other main powers forming an alliance when King Louis XIV attempted to extend his borders beyond the Rhine. The Nine Years War, also known as the War of the Grand Alliance or the War of the League of Augsberg (1688–1697), was subsequently triggered. It was a conflict between King Louis XIV's France and a European Alliance of the Holy Roman Empire, led by Austria, but also included the Dutch Republic, Spain, England and Savoy, in what was a powerful coalition.

The main fighting took place around France's borders in the Spanish Netherlands (modern-day Belgium), but also in the Duchy of Savoy (now part of France, but including parts of modern-day France, Italy and Switzerland), the Rhineland and Catalonia (now part of Spain). The war also encompassed the Williamite Wars in Ireland, a Jacobite Rising in Scotland, and Queen Anne's War in North America.

The exiled James II and his supporters had not gone away and still intended to win back the throne. Jacobite support came mainly from the Highlands of Scotland, Ireland and France. Many non-Catholics in Scotland also became Jacobites as many believed that the Stuarts were the rightful heirs to the throne. They also believed that as James was part of the native Stuart dynasty which had ruled Scotland for over 300 years it was not for Parliament to interfere with that succession. However, for most Jacobite Highland clansmen it was simply clan loyalties that tipped the scales. If a Scottish clan chief was a Jacobite, his clansmen were obligated to follow him into battle as they were effectively tenants of the chief and in lieu of paying rent acted as his own private army. Moreover, severe retribution often followed if clansmen failed to follow their chief into battle.

Another factor in the mix was that the deposing and exile of James II also had an effect on the churches of England, Scotland and Ireland. Clergy were mandated to swear an oath of allegiance to William and Mary as a stipulation of office, and those who refused to do so were known as Nonjuring, from the Latin verb *juro* meaning to swear an oath. The resultant split in the church became known as the 'NonJuring Schism'. Also, among James II's allies in England were high-placed Catholics and members of the Tory party, who believed that the line of succession of the crown shouldn't be interfered with.

However, it was Ireland where James and his supporters turned their attention to first, and within a month of William and Mary's coronation James initiated the Williamite Wars (1689–1691). A month later, the first Scottish rising was launched in support of the Williamite Wars. It was the first in a series of Scottish rebellions that continued until 1746.

Chapter 3

The Williamite Wars in Ireland (1689–1691)

In 1687, before the 1688 Glorious Revolution had taken place in England, James II had appointed the Catholic Richard Talbot, Earl of Tyrconnel, to rule as Viceroy of Ireland. He had also readmitted Catholics to the Irish Parliament, and to positions of high public office, as well as replacing Protestant army officers with Catholics, resulting in the army becoming Catholic controlled.

The Irish public were mostly Catholic and supported James II. He had offered concessions to Catholics and had promised Ireland the right to become a sovereign state. Therefore, in 1689, after the Glorious Revolution, it was to Ireland that James II turned first in his attempts to regain the crown from William. However, the Protestants of Ulster viewed James as a tyrant in the mould of his cousin, the French King Louis XIV. They resisted the Catholic authorities as they were apprehensive of a Catholic dictatorship, and feared a repeat of the massacres of the 1641 Irish Rebellion (part of the Irish Confederate Wars).[1]

King Louis XIV of France sent 6,000 French troops in support of the Irish Jacobites. As far as he was concerned, having the Catholic James II on the English throne suited his ends better than having William, his arch enemy, as the sovereign. Meanwhile, William viewed the ensuing war in Ireland as another front in his overall crusade against King Louis XIV of France. He called on troops from England, Protestant troops from Scotland and the Ulster province of the north of Ireland, as well as Dutch troops and those from other Protestant European countries of the Grand Alliance, including Danish, German and French Protestants.

During this period, Richard Talbot, 1st Earl of Tyrconnell, continued to rule Ireland on behalf of James II, and he despatched Alexander Osbourne to offer the Hillsborough Council of Ulster a pardon in return for the ending of Ulster Protestant resistance and surrender. The offer was immediately rebuffed, so, on 8 March 1689 Tyrconnell sent

Lieutenant-General Richard Hamilton, an experienced soldier who had previously served with the French army from 1671 to 1685, with a force of 2,500 men from Drogheda to bolster Jacobite forces in the predominantly Protestant region of north-east Ulster, with the intention of bringing Ulster completely under Jacobite control.

The first skirmish of the conflict was the Break of Dromore ('break' is the Scottish term for a rout) on 14 March 1689, which took place near Dromore, County Down. Richard Hamilton crossed the River Bann and attacked Lord Mount Alexander's Williamite cavalry, who were taken by surprise and fell back before being completely overrun by the charging Jacobite dragoons, who then chased and slaughtered the Williamite foot as they fled towards Dromore. The Jacobite victory at the Break of Dromore meant that James' army now controlled the entire island of Ireland, except the Protestant towns of Londonderry/Derry and Enniskillen in Ulster.

Lord Mount Alexander escaped to England, while many other Protestants also fled to northern England or Scotland. Meanwhile, Hamilton's men went on to capture Hillsborough, along with money, supplies, arms and ammunition. However, the majority of the Protestant militia under Rawdon and Henry Baker managed to escape to Londonderry/Derry, to help in the defence of that city.

The walled city of Londonderry/Derry – the London being added when James I gave it a Royal Charter – was being guarded by a predominantly Protestant army unit commanded by Viscount Mountjoy. To rectify that situation, Tyrconnel intended to replace Mountjoy's unit with Lord Antrim's Catholic regiment of Scottish mercenaries known as the 'Redshanks'. He initiated the plan by ordering Mountjoy to march to Dublin on 23 November 1688, which left the city temporarily unguarded. However, Tyrconnel's plan was foiled as the former governor of Londonderry/Derry, George Phillips, spotted the Redshanks en route and sent warning to the city.

By 7 December 1688 Antrim's Redshanks had got as far as the banks of the River Foyle and their close proximity caused consternation among the civic leaders of the city, who hesitated in indecision. However, as they dithered, thirteen apprentice boys seized the initiative, as well as the city's keys, and locked the gates of the city walls to keep them out. In effect Londonderry/Derry was now in open rebellion against Tyrconnel and James II.

On 9 December George Phillips returned to the city and was welcomed back by the inhabitants to oversee defensive operations. Meanwhile, when Tyrconnel heard that Antrim had been repulsed, he ordered Mountjoy to cease his march to Dublin and return to Londonderry/Derry. He reached the city on 21 December 1688, and struck a compromise deal with the rebel inhabitants whereby only the two Protestant companies within his unit would come in. One of these was commanded by Lieutenant Colonel Robert Lundy; the other by Captain William Stewart.

Once within the city walls, Mountjoy appointed Lundy as governor of the city instead of Phillips. This situation was allowed to continue for a few months, but Tyrconnel had the intention of bringing Londonderry/Derry back under his Catholic rule. In the meantime, James II sailed to Ireland on the flagship the *Saint Michel* as part of a French fleet of thirty men-of-war commanded by Jean Gabaret, and landed on the south coast of Ireland at Kinsale. He was accompanied by D'Avaux, the French ambassador, and many English and Irish exiles, plus a hundred French officers. King Louis XIV was reluctant to spare any more as they were needed on the Continent for the Nine Years War.

From Kinsale James moved on to Cork, where he had a rendezvous with Tyrconnell. He then left Cork on Wednesday 20 March 1689 and arrived in Dublin on Palm Sunday, 24 March 1689. He stayed in Dublin Castle and hosted a council of war, which included D'Avaux, Tyrconnel, John Drummond, the Earl of Melfort and Conrad Rosen.

Around this time, another member of the Hamilton dynasty, James Hamilton, who was a nephew of Richard Hamilton but on the opposite Williamite side of the political and religious divide, arrived in Ulster from England with two ships, the frigate HMS *Jersey* and the merchantman *Deliverance*, both of which brought gunpowder, munitions and cash for the defenders of Londonderry/Derry. The cargo also included the commission from King William and Queen Mary that confirmed Colonel Lundy as the governor of the town.

On 2 April 1689 the French Jacobite Major-General Jean Camus, Marquis de Pusignan, made his way northwards with five regiments of foot to bolster the Jacobite strength in Ulster to approximately 12,000. He was later followed by James and d'Avaux and the Earle of Melfort, on 8 April 1689.

On 13 April 1689 Jacobite cavalry were seen approaching Londonderry/Derry, and Lundy formulated a plan to cut them off at the Passes of the River Finn. A skirmish ensued at Castlefinn, where the Jacobites were driven back by Colonel Skeffington's regiment, commanded by Mitchelburne. However, at Clady the Jacobite cavalry, under the command of Richard Hamilton, managed to get across the river and inflict a heavy defeat on the Protestant defenders.

Three days later Colonel Cunningham and Colonel Richards sailed into Lough Foyle with the Royal Navy frigate HMS *Swallow* and nine transport ships. They carried two regiments, amounting to 1,600 men. Cunningham, who was the commander of the fleet, had been informed that he was subordinate to Lundy, the governor of Londonderry/Derry.

After the defeat at the passes, Lundy was of the opinion that the city could not be successfully defended and held a council of war, from which the local commanders were excluded. At the meeting he took the decision that the troops should not land and the town should be abandoned, citing that there was insufficient provisions to defend it. Lundy kept his craven course of action secret from the natives, but the outcome soon became obvious to them when various officers and gentry who had been present at the meeting were seen preparing to leave. Lundy himself escaped, disguised as an ordinary soldier, and took a ship to Scotland. Cunningham's ships were also ordered to leave the arena and return to England.

Having broken through the pass at Clady, Richard Hamilton reached Londonderry/Derry on 18 April 1689 and demanded that the city surrender. The city asked for two days grace, before meeting again to discuss the surrender possibilities. They also insisted that the Jacobite army should not come further forward than St Johnston whilst they deliberated.

In the meantime, James II had joined up with the Jacobite army outside Londonderry/Derry, where, on 18 April 1689, he approached the walls with a force of Irish and French Jacobites, believing the inhabitants would obey their king and unlock the gates. This act only succeeded in enraging the populace, who saw it as a breach of the agreement. Accordingly, James was given short shrift, as cannons, including the city's largest, the 'Roaring Meg', were fired at him amidst cries of 'No Surrender'. Although the defenders failed to hit James, one of his aides de camp was killed.

On the same day as James was rebuffed from the walls, Adam Murray and his Williamite reinforcement troops arrived at the city, having fought at the passes. He had managed to break through the Jacobite lines at Calmore and reached Shipquay Gate, which Captain Morrison duly opened for him.

On 19 April 1689 the town council selected Henry Baker as the new governor of Londonderry/Derry, who in turn appointed Reverend George Walker to be in charge of stores.

On 20 April 1689 King James sent Claude Hamilton, 4th Earl of Abercorn, with a final proposal to the defenders at the walls. He spoke with Murray, who rejected the offer. James II and Rosen then returned to Dublin, leaving Lieutenant-General Maumont and Richard Hamilton in command at Londonderry/Derry. They were of equal rank and friction soon developed.

The besiegers then mounted a series of offences on the wall, which were all rebuffed by the defenders, causing the Jacobites to resort to trying to starve the defenders out. Eventually, disease and hunger started to take their toll, and it became evident that the city would struggle to hold out for much longer. However, in retaliation, the besieged, led by Murray, made numerous sorties to Pennyburn Hill to skirmish with the enemy. On the 21 April 1689 De Maumont was killed at one of these battles, and then, during another sortie on 25 April 1689, De Pusignan was also killed, among others.

On 26 April 1689 nearby Fort Culmore, which guarded the mouth of the River Foyle, was captured by the Jacobites, and shortly after this, on 6 May 1689, ramparts were also erected to the south of the city, by a company of besiegers commanded by an English officer, Brigadier General Ramsay. Cannons were then mounted on this structure, bringing the city walls within range of cannon fire for the first time. These were worrying developments for the Williamites; until now, the skirmishes had been at Pennyburn Hill to the north of the city, from where the besieger's cannon shot had failed to reach the walls. However, the defenders didn't take this lying down, and as they were being organised into an attacking party by Baker, the men broke ranks and ran at the enemy, attacking them with great fury, slaying General Ramsey and successfully putting his company to flight. Baker then oversaw the construction of a temporary defensive fortification on the ridge of the hill, which was then manned by the defenders throughout the siege.

On 7 May 1689, whilst the siege of Londonderry/Derry was in full swing, King William of Orange formally declared war on France, which had the affect of officially sanctioning the death of the two French Generals, Du Maumont and De Pusignan. On the other hand, France refused to declare war on England, because as far as King Louis XIV was concerned, James was the rightful king and the Williamites were nothing more than upstart rebels. However, although King Louis hadn't declared war on England, it didn't stop him sending a French fleet comprising forty-four ships with equipment and troops, which landed at Bantry Bay in south-west Ireland, where they fought an inconclusive battle against an English fleet on 11 May 1689.

Towards the end of May 1689 the French Chief of Artillery, Jean Bernard Desjeans Sieur de Pontis, constructed a boom or floating barricade across the River Foyle (just to the north of the location of the present Foyle Bridge), to prevent any relief ships from reaching the city. Then, to add to the defender's woes, in early June the besiegers received a consignment of siege guns and mortars, which coincided with the arrival of the Fitzgerald Regiment from Trim, along with a Lithuanian named Conrad Rosen, who was a Marshall General in the French army. He had been sent by James to accelerate the siege and he immediately began intensifying the bombardment.

Shortly before Rosen's arrival on 4 June 1689, a Jacobite force under Richard Hamilton stormed the walls and breached them in some places, before being finally beaten back. Meanwhile Cunningham and Richards, the captains of the two frigates that Lundy had sent away, had returned to England, bringing the message from Lundy that defence of the city of Londonderry/Derry was not possible.

However, King William realised that it was imperative to relieve the city and he gave the task to Kirke, the same cruel, vicious thug whose men had inflicted so much carnage on the survivors of the Battle of Sedgemoor only four years earlier. Kirke despatched HMS *Greyhound* from Hoylake to investigate further. He ordered Captain Guillam to get into the city if he could, but not to pass Fort Culmore if it could not be done without losing men. Consequently, on 8 June 1689, as HMS *Greyhound* approached Fort Culmore, she came under heavy fire and ran aground.

However, the ship eventually broke free and escaped to undergo repairs at Greenock in Scotland, before returning to England.

On 11 June 1689 HMS *Swallow*, HMS *Bonaventure* and HMS *Dartmouth*, along with twenty-four transport ships, carrying four regiments amounting to approximately 3,000 men between them, arrived in Lough Foyle, where they could be seen by the besieged from the cathedral tower. Two of the regiments were those commanded by Cunningham and Richards, who had previously departed the theatre of war on Lundy's orders.

In the second week of June, Kirke sent an exploratory force of four ships to explore the mouth of the River Foyle, to find out if it was possible for ships carrying supplies to get through. The ships subsequently withdrew as Kirke believed that he had insufficient troops to mount a serious challenge to the besiegers, and the previous incident with HMS *Greyhound* seemed to show that it was too risky to approach the city by river. Accordingly, the fleet sailed into nearby Lough Swilly, where they were able to establish communications with those inside the city walls by semaphore.[2]

On 28 June 1689 Lord Clancarty came up from Munster to Londonderry/Derry with his regiment to reinforce the Jacobites, and as soon as he arrived, he led an audacious attack on the Butchers Gate, which took the defenders by surprise. Yet again they withstood the onslaught and were able to repel the attackers.

At the beginning of June, Governor Baker had become unwell and on 21 June 1689 a council of war was held in which a successor in the form of John Mitchelburne was appointed. He subsequently took over as governor of Londonderry/Derry on 30 June 1689, when Baker succumbed to his illness and passed away.

On 2 July 1689 Rosen placed Protestant civilians against the walls as human shields to try and elicit a surrender from those within. The besieged retaliated by threatening to kill all of their Jacobite prisoners. Even James found Rosen's tactics distasteful and called him a barbarous Muscovite, despite the fact that he was actually from Lithuania.

The final skirmish of the siege took place on 17 July 1689 and was a desperate attempt by the defenders to obtain some food to relieve the starvation within the walls. The aim was to seize the cattle which grazed in the fields between the city and Pennyburn Mill. The defenders attacked Sir John Fitzgerald's regiment and killed and wounded many including

Fitzgerald himself. However, the besiegers reinforced their beleaguered colleagues and the attacking party went away empty handed.

After the failure by the defender's raiding party to obtain food, the starvation situation within the city walls was becoming even more desperate. Towards the end of July William appointed Frederick de Schomberg as commander in chief, who in turn ordered Kirke to make another attempt to breach the boom. Accordingly, the ships in Lough Swilly were ordered by Kirke to return to the mouth of the River Foyle at Culmore Point and attempt to break through the boom and break the siege.

At the vanguard of the fleet on 29 July 1689 was a small local boat, whose crewmen set about the boom with axes and managed to severely weaken it. The other ships in the fleet were HMS *Dartmouth* and three merchant ships: the *Mountjoy* from Londonderry/Derry; the *Phoenix* from Coleraine; and the *Jerusalem*.

HMS *Dartmouth* drew the fire from the shore batteries and provided covering fire while *Mountjoy*, commanded by Michael Browning, a Londonderry/Derry man, rammed the boom. The ship bounced off the boom and Browning was killed by Jacobite fire.[3] Undeterred, the *Mountjoy* tried again and this time successfully breached it, enabling the *Mountjoy* and the *Phoenix* to deliver many tonnes of food via the Shipquay Gate to the grateful inhabitants. Three days later the besieging troops, realising they could no longer starve the inhabitants out, conceded defeat and moved away.

The Siege of Londonderry/Derry lasted from 7 December 1688 to 1 August 1689 and was a pivotal point in the Williamite Wars of Ireland. The Protestant population of Ulster could have been decimated if the defenders failed to hold out. The siege is still celebrated annually by the Protestant community of Northern Ireland.

However, whilst the siege of Londonderry/Derry was in progress, Enniskillen was also under threat. The townsfolk of Enniskillen had already been involved in a siege in early 1689 involving Crom Castle, about twenty miles away from Enniskillen and five miles from Newtownbutler. On that occasion, they shut the gates of the town and rode out the storm, despite only having very meagre supplies. The available manpower was very limited but was bolstered by Protestants from the surrounding area. They managed to hold out until a relieving force under the command of Enniskillen's governor, Gustavus Hamilton, eventually arrived and managed to defeat Lord Galmoy's attacking force.

Since then, Enniskillen's Williamite civilians had formed themselves into a formidable irregular military force colloquially called the Enniskilleners. Lundy had ordered the Enniskilleners to fall back to Londonderry/Derry, but they had ignored that order, preferring to launch guerrilla attacks instead from their base at Enniskillen. Then in July, Crom Castle came under siege again as a Jacobite army led by Justin McCarthy Viscount Mountcashel, consisting of three regiments of foot and two of dragoons, moved out from Dublin to oppose the Enniskilleners and bombard the castle. Two days later a force of 2,000 Enniskilleners under Colonel Berry confronted Mouncashel's Jacobites in an ambush near Lisnaskea. Mountcashel's men fought off Berry's cavalry, but then, on 31 July 1689, came under attack from the main force of the Williamite army in County Fermanagh, near Enniskillen, at the Battle of Newtownbutler.

The Williamite force skilfully lured the Jacobites into a boggy area and cut them down with withering crossfire as they advanced through it. The Enniskilleners foot regiments then advanced through the bog, seizing the enemy cannons. The Jacobite cavalry, realising that defeat was imminent, galloped away, abandoning their foot regiments, who then had no other option but to flee themselves. The battle, which was a rout, is still commemorated by the Orange Order in Northern Ireland, and is mentioned in the traditional Unionist song *The Sash my Father Wore*.[4]

The Protestant victory at the Battle of Newtownbutler ensured that the Duke of Schomberg, who William had appointed as Commander-in-Chief of the government forces in Ireland, could now safely land further Williamite reinforcements and that they could now be used in an offensive capacity. Accordingly, a force of six cavalry and nine infantry regiments departed from Hoylake on 12 August 1689 and sailed for Belfast Lough, where they landed unopposed and joined with the Protestant forces of Londonderry/Derry and Enniskillen.

The arrival of the Williamite reinforcements and the consequent threatening presence of large numbers of Williamite forces meant that the Jacobites had effectively lost control of Ulster. Consequently, Thomas Maxwell, the Jacobite commander in the north, was forced into an ignominious retreat, operating a scorched earth policy as he withdrew to Newry. Meanwhile, the Jacobite garrison at Carrickfergus Castle was ordered to delay Schomberg's force for the maximum time possible.

Carrickfergus Castle had become a refuge for the Catholic population of the area as the Ulster uprising against the Jacobites gathered momentum. Meanwhile, Schomberg was anxious to quickly take Carrickfergus so he could march to Dublin before the winter arrived. He marched through to Belfast, which was quickly vacated by the Jacobites, and in turn was swiftly taken over by Henry Wharton's English regiment, who then patrolled the surrounding area to prevent plundering by the retreating Jacobites.

On 14 August 1689, as the Williamite forces approached Carrickfergus, the Jacobites set fire to the parts of the town beyond the city walls to deny the attackers any cover. Then, on 20 August 1689, Schomberg duly arrived with twelve regiments and General Percy Kirke also arrived with his Enniskillen troops. Several skirmishes ensued in the surrounding area and Schomberg gave the town the opportunity to surrender. The defenders requested time to get a message to King James, which was rejected as a ruse to delay proceedings.

In an attempt to find some cover and move closer to the walls, the Williamites then dug trenches during the night, and from their new vantage points subjected the town to a heavy bombardment. They also trained their fire on Carrickfergus Castle, which they had initially held back from doing as they were intending to use it themselves once they had claimed it.

A request came from the besieged asking if they could be allowed to surrender with the honours of war and thus decamp to the next nearest Jacobite garrison. But this was rejected and Schomberg insisted on an unconditional surrender. Royal Navy ships then arrived in the harbour to add their fire power to the bombardment. This proved to be the last straw and finally, having achieved their aim of considerably delaying the Williamite forces, the Jacobites raised the white flag.

Schomberg then granted the Jacobite defenders the honours of war in a reversal of his previous stance, and they were allowed to march to Newry Garrison. However, the local Protestant population didn't allow them to go unmolested and robbed them of their supplies as compensation for the hardships they had suffered during the Jacobite occupation. In the end, Schomberg had to ride amongst them with his pistol drawn to allow the Jacobites to get away.

The Williamite Wars in Ireland (1689–1691)

Schomberg left Henry Ingoldsby's regiment in charge of Carrickfergus as the main Williamite force left the town on 28 August 1689. However, a lack of supplies slowed Schomberg's progress southwards and he had to stop at Dundalk camp on 7 September 1689, where the army garrisoned for the winter. Whilst in Dundalk, the Williamites suffered dreadfully with illness; thousands died and many of the sick were shipped via Carrickfergus to receive hospital treatment in Belfast.

King William of Orange had now decided to involve himself personally in Ireland and the Williamite victory at Carrickfergus provided a secure port for him to land on 13 June 1690, with the largest invasion force the country had ever seen. He headed south to join Schomberg and his troops, who were moving to threaten James' Dublin citadel, on the campaign trail that would lead to the Battle of the Boyne the following month.

They encountered the Jacobite army on 1 July 1690 (in the old-style Julien calendar), thirty miles north of Dublin, just outside the town of Drogheda on Ireland's east coast. The armies faced each other across the River Boyne. The Jacobite army consisted of a mixture of experienced Irish cavalry and untrained, poorly equipped, infantry conscripts, who were reinforced by 6,000 French troops to make up a force of approximately 23,000. They were faced across the river by a Williamite army of 36,000 professional soldiers, with far superior firepower, drawn from Ulster, England, Scotland, the Netherlands and Denmark, as well as a large number of Protestant French Huguenot troops.

William initially sent a detatchment of cavalry and infantry totalling 9,000 men to cross the river at Roughgrange, in an attempt to outflank the Jacobites. To combat this, James sent about half of his army to challenge them, which diverted his troops from the main battle area, giving William a massive superiority in that main arena. However, what neither side appreciated was that there was a deep ravine in the area of Roughgrange which kept those two detatchments apart, and, therefore, unable to participate in the battle. This worked to William's advantage as he was less committed there than the Jacobites, and the main body of the Williamite infantry were able to cross the river near the village of Oldbridge and force the Jacobite infantry to retreat.

Over three-quarters of the casualties were from the Jacobite side. William had won a crushing victory in what was the largest pitched battle fought in the British Isles, and the last time two crowned kings of England, Ireland, Wales and Scotland met in battle.

James II fled to France immediately after the battle, leaving his demoralised troops behind. Some of the senior Jacobite commanders, particularly Richard Talbot, 1st Earl of Tyrconnell, thought it best to surrender. However, the majority of the Jacobite officers including Patrick Sarsfield opposed the surrender option, due to the harsh surrender terms offered by William. A pardon was offered only to the rank and file and not to officers, so the Jacobites split acrimoniously into two factions - those in favour of surrender and those against.

Protestant Orange Order folklore tends to glorify the Battle of the Boyne as being the most decisive battle of the Williamite Wars. But though King James II fled to France after the battle, the Jacobites did continue to fight on after his departure, although they were definitely on the back foot at this stage. However, they were able to draw some encouragement from William's continued inability to take the city of Limerick.

The Jacobites appealed directly to King Louis XIV for more support. He was receptive, as the battle had caused shockwaves throughout Europe, and put a severe dent in his Catholic expansionist plans. He sent General Saint Ruhe, one of his most experienced generals, to Ireland to take overall command and assess the situation. Meanwhile, William and his troops entered Dublin two days later.

As a consequence of their victory at the Boyne, the Williamites now controlled the eastern part of Ireland. The Jacobites had abandoned Dublin and fallen back, making the River Shannon the new front line as the Jacobites were still in control of the castles of Athlone and Limerick.

The first castle that the Williamite force – under the command of the Scottish general James Douglas – turned their attention to in July 1690 was in the strategically positioned town of Athlone, which sits on the River Shannon, right in the centre of Ireland. The Williamites, who were without siege guns, offered surrender terms, to which Grace responded by firing his pistol and announcing, 'That's the only negotiation I want.' He had, in effect, called General Douglas' bluff by this action as Douglas was loathe to cross the Shannon, knowing that to do so would result in many casualties. Once he realised that the besieged had reinforcements on the way, he decided to withdraw, meaning that Grace and his garrison's actions had enabled the Jacobites to continue to successfully hold the line between the east and the west of Ireland at the River Shannon, thus allowing them to continue fighting the war for another year.

William was keen to bring the war in Ireland to a conclusion. He was anxious to return to the Netherlands and get on with the main business of the War of the Grand Alliance against the French. He arrived at Limerick on 7 August 1690 with 25,000 men and occupied Iveton's and Cromwell's forts outside the city[5], before launching an all-out assault. However, he only had field artillery, as his siege guns had yet to arrive from Dublin.

The lack of siege guns at this stage of the campaign was proving problematic for the Williamite army. The reason for this was that Sarsfield's cavalry had intercepted the siege guns en route and destroyed them in an action known as the Ballyneety Raid, meaning there was a delay of ten days whilst alternative siege guns were moved from Waterford.

When the siege guns finally arrived in Limerick on 27 August 1690, the walls of the 'Irish Town' area of the city were breached and Danish troops stormed through. However, the French Jacobite officer Boisseleau had built further fortifications within the walls and had also barricaded the streets, meaning that the Danes came under a fierce onslaught from the Jacobite soldiers as they broke through. The civilian population also got involved and hurled bottles and stones at the Danes. Meanwhile, a regiment of Jacobite dragoons also attacked the Williamites outside the perimeter. After several hours of fierce fighting, William was finally forced to abandon the assault. His men had suffered heavy casualties, and many of his Dutch, Danish, German and Huguenot regiments were now seriously depleted, whereas the Jacobites had only lost 400 men in the battle. After this, William decided to return to the Continent and take control of allied forces in Flanders, leaving the Dutch general de Ginkel in charge of his forces in Ireland.

General de Ginkel instigated the second siege of Athlone in June 1691, in which he quickly overran the lightly defended East Town. However, the Jacobite general Saint Ruhe then withdrew his men out of the eastern town, across the bridge dividing the east and west sectors, in order to concentrate his defensive effort on the western section of the town. After having crossed the bridge, his Jacobite troops destroyed it, thus denying de Ginkel access to the West Town. In response, de Ginkel bombarded the West Town with cannon and mortars.

De Ginkel's Williamites did eventually break through after launching a well-executed surprise attack across the Old Ford, which allowed de Ginkels's men to take control of the town, leaving Saint Ruhe no option but to withdraw west with his army, where he continued to hold a defensive position around Limerick while he waited in hope for aid from France to arrive. In order to prevent this, the Williamites marched on Limerick, but found their way blocked at Aughrim, County Wicklow, on 12 July 1691 (in the old-style Julien calendar).

At Aughrim, both armies were approximately 20,000 strong and the Jacobites held a formidable position on the brow of Kilcommadon Hill. Saint Ruhe couldn't have chosen better ground as stone walls and hedgerows provided cover. There was also a bog in front of them, with only one pathway through it, which the Williamite forces would have to cross in order to attack them.

The Williamite commander, Hugh MacKay[6], initiated the battle by attacking the Jacobite flanks, and then led a full frontal assault on the Jacobite lines. The Jacobites, as planned, retreated to the next defensive line, from where they were able to beat the Williamite forces back as they struggled to cross the bog.

The battle was going well for the Jacobites, who were fighting with great fortitude and courage as they mounted an infantry counter charge. They forced the Williamites back into the bog where many drowned or were killed, but just as it seemed the Jacobites may be able to pull off an unlikely victory, Saint Ruhe was decapitated by a cannon ball.

Now the English cavalry, which had been kept in reserve, entered the fray and the ensuing charge created a confusing melee and great uncertainty. The Jacobite command structure was now rudderless and the order to mount a counter cavalry charge never came. Meanwhile, the English cavalry continued to smash into the Irish infantry. This in turn allowed the Williamites to gain the upper hand and turn the tide of the battle in their favour, eventually snatching victory from the jaws of defeat in what is regarded as one of the bloodiest battles ever fought in the British Isles. Although the city of Limerick continued to hold out until the autumn of 1691, the Battle of Aughrim is considered by many to have effectively ended the Williamite War and Jacobitism in Ireland, leaving subsequent Jacobite risings to be fought only in England and Scotland.

By the time of the second siege of Limerick (August to October 1691), Jacobite morale had reached breaking point. Over 40,000 Jacobites had been killed at the Battle of Aughrim, including their commander Saint Ruhe, and thousands more had either been taken prisoner or deserted. However, in July 1691 the city of Limerick was bolstered by Jacobite reinforcements, due to the garrison at Galway surrendering and the inhabitants being accorded the articles of war, which allowed them to retain their weapons and move on to Limerick.

When the Williamites reached Limerick, a surprise assault drove the Jacobite defenders from Thormond bridge at the north-eastern extremity of the English Town, forcing them back towards the sanctuary of the inside of the city walls. However, the French defenders within refused to open the gate for the Irish and about 800 of them were shot or drowned in the River Shannon. After seeing this, Patrick Sarsfield ousted the French commanders, Chevalier de Tesse and the Marquis d'Usson, and started negotiations for surrender.

The Treaty of Limerick of 3 October 1691 promised to respect the Catholic religion in Ireland and provided a guarantee that Catholic-owned land would not be confiscated. However, the Protestant-dominated Irish Parliament did not fully honour the agreement and Catholics continued to suffer from penal laws designed to underpin Protestant supremacy and to ensure the survival of the Protestant-English speaking areas.

The treaty also made provision for Sarsfield and his fully armed Jacobite army to withdraw to France. So, a year later, Patrick Sarsfield's 10,000 strong army put themselves at the disposal of King Louis XIV, in what was known as the 'Flight of the Wild Geese'. This was part of a reciprocal understanding that the Irish would supply troops for France in the Nine Years War against the Dutch in return for the French troops that King Louis XIV had sent to Ireland to aid the Jacobites in 1690.

Chapter 4

The 1689 Jacobite Rebellion and the Subsequent Events that Led to a Further Jacobite Rebellion in 1715

This Scottish Jacobite rising was designed to coincide with the Williamite Wars in Ireland and was also part of the wider conflict known as The Nine Years War (1688–1697), also known as the War of the Grand Alliance or the War of the League of Augsberg.

The main protagonist, John Graham of Claverhouse, 1st Viscount Dundee (1648–1689), was a Scottish Lowlander born in Angus. He was the elder son of Sir William Graham and Lady Madeline Carnegie and was educated at the University of St Andrews in the 1660s. His family owned the estate of Claverhouse near Dundee and he first distinguished himself as a soldier at the Battle of Seneff in Belgium, whilst serving in the French army in the Dutch Wars against the Netherlands.

On his return to Scotland in 1678 he was tasked by Charles II with dispersing the Lowland Presbyterian meetings held by the Convectiles, which were deemed subversive. His enthusiasm in this task earned him the moniker of 'Blaidy Clavers, the scourge of the Covenanters'. He was defeated by the Covenanter army at Drumclog on June 1 1679 (see Chapter 1), but then was involved in the Duke of Monmouth's victory over the Covenanters at Bothwell Bridge (see Chapter 1). His subsequent ruthless campaign against the Covenanters during the 'Killing Time' (1679–1688) had also earned him the approval of James II, which proved to be the catalyst for a spectacular ascent, which saw him appointed as sheriff of a number of areas of south-west Scotland as well as a colonel of a new Scottish regiment. He also was appointed a Hereditary Constable of Dundee in 1683, as well as being appointed to the Scottish Privy Council, and as the Provost of Dundee. He lived at Dudhope Castle near Dundee from 1685 until the Glorious Revolution of 1688, when he sought exile in France. It was during his exile that James II appointed him as the commander of his forces in Scotland.

He was also to prove ruthless in his love life. In 1679, when Claverhouse was thirty-one years old, he attempted to woo Helen Graham, who was the cousin of the childless Earl of Montieth. The earl was heavily in debt and Helen was liable to inherit the debts but not the titles. Some cynics were of the opinion that Claverhouse's main interest in Helen, who he had only corresponded with but never met, was to take on the debt and then eventually acquire the titles. However, when the Earl of Montieth – who was childless – died, the titles went with him, leaving Claverhouse to prove the cynics right and turn his attentions elsewhere. Although, in fairness to him, he was being thwarted at every turn by the potential mother-in-law from hell.

Not long afterwards, Claverhouse met an Ayrshire girl by the name of Jean Cochrane, who, at the age of twenty, was sixteen years his junior. The liaison was controversial to say the least as her family were one of the leading Covenanter families in Scotland. Claverhouse was, of course, the scourge of the Covenanters and to say that neither family approved of the subsequent marriage would be a huge understatement. At the wedding in Paisley, on 9 June 1684, Jean's parents refused to attend and the ceremony was a total debacle anyway as Claverhouse was called away early from the celebrations to break up a convectile.

In 1689, when the Scottish Parliament declared that James had forfeited the Scottish throne, Claverhouse, a staunch Episcopalian, sought to overturn the decision through the courts, and when this failed he began to gather the clans to take on King William.

* * *

Scotland's clan system was actually initiated by the English Saxon queen of Malcolm III, who, after they were married in 1069, introduced the idea of the feudal system of land tenure. Under this system the land belonged to the king, who distributed it in exchange for military allegiance. However, in time, the clan chiefs became rulers of their own tribal kingdoms, with the power of life and death over their clansmen. The clan was like an extended family and members were related by blood. The chief was the 'father' of the clan and responsible for administering justice. The clan members didn't pay rent to live on the chief's land, but instead were the chieftain's private army. The clansmen were, in effect, slaves, whose only allegiance was to their chief. This positively feudal system, known as 'heritable jurisdiction', was highly prized by the chiefs and the Highland clans were a law unto themselves. They spoke their own language (Gaelic) and had their own unique culture. They dressed in their own way and enjoyed their own distinctive style of music and dancing.

Clans loyal to the Jacobites and those loyal to the British government controlled their clansmen, with an underlying threat of violence if their demands were not met; although in many cases the men joined the respective causes with enthusiasm. So, for instance, in 1745 Bonnie Prince Charlie would order a clan chief to supply a certain number of men per merkland (a merkland being a unit of land for taxation purposes). Similarly, William Sutherland of the pro-government Sutherland clan ordered the officers of his Highland Independent Companies to supply men for the Skirmish of Little Ferry, against the threat of burning their houses and slaughtering their cattle if they didn't comply (see Chapter 10). However, the Sutherland clansmen involved in that skirmish acquitted themselves well against the Jacobite clansmen of George Mackenzie, 3rd Earl of Cromatie, in what was arguably the last conflict fought entirely by clan levies in Scotland.

At the time of the Jacobite Rebellions, the system of the 'Fiery Cross' as a means for the chiefs to summon their clansmen to battle would have been in use. It was used most frequently during the 1715 Rebellion, and involved a burning cross typically made from the branches of a yew or hazel tree. The four ends of the burning cross then had their flames extinguished by being doused in the blood of a goat, specifically slaughtered for the purpose by the chief. The cross was carried to the first village by a messenger who gave the appointed place for the clan to meet. A messenger from that village would then take the cross on to the next village, and all the villages where that clan dwelled were informed via this relay system. Every man between the ages of sixteen and sixty was expected to respond to the call, and failure to do so would result in him meeting the same gruesome fate of the goat; i.e., he would be killed and his family's home would be destroyed by fire. This Highland symbol of war was thought to have last been used in 1812 during the Anglo-American War, when members of the Glengarry MacDonnell clan, who had emigrated to Canada en masse as a result of the Highland Clearances (see Chapter 15), were summoned to action by this method.

So, in 1689, the clan levies of the Jacobite clans were duly raised for Claverhouse. He became known by the Highland clansmen as 'Bonnie Dundee' and he raised the Jacobite standard on the highest point in the city – the top of Dundee Law – to signify the beginning of the first Scottish Jacobite Rising.

William's military commander in Scotland, and Claverhouse's opponent, was General Hugh Mackay (1640–1692), who was a Highlander from Scourie, Sutherland. He enlisted initially as a mercenary soldier fighting for the French army against the Dutch, but the situation changed when England and the Netherlands joined forces and McKay met his Dutch Protestant sweetheart, Clara de Bie, who was the daughter of a rich Amsterdam merchant. They married in 1673 and it was her influence which caused him to change sides and become a major in the Dutch Scottish Brigade, which was one of the premier regiments to arrive with William of Orange's army at Torbay in the Glorious Revolution of 1688. He was promoted to the rank of General and his army of 4,000 troops in Scotland in 1689 consisted of the clan regiments of Mackay, Balfour and Ramsay, the English Hastings Regiment and two newly raised Scots units, as well as 1,100 men from the Dutch Scots Brigade.

On the completion of the campaign against the 1689 Jacobites in Scotland, he joined the fight against the Jacobites in Ireland, where he was instrumental in the Protestant victory at the Battle of Aughrim (see Chapter 3). After the Irish campaign, he returned to the Netherlands as commander of the British Division fighting France in the War of the Grand Alliance, where he was killed at the Battle of Steenkerque on 3 August 1692.

In addition to the clan levies raised for Claverhouse that had gathered at Dundee Law, Ewen Cameron of Lochiel also raised an army of clansmen for the Jacobite cause in April 1689 and took his force of around 1,800 Highlanders to Glenroy, where he linked up with Claverhouse and his forty companies.

On 16 May 1689 the Jacobites marched out and attempted to bring Mackay to battle. However, Mackay cunningly avoided major pitched battles, as he was light on numbers at this stage, and being a Highlander himself, was well aware that the clansmen tended to favour short-term warfare, which enabled them to return to their glens and their families. He opted instead to become involved in guerrilla warfare and minor skirmishes.

One such minor skirmish was the Battle of Loup Hill on 27 June 1689, in which Jacobite sympathisers had previously taken control of northern Kintyre but were then ambushed on the slopes of Loup Hill as government troops retook the Kintyre peninsula. In the aftermath of the battle, Claverhouse asked for reinforcements, but the loss of Kintyre now made resupply from Ireland extremely difficult, and it was during this period, on 14 June 1689, that Edinburgh also surrendered to government troops.

Claverhouse's requests for additional resources were denied partly due to an internal dispute with the Catholic Non-Compounders who dominated James' court in Ireland and who urged James to refuse any concessions to regain his throne. Claverhouse and other Scottish Jacobites were mostly Compounders, for whom concessions were essential, and consequently were viewed with suspicion by the Irish. Accordingly, only a paltry 200 Irish soldiers were sent to Scotland as reinforcements. They were commanded by Alexander Cannon and landed near Duart Castle, on the Isle of Mull, on 21 July 1689.

Blair Castle has historically been the ancestral home of the Chief of Clan Murray, the Duke of Atholl, and its strategic position has ensured that it has featured prominently throughout Scottish history. Its location in Glen Garry controlled the mountain passes and guarded the southern gateway of the Cairngorns, as well as access to the Lowlands and the main route to the north through the Pass of Killiecrankie. In 1689 the castle was under Jacobite control. Though the Duke of Atholl, John Murray, was loyal to the government, he was unable to prevent his brother, James Murray, taking command of his clan and bringing them out for the Jacobites. Meanwhile, his factor, Patrick Stewart of Ballechin, had taken control of the castle and had allowed Claverhouse to garrison his troops there. In response, John Murray set about trying to reclaim his own home and laid siege to it, whilst General Mackay made haste northwards to assist him with a force of between 3,000 and 5,000 troops.

Claverhouse saw this as the opportunity he had been craving to bring Mackay to battle. He relieved the castle, and then when he learned that Mackay's forces were heading towards the Pass of Killiecrankie – a splendid, wooded gorge of just over two miles alongside the River Garry, three miles north of Pitlochry, lying between Ben Vrachie and Tenandry Hill in Perthshire – he set out to confront MacKay with the force he had at his disposal while the Duke of Atholl's sons, who were also Jacobites, were sent to raise further clansmen for the Jacobite cause.

On the morning of 27 July 1689 Claverhouse held a council of war, at which he discussed with his senior commanders whether to catch Mackay in the pass or attack him at a later date when the promised extra clansmen had arrived in support. The consensus was to take a gamble and attack Mackay's Williamite army whilst they were still in the pass and hopefully gain a decisive victory, which would then attract further support for the cause.

Claverhouse sent Sir Alexander Mclean and 400 men to combat Mackay's advance guard, while Claverhouse and the main body of his troops formed into columns on the high ground of the lower slopes of Creagh Eullich, north of the pass, overlooking the exit.

As Mackay's troops progressed through the narrow, treacherous pass, they were shadowed by a lone Atholl hunter, Ian 'Ban Beag' Mac-Rath, who, with his only bullet, killed a Williamite cavalry officer. The gulley from where he took the shot is now known as 'Trooper's Den'.[1] After the single shot rang out, Mackay had an awareness of Jacobite troops in the vicinity, and so deployed his men in a long line only three men deep to achieve maximum fire power. The most experienced men of the Dutch Scots Brigade under Balfour and Launder were placed on the left, to give them the best firing opportunities. Meanwhile, Claverhouse organised his wild Highlanders in battle formation, clan by clan, as an uneasy stand-off took place.

Claverhouse and his Jacobite Highlanders, who were outnumbered two to one, waited until sunset, just after 8pm, to launch the attack. He gave the order to charge and the Jacobites rushed headlong downhill at the enemy. As they charged, Balfour's Dutch Scots Brigade in the front line fired three murderous volleys which killed nearly 600 Jacobite Highlanders. However, their fire was partly masked by a shallow terrace on the hillside, which also prevented the regiments to their right from shooting. Another problem was that the government gun carriages collapsed and broke after the third volley. Consequently, the gunfire did little to halt the fabled Highland Charge and the Jacobites got amongst the government troops with their broadswords and claymores, resulting in the mainly inexperienced government troops freezing in terror and panic.

The speed, ferocity and sheer commitment of the Highland Charge was a lethal weapon that had regularly struck horror into the hearts of the English since the days of Robert the Bruce. The clansmen would fire a volley with their rifles, from about 60ft away and then run full tilt at the enemy, brandishing their broadswords and claymores[2], whilst shouting the blood curdling Gaelic battle cry *'claidheamh'* (claymore, or 'great sword'). The charge was usually so ferocious that it would frequently cause enemy troops to break ranks before contact, leaving gaps which were exploited to 'roll up the rest'. It had often resulted in routs in double quick time, such as at Killiecrankie, Prestonpans and Falkirk. However, if the charge failed for any reason, as it did at Culloden, they were then over committed and unable to hold their ground.

At Killiecrankie the government troops had an added problem in that they had been supplied with plug bayonets. This was the first time they had been used by British troops[3] and the idea of them was that a soldier would have a weapon which combined as both a musket and a lower grade version of a pike (a musket with a bayonet attatched), thus eliminating the need for specialist pikemen. However, although the plug bayonet could be used for either task, it had its limitations. In order to fire the musket, the bayonet had to be unplugged and vice versa, meaning that the bayonet was not fixed until the last possible moment. This issue was seriously exposed at Killiecrankie, as the task of plugging in the bayonet proved almost impossible to perform in the high-pressure situation of thousands of bloodthirsty Highlanders bearing down at speed. Many simply couldn't manage it as they fumbled with trembling hands, and they fled rather than stand there defenceless against the clansmen's fearsome double-edged broadswords and claymores.

The Jacobites secured a resounding victory as they inflicted heavy casualties and routed the government troops in a few minutes. But victory came at a heavy cost, as nearly a third of the Jacobites were also killed, including Claverhouse. As victory beckoned, Claverhouse led a cavalry charge against MacKay's centre and was shot beneath the breastplate. According to Highland legend, he must have been killed by a silver button from his own coat being pushed into the wound, as he was indestructible to bullets, having made a pact with the Devil. There is a standing stone

The 1689 Jacobite Rebellion and the Subsequent Events 67

in a field near Killiecrankie that Claverhouse is said to have leant against when he died which has since become known as Claverhouse's Stone. He was a fanatical Jacobite right to the end, and as he died he is quoted as saying 'My death matters less for me than seeing that the day goes well for my master.' After his death, he was taken to Blair Castle and was subsequently buried at the Parish Kirk of St Bride in the castle grounds.

There is also a stone in the pass dedicated to Balfour which is reputed to mark Balfour's grave and which reads, 'Here Brigadier Barthold Balfour of the Dutch Brigade, who commanded the left wing of General Mackay's army was killed in the subsequent rout by the Atholl men.'

After the battle a lone sentry by the name of Donald MacBean, whom Mackay had posted to guard the pass, was confronted with the unenviable sight of the Highland hordes charging at him. The adrenalin must have certainly been pumping within him, which maybe explains the superhuman feat he managed of jumping 19ft to safety across the rocky chasm of the raging River Garry. The feat is all the more remarkable considering that, due to the terrain in the area, the jump must have been from a standing start. The spot is still known as 'Soldier's Leap'.

Mackay managed to reform his regiments, amounting to approximately 800 men, and made it back to the safety of Stirling Castle, where many stragglers also arrived in the course of the next few days. In total, the government losses were in the region of 2,000 killed, wounded or missing. Among those killed were James Mackay, Hugh's younger brother.

After Killiecrankie, Blair Castle remained in Jacobite hands for some time. However, the loss of the Jacobite leader, John Graham of Claverhouse, 1st Viscount Dundee, resulted in Alexander Cannon taking over as leader of the Jacobite forces in Scotland. He had been the leader of the recruits from Ireland, meaning that the renowned Highland Chief, Sir Ewen Cameron of Lochiel, was passed over. Cameron took this as a personal slight and left, taking his clan with him.

Cannon soon found the same problems as his predecessor, Claverhouse, in that his options were limited as he lacked supplies. He also lacked siege equipment which meant he was unable to capture a port from which to resupply, and he was also vulnerable as he lacked cavalry. These factors played into the experienced Mackay's hands, and he adopted the same tactic as before the Battle of Killiekrankie, whereby he disrupted Jacobite strongholds but avoided major pitched battles.

General Mackay also built a new fort by order of King William. It used the earth and wooden fortifications that were originally erected by Oliver Cromwell in 1654, and was strengthened by the addition of stone ramparts. The virtually impregnable stronghold, which housed 1,000 government troops, became known as Fort William, as did the town that grew up around it.

Immediately after the Battle of Killiecrankie, the Scottish Privy Council ordered the newly formed Cameronian Regiment, under the command of William Cleland, to move north from Perth and to hold Dunkeld at all costs. The regiment took its name from the Lion of the Covenant, Richard Cameron. Meanwhile, 5,000 victorious Jacobite Highland clansmen couldn't believe their luck on hearing this news and were delighted to have the opportunity of confronting their Cameronian Covenanter enemies in battle.

Dunkeld was not a walled town, so the Cameronian Lieutenant-Colonel William Cleland ordered his troops to take up defensive positions in the grounds of the Marquess of Atholl's mansion, Dunkeld House, as well as the grounds of the cathedral, both of which were surrounded by walls.

On 21 August 1689 the Jacobites, who vastly outnumbered the Cameronians, stormed the town from all directions and had some initial success, but they had a problem in that the confined streets of the town were not conducive to the traditional Highland Charge.

The Cameronians lost their seasoned colonel, and stalwart of the Cameronian Covenanter cause, William Cleland in the early stages of the battle. He was conscious of the deleterious effect his death could have on the morale of his men, so as he was dying he dragged himself away from the battle so that his men wouldn't see him fall.

William Cleland (1661–1689) had fought for the Covenanters at the battles of Drumclog and Bothwell Bridge (see Chapter 1). He was credited with implementing the decisive manoeuvre which led to victory at Drumclog and after which a royal proclamation of 16 June 1679 described him and his brother James as the ringleaders. He subsequently escaped to the Netherlands, but returned to Scotland with Argyll's Rising in 1685, after which he again escaped to the Netherlands, only to return to Scotland again in 1688 with William of Orange's Glorious Revolution. He eventually became a lieutenant-colonel of the Cameronian Regiment, which consisted mostly of Western Covenanters, and was finally laid to rest at Dunkeld Cathedral, the scene of his last battle.

Cleland's death during the battle was a grave loss for the Cameronians and the situation was compounded by the serious wound suffered by the regiment's major, which also necessitated his removal from combat, and meant that command now fell to Captain George Munroe of Auchinbowie.

A terrible battle raged for sixteen hours, during which the Cameronians grimly held on. They ran out of ammunition, but improvised by stripping lead from the roof of Dunkeld House and elsewhere. Meanwhile, the Jacobite Highlanders barricaded themselves into the houses, but many were burnt alive when nearly every house was torched. Somehow, the stand-in Cameronian commander, George Munro, led his troops to victory and forced the Jacobite Highlanders to eventually give up the struggle and retreat.

Holes caused by musket balls are still visible in the east gable of Dunkeld Cathedral and they provide an enduring memento of this hard-fought battle, in which the Cameronian Covenanters claimed a victory that virtually ended the Jacobite Rising of 1689.

As far as William III was concerned, the death of Claverhouse and the subsequent Battle of Dunkeld had extinguished James's hopes of regaining Scotland, so he refused to send reinforcements, saying, 'Armies are needless, the war is over with Claverhouse's life'. William was more concerned with the wider conflict in Europe, and though the 1689 Jacobite Rising stuttered on a little longer, it essentially went nowhere after the Battle of Dunkeld, prompting Alexander Cannon to temporarily bring an end to the campaign.

Many of the Highland clansmen returned despondently to their homes, while Sir Ewen Cameron took temporary control of what remained of the Jacobite army until James' new appointment, Major General Buchan, duly arrived as the new commander-in-chief of the Jacobite forces in Scotland, along with more arms and ammunition. However, on Buchan's arrival a meeting of the clan chiefs took place, where it was decided that the Highlanders should return to their homes for the winter to rest up and take shelter before continuing the war in the spring.

In the spring, Buchan, who had 1,200 infantrymen at his disposal, embarked on a campaign of disruption of the enemy. He advanced along the River Spey, but by the time he had gone as far south as Cromdale, where he set up camp, he had lost a quarter of his men due to desertions. He was then intercepted at the Haughs of Cromdale by a force commanded by Sir Thomas Livingstone of the Williamite garrison at Inverness. Livingstone's cavalry approached from the opposite bank of the Spey, before crossing the river to defeat the outnumbered Jacobites at the Battle of Cromdale between 30 April and 1 May 1690. However, many Jacobites were saved by a thick fog that enveloped the mountain and allowed them to escape. A piper's stone exists at the site today and is said to be where a mortally wounded piper continued to play the pipes to encourage his fellow warriors.

A further group of Jacobites crossed the River Spey the next day, only to be pursued by Livingstone's troops, who killed some and dispersed the rest on the Moor of Granish near Aviemore. The same group of Jacobites then attempted to steal cattle from land that was owned by the laird, James Grant of Loch an Eilean Castle, in the Rothiemurchus Forest. They also made an attempt to seize the castle with the intention of taking refuge within it. James Grant was absent at the time, and it was Grizzel Mhor, his wife, who found herself organising the resistance as she and her fellow defenders managed to repel the invaders by driving them off with volleys of musket fire.

Another Clan Grant castle that was under siege by the Jacobites both before and after the Battle of Cromdale was Urquhart Castle on the shores of Loch Ness. Despite a chronic lack of weapons and supplies, the 200 government soldiers garrisoned within managed to hold out against a force of 500 Jacobites until after the defeat of the main Jacobite army at Cromdale. When the government soldiers finally left in May 1690, they blew up the castle to prevent occupation by the Jacobites.

In the Highlands of Scotland at this time almost half of the population was Episcopalian. However, the decisive role played by the Scottish Covenanters at the Battle of Dunkeld meant the Covenanter views held sway in the political settlement that followed, and in 1690, with the approval of William, the Church of Scotland, or Kirk, removed Nonjuror Bishops and expelled Episcopalians, resulting in the elimination of Episcopacy.

Presbyterianism, which advocated church rule by ministers and elders as practised by the Church of Scotland, therefore became the national religion, as opposed to the Episcopalian method of worship, whereby church rule was administered by bishops and the head of the church, who was the reigning monarch. Both Catholics and Episcopalians tended to be Jacobites, and they strongly rejected Presbyterianism, as well as the fact that they were now unable to practice their own religion. William was anxious to reallocate troops to the war against France, but these issues resulted in the fermentation of further trouble closer to home in the Highlands of Scotland, where rebellion was still very much in the air. In order to pacify the rebel clan chiefs, a summit was called by Lord Stair at Achallader Castle in June 1691.

John Dalyrymple, Lord Stair, had been appointed Secretary of State for Scotland by William, and had complete control of affairs north of the border. Also present was the Earl of Breadalbane, a member of the Campbell Clan and Lord Treasurer of Scotland. He was a Lowlander and was known to be duplicitous and crafty, and was also said to have had an intense dislike of Jacobite Highlanders.

The purpose of the meeting was to persuade the Jacobite clan chiefs to swear allegiance to William, and they did finally agree to do so, in return for royal pardons for their part in the Jacobite uprising of 1689 and the sum of £12,000. The allegiance had to be sworn by 1 January 1692, and William had promised severe reprisals if the allegiance was not signed.

However, many Jacobite clan chiefs were reluctant to swear allegiance to William until they had sought permission from James himself. Word was sent to their exiled king, and he dithered for several months before finally replying just as the deadline was looming with a letter stating that, 'For their own safety the chiefs should sign the agreement.'

The letter only reached Edinburgh on 15 December 1691, which only left sixteen days for the information to be passed on to those Highland clans that were pro-Jacobite, meaning that some of the clans in more remote areas were struggling to comply in time.

The seventy-year-old, clan chief of the Macdonald's of Glencoe, MacIain MacDonald, only received the news on the 29 December 1691, and immediately set off on horseback for Fort William to swear his clan's oath of allegiance. He was further hampered by a snowstorm, but just made it to Fort William in time. However, to his dismay, the governor, Colonel John Hill, refused to accept the oath, stating that he did not have the authority to accept it, and that he would have to travel a further seventy miles back across Glencoe to Inveraray for the oath to be sworn by the sherrif of that town. This was an appalling journey at the best of times, as Glencoe is one of Scotland's wildest glens, but in a raging winter storm the journey was even more perilous and he didn't get there until 2 January 1692, only to find that Sheriff Campbell of Ardkinglas was away with his family for Hogmanay. Maclain MacDonald had little choice but to wait it out, and when the sherriff returned, on 6 January 1692, he allowed the oath to be taken, despite its lateness, as he appreciated the mitigating circumstances and the obvious distress MacIain was in. The sheriff then sent the oath with an accompanying letter explaining why it was late.

However, King William and his callous, and canny, Scottish administrators, Lord Stair and the Earl of Breadalbane were a little less forgiving as they had been looking for an opportunity for revenge ever since clans loyal to James II had annihilated government troops at the Battle of Killiecrankie. They saw this as a perfect opportunity to make an example of this small and unpopular clan, believing that it would not ignite general rebellion. As a result, they refused to accept the oath, due to it being six days late, and King William himself is said to have signed an order for reprisals to be exacted.

Later, in the bitter snow of January 1692, 120 red-coated soldiers from the Earl of Argyll's Regiment of Foot, drawn mostly from the Campbell Clan, under the command of Captain Campbell of Glenlyon, were billeted among the crofter's cottages of Clan MacDonald in Glencoe, on the pretence that their barracks at Fort William had no room for them.

Clan Campbell, with their tribal territory of Argyll, have historically been the largest and most dominant of the Scottish clans, and their two main castles in the region, Kilchurn and Inverary, reflect their sheer power. The Campbells were great advocates of the Protestant Reformation and had always tended to side with the English Crown in pursuit of a Protestant Scotland. Accordingly, they had often assisted the English in putting down rebellion among other clans. Consequently, the Duke of Argyll's Campbell Clan Regiment were chosen by Lord Stair and the Earl of Breadalbane to do their dirty work; the fact that they had a blood feud with the MacDonalds was also a factor in this choice.

Despite the long running feud between Clan Campbell of Glenlyon and Clan Macdonald of Glencoe, the Campbells were welcomed, due to the Highland tradition that even the fiercest feud between guest and host must be left aside to provide a guest with shelter and hospitality. However, after a fortnight of feasting, the sickening order came to put their hosts to the sword. The orders stated that the soldiers should take special care not to spare that old fox MacIain and his sons. Captain Campbell was dismayed at the order, which threatened him with hanging if he didn't comply. As a Highlander himself, he also found it particularly distasteful to go against the ancient Highland code of hospitality.

At 5am on the bitter winter morning of 13 February 1692, the massacre began. Many of the rank and file soldiers were also sickened by the orders; many refused to carry them out and others helped the MacDonalds escape. The massacre took place near the village of Glencoe, and in various parts of Glencoe at Inverrigan, Invercoe, Carnoch, Auchnaion and Achtriochtan. Both of MacIain's sons escaped, but thirty-eight men, women and children were initially slaughtered. And of those who escaped into the hills and glens after being alerted by the piercing screams, many perished due to starvation and exposure as their homes were burnt to the ground.

The deadline for the allegiance had been cynically set in the middle of winter, as Stair had argued that 'This is the only season in which we are sure the Highlanders cannot escape and carry their wives, bairns and cattle to the hills. This is the proper time to maul them in the long winter months.'

Since this incident, Glencoe is also known as the 'Glen of Weeping', and a monument to the murdered chief, MacIain, stands near the entrance to the glen. But if the idea of the shameful massacre of Glencoe was intended to make the clan chiefs loyal towards King William, then it was an unmitigated disaster. Though the MacDonalds of Glencoe were considered to be a bunch of murderous cattle thieves and unpopular with neighbouring clans, no other single event did as much to strengthen Highland loyalty to the exiled James II and his Stuart Jacobite descendants as the massacre, and it was no coincidence that the MacDonalds of Glencoe featured strongly in all future Highland Jacobite uprisings.

The government attempted to suppress news of the Glencoe massacre, but it was leaked by Jacobite supporters to the *Paris Gazette* and copies subsequently reached London. Eventually, after three years, King William was shamed into initiating a public enquiry, which was a total whitewash. Nobody was ever brought to justice and the only thing that happened was that Lord Stair resigned from his post after receiving a king's pardon and an additional pension.

Jacobite support was not restricted purely to the Highlands of Scotland and Ireland, and the next significant Jacobite activity after the Scottish Rebellion of 1689 involved the Ailesbury Plot (1691–1692). The plotters were mostly peers of the realm from the south of England, led by the Earl of Ailesbury. The plan involved a French invasion fleet sailing to England under the command of James II and was the idea of James' secretary of state, the Earl of Melfort. However, the government became aware of the plan and despatched the Royal Navy to put a stop to it.

Then, in early 1692, a large military contingent under the command of James II started to assemble in northern France, making preparations to invade England. The predominantly French force included Sarsfield's Wild Geese and Mountcashel's Irish Brigade. On 17 May 1692 the French fleet left the port of Brest, but immediately came under attack from an Anglo-Dutch force commanded by Admiral Russell off Cape Barfleur. The Battle of Barfleur ensued, from which the French escaped relatively unscathed, although a few days later the Royal Navy destroyed three French ships, including their flagship the *Soleil Royal* in Cherbourg Harbour.

Subsequently, on 23–24 May 1692, the Battle of La Hougue took place, in which the Royal Navy destroyed twelve more French ships in the harbour of La Hougue, bringing James to the realisation that if he were unable to even leave France, he had no chance of regaining the throne. However, both Sarsfield's Wild Geese and Mountcashel's Irish brigade later regrouped back in France to fight another day.

The next Jacobite activity was the Fenwick Plot of 1696, which involved Sir John Fenwick, 3rd Baronet of Fenwick, who was part of James' inner circle and his advisor on English affairs. After Queen Mary's death in 1694, he began to consider a Jacobite insurgency in England and received finance from France for that purpose in April 1695. His plan involved securing a port on the south coast of England that would be suitable for a French army detatchment to arrive, before making their way to London with Fenwick and his associates to capture William. However, a Catch 22 situation developed, whereby Fenwick refused to seize a port until the

French were prepared to sail and the French refused to prepare to sail until a port was captured.

In June 1692 Fenwick was arrested for being involved in pro-Jacobite riots and that seemed to be the end of the plot. However, Sir George Barclay then took over the role of coordinating an invasion force. He quickly dismissed Fenwick's original plan and instead instigated the Assassination Plot of 1696, which involved assassinating William.

Barclay had analysed the habitual route that William took when returning in his royal coach from hunting in Richmond Park in London, and he noted that he crossed the Thames at Kew and then took a path between Turnham Green and Brentford. The intention was to install three sections of armed men at a narrow point in the lane, where the coach would be unable to manoeuvre. One section was tasked with assassinating the king and the others to deal with the armed guards. Some forty armed men were ready to carry out the attempt and were in position on both 15 February and 22 February 1696. However, William didn't show up on either occasion and the would-be assassins eventually received the news that the plot had been discovered. The king was subsequently given details of the forty conspirators. Fenwick was among the accused and he in turn implicated many leading figures in the establishment and the Whig government. This issue of disloyalty to the Crown amongst Members of Parliament resulted in subsequent Members of Parliament being obliged to swear an oath of loyalty to the monarch. This is still a requirement today.

A long succession of trials relating to the plot then took place, resulting in many of the plotters receiving the death sentence. On the execution date of 13 April 1696 the conspirators were attended to on the scaffold by three Nonjuror priests, and just prior to their executions the clergymen announced that the prisoners were absolved of their sins. In doing so they had effectively affirmed that the guilty were justified in their actions, whilst also carrying out a religious ceremony that was not acceptable to the Church of England. Accordingly, the Nonjuror priests also found themselves convicted of treason, before they were later released. In total, nine Jacobite conspirators were executed, including Fenwick.

George Barclay successfully escaped to the Continent, but seven others were imprisoned without trial. The last survivor died in 1738 while still in Newgate Prison.

The Nine Years War eventually concluded with the treaty of Ryswick in 1697, in which Louis XIV retained the whole of Alsace but was forced to return Lorraine and give up the gains he had made beyond the Rhine. The Dutch were able to preserve their borders, and Louis XIV was also forced to accept that William III, whom he had previously refused to recognise as such, was the rightful king of England, Ireland, Wales and Scotland.

In June 1701 the Act of Settlement, which permitted only Protestants to be on the English throne and was partly in response to a fear of the Catholic superpowers of mainland Europe, came into being. The act, which still applies today, was intended to ensure that if William III and Princess Anne (later Queen Anne) should die without heirs, the succession to the throne would pass to Sophie of Hanover, granddaughter of James I, and to her heirs, as long as they were Protestant.[4]

Later in 1701 James Francis Edward Stuart (1688–1777), the Old Pretender, took up the baton of the Jacobite cause after the death of his father, James II, at Saint Germain, France, on 16 September 1701. He was the son of James II and Mary of Modena and was brought up as a devout Catholic, having been raised in exile in France at the court of King Louis XIV. It was his birth, on 10 June 1688, which had triggered the Glorious Revolution, resulting in King William of Orange relieving King James II of the crown. He announced his claim to the English, Welsh, Scottish and Irish throne as James III of England, Wales and Ireland and James VIII of Scotland. King Louis XIV of France then added fuel to the fire by recognising James as the rightful heir, much to the chagrin of King William and then Queen Anne, as tensions mounted in Europe again in the build-up to the hostilities of the War of the Spanish Succession.

Shortly after James II's death in 1701, legend has it that, in 1702, King William, who by now had become a shambling drunk with deteriorating health, was riding at Hampton Court when his horse lost its footing on a molehill causing William to fall. It is said that from this he developed pneumonia, after fracturing his clavicle, which ultimately led to his death on 8 March 1702. To this day Jacobite supporters still toast, 'The wee gentleman in the black velvet waistcoat', in honour of the mole and the molehill.

Queen Anne (r. 1702–1714), Mary's Protestant sister, duly became the new monarch, in accordance with the previously laid-out constitution. She was born on 6 February 1665 at James's Palace. She was the second daughter and fourth child of James II and his first wife, Anne Hyde. It was said that Anne was more like her mother, while Mary was more of a Stuart like her father.

At the age of seventeen, after she had been involved in a scandal which culminated in John Sheffield, Lord Mulgrave, being expelled from court for attempting to seduce her, the decision was taken to find Anne a husband. Her first suitor was George Louis, Prince of Hanover, who was Anne's second cousin. The two formed an instant dislike and he was sent packing. Ironically, he was to later return to England as George I, Anne's successor to the throne.

Anne eventually married Prince George of Denmark, the youngest son of King Frederick III, in the Chapel Royal at St James's Palace on 28 July 1685. Anne and Frederick lived at the palace with her father, James II, and his second wife, Mary of Modena. However, when James and Mary's son, James Francis Edward, was born in 1688, Anne was instrumental in her father's demise as she didn't dispel the rumours that the baby had been switched in order to propagate the Catholic dynasty. She also colluded with William and Mary about the possibility of a coup d'état (The Glorious Revolution 1688).

By the time she succeeded her brother-in-law, William, to the throne, at the age of thirty-seven, she had endured seventeen pregnancies in sixteen years, which had still left her without an heir, meaning that she was already struggling with her health at her coronation at Westminster Abbey on 23 April 1702, and on the day had to be carried in a chair as she was suffering with gout, a condition that was not helped by her fondness for brandy (hence her nickname of Brandy Nan).

Anne was popular with her subjects. She displayed certain characteristics that people could identify with, which gave her the common touch. For instance, she had a dislike of the French and Catholics; she also lacked education or intellect and loved drinking, hunting, and gambling. For many, this was a pleasant change from the ever-so-sophisticated Stuarts.

Anne had a very close relationship with Sarah Jennings (1660–1744), who had been a great friend and confidant of Anne ever since childhood, when Sarah first entered the court of Anne's father, the Duke of York, later to become James II. It was at court that Sarah met her husband-to-be, John Churchill, who subsequently became the Duke of Marlborough. The wedding took place in secret, with the aid of the Duchess of York,

Mary of Modena, as both sets of parents were against the match. However, the marriage was a great success, and the couple were devoted to each other.

Sarah's friendship with Queen Anne made her the second most powerful woman in the country and the pair were so close that in order to dispense with formality, they addressed each other with joke names, Mrs Morley and Mrs Freeman. However, one potential issue with their friendship was Sarah's younger sister, Frances Jennings (1649–1731), who, like her sister, was born into the Protestant faith and was noted for her beauty. After Frances' first husband, George Hamilton an officer in the Life Guards, was killed in action, she married the Catholic Richard Talbot, Earl of Tyrconnell, Viceroy of Ireland and leading Jacobite in Ireland during the Williamite Wars. He had been an old suitor of hers and they lived together in Dublin. Accordingly, she then became Countess Tyrconnell and then later, after the arrival of James II in Ireland on 20 March 1689, Tyrconnell was made a duke and she became a duchess.

Tyrconnell died of a stroke in 1691 during the Siege of Limerick, shortly before the Jacobites were defeated in the Williamite Wars. After his death, Frances was regarded as a Jacobite outlaw, her estates were confiscated and she escaped to exile in France. However, following the accession of Queen Anne, Frances was able to recover some of her husband's property and wealth, probably due to the influence her sister had with the queen.

Anne stated that she knew in her heart that she was entirely English, which played well with her English subjects, but touched a nerve among the Scots, particularly after the Act of Union of 1707. Meanwhile, trouble was brewing in Europe with King Louis XIV of France at the centre of it. The War of the Spanish Succession (1701–1714) was triggered by the death of Charles II of Spain in November 1700. He was the last Habsburg Monarch of Spain and had presided over a vast empire for over forty years, comprising Spain, Naples, Sicily, Milan, the Spanish Netherlands (modern-day Belgium) and numerous gold-rich Spanish colonies of Central and South America. He had no children and therefore no direct heirs to the kingdom and his closest heirs were members of the ruling families of the Austrian Habsburg and French Bourbon dynasties. Acquisition of the Spanish Empire was coveted by both dynasties, and the prize was particularly sought after by King Louis XIV of France.

Charles had actually bequeathed Spain to Louis XIV's grandson Philip, who was a member of the French Bourbon family, and he became King of Spain on 16 November 1700. This decision seemed to make an already dominant France an even more powerful entity in Europe under their tyrannical leader, King Louis XIV, who was already hellbent on further expansion. For this reason, the English and Dutch favoured the Hapsburg candidate, Archduke Charles of Austria, and became part of the alliance against France when King Louis invaded the Spanish Netherlands.

As war in Europe was on the horizon again, one of Anne's first actions as monarch was to appoint the brilliant and experienced John Churchill, who had earlier been involved in the Monmouth Rebellion and Battle of Sedgemoor, as the overall commander of English forces; she also simultaneously made him the Duke of Marlborough.

The first decisive action occurred on 13 August 1704, when British troops fighting as part of the alliance against France won one of their greatest ever victories, at the Bavarian village of Blenheim, when John Churchill, the Duke of Marlborough, shattered the legend of French military invincibility and put King Louis XIV on the back foot for the first time.

Initially, the focus of the war was the Netherlands, but in 1704 King Louis XIV set his sights on Vienna, the capital of England's other ally, Austria. This was a concern to the Duke of Marlborough, as the fall of Vienna would weaken the alliance. He ignored Dutch pleas that he should continue defending the Netherlands and instead marched his army halfway across Europe to defend Vienna.

Marlborough's army was then joined by the army of Prince Eugene of Savoy, and they blocked the path of the French and Bavarian army marching towards Vienna. Prince Eugene was a highly competent general and his skills and experience combined well with those of Churchill.

Marshall Talland, the French commander, took up a strong position on the western bank of the River Nebel, a position which was afforded protection by both the River Nebel and the River Danube, close to the fortified village of Blenheim. He had wrongly assumed that Churchill and Eugene would not risk attacking such an impregnable position, so had a shock on the morning of 13 August 1704 when he awoke to see the Allied army preparing to cross the river.

The French immediately started pounding the Allies with a relentless artillery bombardment, but Prince Eugene's army managed to navigate the river and reach their position on the flank. Once they had done so, Marlborough gave the order for his forces to attack.

The French commander in Blenheim, the Marquis de Cerumbault, panicked, and instantly called up eighteen battalions of reserves, which caused the fortified city to become severely overcrowded and enabled Marlborough to simply order a contingent of his troops to hem them in whilst directing fire onto them. The main fighting, however, was taking place outside Blenheim, and Marlborough was giving a masterclass in how to combine infantry and cavalry into a devastating force. The French lines fell back and eventually crumbled as the Allied cavalry thundered into them, causing devastating French losses.

Marlborough had been immense, and it was said that the glory of their greatest enemy, Louis XIV, departed that day. The Battle of Blenheim is considered to be one of the turning points in European history. It was the most decisive battle in the War of the Spanish Succession, and one that prevented France invading Austria and dominating Europe. As a reward, a grateful Queen Anne gave Marlborough a mansion near Oxford named Blenheim Palace, which also became the birthplace of his descendant, Winston Churchill. However, the war did continue to rumble on until 1713.

After the disastrous defeat at Blenheim, 1705 brought some respite for the French. The Duke of Marlborough's intention was to invade France through the Moselle valley and press home his advantage, before persuading King Louis of France to make peace. But to his intense disappointment, the plan was thwarted by various factors, and he was unable to bring the French into a direct engagement.

His frustration was then compounded when the French began to regain the ascendancy to some degree. Marshal Villeroi, the French commander, took the town of Huy on the Meuse on 10 June 1705, before moving on towards Liege, whilst Marshal Villars was in an impregnable position on the Moselle. Meanwhile, Marlborough's supplies were running short, meaning he had to temporarily abort his campaign on 15 June 1705.

However, King Louis XIV, realising after the defeat at Blenheim that the campaign couldn't be won, wanted peace, but on favourable terms. Therefore, in 1706 France went on the offensive, and accordingly, King

Louis ordered Marshal Villeroi to set off from Lourain at the head of 60,000 men and march to Tienen, from where he threatened the town of Zoutleeuw. The Duke of Marlborough saw his chance and assembled 62,000 Dutch and British forces near Maastricht.

The two armies locked horns between the Mehaigre and Petite Gheete rivers, close to the small village of Ramillies, on 23 May 1706, where the brilliant duke tactically out-thought the opposing commanders at every turn. It took Marlborough's Dutch, English and Danish force less than four hours to rout the French.

The Allies were then able to push home their advantage as they went on to take the towns of Brussels, Bruges and Antwerp, driving Villeroi's army from most of the Spanish Netherlands. This, along with Prince Eugene's success at the Battle of Turin, accounted for the Allies greatest territorial gains during the war.

Meanwhile, back in the British Isles there were still rumblings of Jacobite discontent, not least from the Jacobite Highland clans, who were still smarting from the Glencoe massacre. However, there was also resentment among the people of the Lowland Scottish towns and cities at the harsh trading embargoes imposed by England.

After the death of King William the Scottish Parliament passed an Act of Security, which prohibited an English monarch from ruling Scotland unless equal trading, political and religious rights were guaranteed. Worryingly, it also allowed an independent Scottish army to be raised, increasing the likelihood of war between the two nations. This prompted the English Whig government to make concessions to the Lowlanders and mastermind the 1 May 1707 Act of Union, which was passed by both Scottish and English Parliaments, and meant that England and Scotland were now united within the Kingdom of Great Britain, with a uniform system of taxation, trading and coinage. Scotland joined Wales and Ireland, who had already been declared part of a union with England by Henry VIII in 1536. However, the Scottish legal system and Scottish Church remained separate entities.

The Jacobite Highland clansmen, who were still unwavering in their loyalty to King James II and his descendants, were disgusted with this outcome. They felt that Scotland had pledged loyalty to Queen Anne for commercial benefit, 'We are bought and sold for English gold,' they sang, and this particular sentiment appeared many years later in Robert Burns' poetry.[5]

By the end of 1707 the War of the Spanish Succession had reached stalemate. Despite victories in Flanders, Allied forces had been unable to break through the French border defences or place their candidate on the Spanish throne. However, the French were facing a far more calamitous military situation as a result of Marlborough's victories in Flanders, and the Jacobite Rising of March 1708, also known as The Enterprise, was a desperate response to this. Indeed, both sides in the War of the Spanish Succession saw the use of internal conflicts as a possible way of breaking the deadlock. For instance, Britain supported the Comisard rebels (Huguenot Protestants) in south-west France in their conflict against King Louis XIV, whilst the Jacobites unwittingly served a similar destabilising function in Britain on behalf of the French.

Jacobite Nathaniel Hooke convinced those in power in France that there was an opportunity for a Scottish rising due to the general discontent in Scotland regarding the 1707 Act of Union. This would also serve the dual purpose of diverting British troops away from Europe. Accordingly, King Louis XIV was keen to launch an invasion that linked up with the Highland Jacobite Scots in order to put James Francis Edward Stuart on the throne of Great Britain.

King Louis XIV provided weapons, money, artillery and ammunition. He also supplied 8,000 French troops, which included the Comte de Ponchartrain, whose role was to preside over the planning of the Enterprise, and Claude de Forbin, who was to be the commander of the naval squadron, with the Comte de Gace in charge of the landing force.

French naval operations often took place during the winter months, when winds and tides made it harder for the Royal Navy to patrol the French Channel ports and enforce a blockade. However, the French privateers were familiar with the awful weather conditions off the intended destination of eastern Scotland and informed De Forbes that the expedition had no chance of succeeding. De Forbin was also concerned that there was no confirmed landing place to disembark troops. This information was in turn passed on to Louis XIV, but planning for the expedition continued and a fleet of five men of war and fifteen transports was assembled at Dunkirk. They were joined by James Francis Edward Stuart, the Old Pretender himself, on 9 March 1708. However, the

British had become aware of the situation and a Royal Naval fleet, with a company of soldiers commanded by Sir George Byng, arrived at the nearby port of Gravelines to scupper the French plans. The French troops disembarked, and as the Old Pretender was ill with measles, they were stood down whilst he recovered.

After a week, Byng had to leave the area to resupply, providing the Jacobites a window of opportunity to set sail on 17 March 1708. Once the fleet set sail, there were severe gales, which had the effect of delaying Byng's pursuit. Despite the gales, De Forbin's fleet kept out to sea rather than hugging the coastline, in an attempt to avoid the pursuing Byng. De Forbin knew he could ill afford to face the British in direct confrontation; he had insisted on using small but fast and manoeuvrable privateers and had sacrificed fire power for manoeuvrability. This improved their odds of avoiding the Royal Navy, but severely compromised their chances in battle if they were confronted.

The French, whose intention was to make for Stirling, were blown further north than they intended, and on 25 March 1708 they anchored near Fife Ness while they tried to locate a suitable landing site. They then spent two days fruitlessly attempting to enter the Moray Firth, which allowed Byng's fleet to close the distance on them. Realising they needed to get away, they then hastily set sail for Dunkirk whilst being pursued by the Royal Navy. They made it back but suffered severe damage and heavy loss of life as the Royal Navy harassed them all the way around the north of Scotland and the west of Ireland.

Although the Enterprise of March 1708 ended in abject defeat for the Jacobites and severely damaged their credibility, the French viewed it as a great success. During this period, they regained large swathes of the Spanish Netherlands, as British resources were diverted away from that arena to deal with the threat that the Enterprise posed.

However, King Louis XIV was still desperate to avenge the defeats of Blenheim and Ramillies, so he released French troops from other theatres into Flanders, with the intention of taking the region. The Allies also wanted to bring the French into a conclusive set piece battle.

Marlborough's army was located just south of Brussels, whilst Eugene's forces were assembled at Koblenz, where the Rhine is joined by the Moselle River. However, in May 1708 the French army moved towards Flanders, reaching the city of Braine, about fifteen miles south of Brussels. Marlborough then sent an urgent communication to Prince Eugene requesting him to make haste from Koblenz.

The French remained in Braine for several weeks, which allowed Prince Eugene time to bring his army up from the Rhine. However, on 5 July 1708 the French took the Allies by surprise by moving westwards and taking the cities of Bruges and Ghent, which only left one British fortress remaining in the area, at Oudenarde. The town was strategically important as it was a crossing point over the Scheldt River and if that was taken, Marlborough would be cut off from the coast. Marlborough was anxious not to become hemmed in, or become involved in a siege situation, so his objective was to position his forces between the French and Lille. This left the French with a choice of either coming to battle or relinquishing the cities of Bruges and Ghent. It also became a race to cross the River Scheldt. General Cadogan of Marlborough's army got there first and set up a defensive position, building several pontoon-style bridges to allow Marlborough's troops, arriving later, to cross. Meanwhile, the French army crossed the Scheldt to the north of Oudenarde.

The two armies then collided at the Battle of Oudenarde on 11 July 1708. The French were in a good position, but a reconnaissance party had come to the conclusion that the ground in front of them was too marshy for cavalry. The French general, Louis Joseph Duc de Vendome, a seasoned and experienced soldier, was against attacking from this position. But the Duc de Bourgogne, who had considerably less experience and owed his position to the fact that he was the grandson of King Louis XIV of France, countermanded this order and gave instructions to attack. Unfortunately, this later order only got through to seven French battalions. They attacked, but because they were too few in number they were cut to ribbons. The remaining French troops then had no alternative but to join the battle, and in contrast to the disjointed efforts of the French commanders, the tactically brilliant Marlborough was able to perform a flanking manoeuvre which routed the French army, causing them to retreat to Ghent, having yet again avoided complete destruction. One of the junior commanders with the Hanoverian cavalry on the Allied side was the Electoral Prince of Hanover, the future King George II of Great Britain, who had his horse shot from under him during the battle. History could have been very different.

By September 1709 King Louis XIV was still seeking to end the war, but was also still looking for better terms than the Alliance had so far offered him, so the war continued to drag on. Marlborough had captured the fortress city of Tornai, in present-day Belgium, and was advancing on Mons, whilst the French, under the Duke of Villars, moved to protect the city, resulting in the armies converging near the border with France at the Battle of Malplaquet on 11 September 1709.

Villars, who was outnumbered, took up a clever position whereby both of his flanks were covered by wooded areas. This was to negate Marlborough's favourite tactic of attacking the flanks with the intention of weakening the centre by siphoning off troops from there. Consequently, Marlborough's inevitable attack on the flanks did not prove very successful and resulted in great loss of life on the Allied side. British infantry then bludgeoned the French centre, before several Allied cavalry charges took place, which were all repelled, resulting in further heavy Allied casualties. The French, realising the battle could not be won, ordered a tactical retreat. However, the Allied army were in no position to follow up and take advantage of their 'victory' as they had been so severely mauled, having lost 20,000 men, twice as many as the French.

Technically, it was an Allied victory, but the massive loss of life on the Allied side did not reflect that, and Marlborough on this occasion had hardly covered himself in glory. Consequently, Malplaquet, which was one of the bloodiest battles of the eighteenth century, proved to be a turning point of the war.

Queen Anne's relationship with her long-term friend and confidant, Sarah Jennings, Marlborough's wife, had already been showing signs of strain due to their differing views on politics, but reached breaking point when the heavy casualties of this battle resulted in Marlborough's dismissal by the queen. The disastrous battle was also instrumental in the Whig government losing power. They were replaced in 1710 by the Tories, who immediately began agitating for a withdrawal from the Grand Alliance.

The War of the Spanish Succession was eventually concluded with the Treaty of Utrecht in 1713, which allowed Philip the Spanish throne, so long as he renounced any claim to France. Britain received considerable gains in territory, particularly in North America, and had emerged as a great naval and colonial power.[6] The treaty also forced Louis XIV to withdraw his support for James Francis Edward Stuart and required him to order him to leave France. In effect, the all-powerful Louis XIV had been humbled by England's greatest general, John Churchill, Duke of Marlborough.

The Treaty of Utrecht subsequently became a series of treaties as the original was followed by the Treaty of Rastatt and the Treaty of Baden, both in 1714. The Treaty of Rastatt was a treaty between the Holy Roman Emperor, Charles VI, and France, which took place on 7 March 1714 in the Baden city of Rastaat, Switzerland. It ended the emperor's attempts to continue the War of the Spanish Succession after the other states had made peace in the Treaty of Utrecht. Later, on 7 September of the same year, the Holy Roman Emperor, Charles VI, made peace in the name of the states of the Holy Roman Empire at Baden in Switzerland.

Queen Anne died, at the age of forty-nine, on 1 August 1714, having previously suffered two strokes. The issue of Anne's successor to the throne had already been decreed by the 1701 Act of Settlement, which stated that 'The throne should pass to the next Protestant heir'. As none of Anne's children had survived, Parliament was now constitutionally bound to hand the throne to her father's Protestant cousin, Princess Sophia, from the House of Hanover, rather than her half-brother, the Catholic James Edward Stuart.

Although Anne detested her Hanoverian relatives, and her previous suitor, George, in particular, she had made an effort to make positive overtures towards them before her death in an attempt to secure a smooth transition of the monarchy into Protestant hands.

Princess Sophia, Electress of Hanover (1630–1714), was the granddaughter of James I and youngest child of Elizabeth (Stuart) of Bohemia and Frederick V of the Palatinate. She was the Electress of Hanover by virtue of her marriage to Elector Ernest Augustus, whom she married in 1658. However, Sophia died in 1714, eight weeks before Queen Anne, so the man who landed at Greenwich in September was Sophia's son, George Elector, Anne's previous suitor and her second cousin. He was crowned King George I (r. 1714–1726) on 20 October 1714 and became Britain's first monarch from a new dynasty, the House of Hanover, thus ending the 343-year-old Stuart dynasty.

George was married to Sophia of Brunswick-Luneberg Celle, who was the only surviving daughter of George William, Duke of Brunswick-

The beach where Monmouth and his army landed at Lyme Regis, Dorset, is now called Monmouth Beach.

The pub sign of the Sedgemoor Inn. In the background, St Mary the Virgin Church, Westonzoyland, can be seen, where rebel prisoners were held after the battle. The Battle of Sedgemoor 6 July 1685, was the last battle to take place on English soil.

Moyles Court: the home of Alice Lisle was given to Lord Feversham by King James II after Alice's execution, as a reward for commanding the Royal Army.

The rooms where Judge Jeffreys lodged at 6 High West Street, Dorchester, during the Dorchester Bloody Assizes, are now the Judge Jeffreys Restaurant and Coffee House.

A statue in honour of William of Orange is situated on the Quay at Brixham, Devon, which cites his vow. 'The liberties of England and the Protestant religion I will maintain'. A replica of Francis Drake's ship the *Golden Hind* can be seen in the background.

The Pass of Killiecrankie, three miles north of Pitlochry, Perthshire, where the Battle of Killiecrankie was fought on 27 July 1689.

Soldier's Leap: the site where Redcoat Donald McBean leapt nineteen feet across the treacherous gorge in order to escape the fearsome Highland hordes.

Loch an Eilean Castle, in the Rothiemurchus Forest, near Aviemore, where after the Jacobite defeat at the Battle of Cromdale, 30 April–1 May 1690, a group of approximately a hundred escaping Jacobites attempted to seize the stronghold, only to be repelled by the absent Laird's wife, Grizzel Mhor, and a handful of other inhabitants.

Urquhart Castle on the shores of Loch Ness was also under Jacobite siege both before and after the Battle of Cromdale.

Glencoe: the site of a shameful massacre of the MacDonald clan committed by government troops on the morning of 13 February 1692.

Eilean Donan Castle: during the Jacobite Rising of 1719, Eilean Donan Castle, which is on an island at the meeting point of Lochs Duich, Alsh and Long, adjacent to the Isle of Skye, served as a Jacobite base, where they left their stores and most of their ammunition, guarded by forty Spanish marines, before pressing on to Inverness.

Glen Shiel: the site of the Battle of Glen Shiel on 10 June 1719. The glen includes a peak named *Spur na Spainteach* or Peak of the Spaniards in honour of the Spanish marines who fought there. It was also the last engagement between British and foreign troops on mainland British soil, as the Jacobites included Spanish marines.

Glen Shiel: the remains of a stone enclosure where the Jacobites stored their ammunition.

Glenfinnan: the site where the Jacobite Highland clans first rallied in support of Bonnie Prince Charlie was marked in 1815 by a monument of a Highland warrior, erected in honour of the Highland clansmen who lost their lives following the Young Pretender.

Carlisle Castle: the Jacobites captured the castle of this English border town on their way south on 15 November 1745, and then returned to the garrison on 22 December 1745 when they retreated back to Scotland. The stronghold was shortly recaptured by government forces on 30 December 1745, and the defending Jacobite soldiers were incarcerated here before meeting their fates of either death or transportation. After Culloden many more Jacobite prisoners were also held within the dungeon, and today a stone can be seen in the cell that has a strange shape. The story is that it became misshapen as moisture collected on it and the Jacobite prisoners licked it to prevent themselves from dying of thirst.

Ruthven Barracks in Badenoch, beside the military road near Kingusie, commanded Strathspey and held a strategically important position with regard to controlling access to the Cairngorns and the main thouroughfare between the Lowlands and Inverness.

Fort William was the only one the three Great Glen forts that had managed to hold out against the Jacobites. However, very little remains of the old fort today.

Drummossie Moor, better known as Culloden Battlefield.

The battle raged around Leanach Cottage, which was used as a field hospital by government troops. It was inhabited until 1912 and has now been restored.

Clan Stewart of Appin headstone at Culloden. Perhaps Charles Stewart of Ardsheal shouldn't have listened to his wife, Isabel Haldene.

Tollbooth Steeple, Inverness. In Inverness, the nearest town to the battle, churches were transformed into jails and prison ships were moored nearby. The old tollbooth was also used as a prison. The steeple and courthouse that are in situ now were built in 1791 on the site of the original medieval steeple and toll booth that housed Jacobite prisoners.

Lancaster Castle. Many of the soldiers from the Jacobite Manchester regiment were confined here after the regiment's capture at Carlisle.

Flora Macdonald's statue outside Inverness Castle was designed by Andrew Davidson. She is scanning the landscape awaiting the return of Bonnie Prince Charlie.

Flora MacDonald's grave in the grounds of Kilmuir Church, Isle of Skye. Some say she was wrapped in the prince's bed sheet and that when she died in 1790, 3,000 mourners attended the funeral.

Crofters Cottages on the Isle of Skye. This style of cottage proliferated the Highlands, but their number diminished rapidly after the Highland Clearances.

Luneberg-Celle, and his wife, Eleonore Desmier d'Olbreuse. George and Sophia were married on 22 November 1682 and lived happily at first, having a son and daughter. However, the situation changed when they both had affairs; George with one of his mother's ladies in waiting, Ehrengard Melusine Von der Shulenburg, and Sophia with Count Phillip Christoph von Konigsmarck.

Count von Konigsmarck, a Hanoverian army officer, disappeared in suspicious circumstances, and as Sophia now refused to live with her husband, a divorce was swiftly arranged to hush any unseemly rumours, while Sophia Dorothea was quietly moved out of the way to semi captivity at Castle Ahlden, in Lower Saxony, Germany, where her movements could be monitored until she died, on 2 November 1726, aged sixty. Many years later, the count's body was discovered under the floor of Leine Palace in Lower Saxony, in what had been George's room.[7]

The Whig party, which had previously opposed the succession of the Catholic King James II, now formed the government. One slight problem, though, was that George couldn't speak any English, and as a result had to rely on the guidance of his ministers more than any other previous monarch. In fact, his place at government meetings had to be taken by a chief or prime minister.

The first prime minister (a term initially used derogatively by other ministers jealous of his pivotal role) was the highly skilled Whig politician Sir Robert Walpole. His policy of 'jaw jaw not war war' was welcomed by the British public who were war weary after the never-ending series of conflicts with France.

However, there was one fly in the ointment – the Jacobite Scots. They were certainly not war weary, and did not accept the Hanoverian king. And so, in 1715 there was another Jacobite rebellion.

Chapter 5

The 1715 and 1719 Scottish Jacobite Rebellions and Further Jacobite Activity until 1737

The death of Queen Anne was the cue for the Jacobite standard to be raised again. The aim of the rebellion, which initially had the backing of Louis XIV of France, was to put Prince James Edward Stuart, the 'Old Pretender', son of James II and Mary of Modena, on the throne. The timing of the invasion was good, as George I was not generally loved in England, and the elections of 1715 had seen numerous riots, apparently in sympathy for the Stuarts.

The two main political parties were the Tories, who supported the established Church of England and believed that the line of succession shouldn't be interfered with, and the Whigs, who were the government in power at the time and who were in favour of Constitutional Monarchy as opposed to Absolute Monarchy and who had been instrumental in the Glorious Revolution of 1688. They also sought Catholic Emancipation, and were in favour of reducing the restrictions imposed on those practicing the Catholic religion, although they were forthrightly against the Roman Catholic Stuart kings and pretenders.

After 1714 the Whigs entered a period of supremacy that lasted until 1760 and this led many Tory MPs to collude with the Jacobites as a means of regaining power, believing that their political interests would be better served by Stuart restoration, even though they were anti-Papist and the restoration of the Stuarts would mean a Catholic monarchy.

The Whig government were fearful of rebellion and sought to quell the riots with brutality, which only had the effect of causing more hostility. The Tories tried to exploit the situation and their leader, Henry St John, Viscount Bolingbroke, planned to wait until discontent in England reached fever pitch and then execute a coup, which would bring the

Stuarts back to the throne. However, Bolingbroke's fellow Jacobites were not prepared to be patient and thought an immediate revolt in Scotland would spark an English uprising, and bring James to the throne.

One disillusioned politician was the Earl of Mar, who had inherited his father's earldom in 1689 and was nick named 'Bobbing John', due to his tendancy to change allegiance from Whig to Tory or Hanoverian to Jacobite as the situation suited him best.

In the reign of Queen Anne, his career had flourished as Secretary of State for Scotland and he had played a pivotal role in the union of the parliaments of England and Scotland in 1707, for which he was rewarded by being made a Representative Peer for Scotland, Keeper of the Signet and a Privy Counsellor.

By 1713, he was serving in the Government as Secretary of State for Britain, but like many Scots had become disillusioned with the Act of Union, despite the fact that he had drafted it, and he sought a proposal to have it repealed. However when George I ascended to the throne, Mar was dismissed from his role and then publicly snubbed by the monarch, despite writing a grovelling letter in which he pledged his loyalty to the king.

These developments resulted in Mar, switching allegiance and he began making plans with other Jacobite conspirators to instigate a rising. The plans were wildly optimistic as the British Army was loyal and experienced, and the people themselves were beginning to accept George I, who also pulled a rabbit from the hat, by re-appointing the previously disgraced Marlborough.

Realising that a Jacobite rising was imminent the Government proactively arrested many leading English Jacobites as a preventative measure. Another key stumbling block for the Jacobites was the death of King Louis XIV on 1 September 1715, which meant French support for the invasion vanished.

Once again, support for the rebellion was strongest in the Scottish Highlands among the Catholic and Episcopalian clans, when on 6 September 1715, the Jacobite Stuart standard was raised in rebellion by John Erskine, 6th Earl of Mar, at Braemar. The Jacobite Highland clansmen were quickly mobilised to the cause and in fact, the fifteen attracted greater support than the subsequent more famous forty five. In no time they had captured Perth and established a base encampment. Meanwhile, the government forces in Scotland, under the command of

John Campbell, Duke of Argyll, were powerless at this stage, as they were too few in number.

Inverness was next on the Jacobite radar and Mackenzie, 5th Earl of Seaforth, a Jacobite commander, and chief of Clan Mackenzie, led a large Jacobite force and captured the town and castle, before moving on the following day and leaving the garrison under the control of his clan kith and kin, John Mackenzie of Coul.

Shortly afterwards, an opposing government force consisting of men from the clans of Sutherland, MacKay, Ross and Munro, under the command of Sir Robert Munro, 6th Baronet, chief of Clan Munro, arrived at Alness on 5 October 1715, en route to Inverness. On learning of this, Mackenzie of Seaforth resolved to confront them.

A council of war took place between the pro-government clan chiefs, and it was decided that, due to their enemy's numerical supremacy, it would be foolish to take them on, so they decided to return to their homelands. However, upon their return home the Munros and Rosses discovered that their lands had been plundered in their absence by Mackenzie's men.

Meanwhile, a separate force of 2,000 Jacobites crossed the border with the intention of recruiting disaffected Englishmen from the north of England to their cause. As they advanced southwards and made their way through Lancashire, they recruited another 2,000 men commanded by Thomas Forster, a Northumbrian gentleman, bringing their total force to 4,000. They faced very little opposition, until they reached Preston in Lancashire, where, on hearing that the Hanoverian General Charles Willis had been despatched to Preston to halt their progress with six regiments from Manchester, the Jacobites barricaded themselves into residential properties.

Upon arrival in Preston on 12 November 1715 Willis launched an immediate attack against the Jacobite barricades and came under intense fire, resulting in the attack being repulsed after both sides had suffered heavy losses. Wills then ordered houses to be set on fire so that the flames spread along to the Jacobite positions, then, as darkness approached, Wills ordered the houses taken as government positions to be lit for identification purposes. This backfired as it provided targets for the Jacobite snipers, who also set the government-occupied houses alight.

On the morning of Sunday, 13 November 1715 more Hanoverian troops arrived and were positioned to surround the town and prevent the now-besieged Jacobites from escaping. Prior to the encirclement of the town by government forces, the Jacobites had suffered heavy losses and had also lost a considerable number due to defection, so, on 14 November 1715, negotiations were opened with Wills to broker an honourable surrender. However, the Jacobite Highlanders – whose intention was to fight on and take the attack to the enemy – knew nothing of this and reacted with fury when they discovered what was, in their eyes, a betrayal. They threatened to kill any Jacobites who wanted to surrender and carried out their promise on many. Accordingly, Wills refused to accept the surrender as he was aware of the Jacobite Highlanders intent. However, eventually the Jacobite Highlanders were persuaded to lay down their arms in the market square and only then did Wills accept the surrender.

After the surrender, the Jacobite Highland clansmen captured at the Battle of Preston were tried in England and jailed or transported, whilst the commanders were executed for treason under the Act of the Attainder.

Meanwhile back in Scotland, Mar's main Jacobite army based in Perth had defeated the Duke of Argyll's men in some minor skirmishes. As a result, they now commanded most of the northern Highlands and were ready to move south to take Stirling. However, local spies had informed Argyll of Mar's intentions and consequently he moved his army to Sherrifmuir near Dunblane, where they met on the battlefield on 13 November 1715, on the same day as the Siege of Preston raged.

At Sherrifmuir, a remote area of heathland lying between Stirling and Auchterarder on the northern edge of the Ochil Hills, near Perth, Mar's 7,000–10,000 Jacobites – with Mar commanding the left flank, James Drummond, 2nd Duke of Perth, commanding his cavalry in the centre, and George Keith, the Earl Marischal, leading two squadrons of cavalry on the right – faced up against a much smaller Hanoverian force of 3,000 men, commanded by John Campbell, 2nd Duke of Argyll and Chief of Clan Campbell.

Argyll was aware that his left flank, under the command of General Thomas Westham, was particularly outnumbered by the Jacobite right wing facing them, so, in order to compensate, Argyll ordered Westham's men to attack. They had some success initially in driving the Jacobite Highlanders back, but then began to be overwhelmed by the greater Jacobite numbers, meaning that Argyll's right flank had to move round to assist. This was the cue for the Highland clans on the Jacobite right wing to initiate the Highland Charge, which caused chaos and drove the Hanoverian infantry back onto their own cavalry and forced a retreat.

Mar ordered the Highlanders to pursue them, but the Jacobite cavalry, under the command of the 2nd Duke of Perth, waited in vain for orders which were not forthcoming. Meanwhile, the Jacobite left wing was being forced back by the musket fire of the government infantry.

By the evening both armies had suffered severe losses and each right wing had prevailed. The Jacobites survivors made their way back to their encampment in the village of Muthill just outside Perth, whilst the Hanoverians returned to their base at Dunblane.

On the morning after, Argyll took to the field again, fearing the worst due to the Jacobite's superior numbers. However, the Jacobites failed to arrive because Mar refused to sustain any more losses.

Although the fighting itself was inconclusive, Argyll had achieved his strategic objective of preventing the Jacobite progress. In effect, the result was a Jacobite defeat, especially as Mar's army was forced to retreat further back to their base in the city of Perth, where they were then trapped. The fact that the Jacobites had failed to achieve a decisive victory, despite their superior numbers, created a demoralising effect, which was further compounded when Mar's French and Spanish troops departed, whilst Argyll's army was increased by reinforcements. The government forces saw the battle as a victory and those regiments that were involved were awarded the battle honour of the White Horse of Hanover.[1]

Another issue that was prominent in November 1715 involved the town and castle of Inverness, which were still under the control of the Jacobite Clan Mackenzie led by Sir John Mackenzie of Coul.

The pro-government clans of Fraser, Rose and Forbes, under the command of Simon Fraser of Lovat, duly arrived in the town to try and bring them back under government control. They assembled on the opposite side of the River Ness to the castle. About the same time, Keppoch MacDonald also arrived with his clansmen to add weight to the Jacobite defenders.

A further group of Jacobites from the Chattan Confederation, a confederation of twelve separate clans, each with their own clan chief but under the umbrella of the Clan Chief of Clan Mackintosh, also arrived to reinforce the defence of the castle. However, Lovat intercepted them and threatened to send his troops south to Mackintosh country and destroy their lands if they proceeded. The threat was enough to cause the clan chief to back down and return with his clan to whence they came.

Lovat then held a council of war amongst his clan chiefs, at which it was decided to take the town rather than try to besiege the castle without the necessary equipment. But before Lovat could initiate the attack, Arthur Rose and a handful of men were already attacking the Tollbooth, which was doubling up as a guard house. Rose then became the only fatality of the siege when he was crushed by the heavy door and simultaneously shot.

The next day, 13 November 1715, Sir John Mackenzie of Coul brokered a surrender in which he was allowed to join the main body of the Jacobite army, and Mackenzie and his men left hastily by boat, anxious to avoid running the gauntlet of the pro-government clansmen outside.

The pro-government forces took over and the medieval castle was repaired. In addition, a new barracks and outer wall were added by General Wade when it was reinvented to become the first Fort George.

Meanwhile, the Jacobites from the Chattan Confederation hadn't gone straight home. Instead, they laid siege to nearby Culloden House, the seat of the pro-government Forbes Clan Chief, Simon Fraser of Lovat. Lady Forbes, the laird's wife, was the only senior member of the family in residence at the time. Along with her servants, she was able to keep the 700 armed marauders at bay, and let the besiegers know in no uncertain terms that if they approached within gunshot range of the house that she would show them she had both the arms and ammunition to support the right and title of George I of Great Britain. The house was under siege for seven weeks before it was relieved by Simon Fraser, the 11th Lord Lovat, whose royalist troops were able to scatter the Chattan Confederation clansmen, who subsequently returned to Perth to join the Earl of Mar and the main body of the Jacobite army.

November 1715 was a disastrous month for the Jacobites – they suffered a serious reverse at the Battle of Sherrifmuir and also defeats at Preston, Inverness and Culloden House. To add to the Jacobite woes, following the Siege of Inverness, where Mackenzie of Coul had been forced to retreat, Sir Robert Munro exhorted his men to avenge the plundering of his lands by Mackenzie's clansmen after their confrontation at Alness. Accordingly, the Munros and other Highlanders loyal to the British government of George I laid siege to Brahan Castle, seat of William

Mackenzie, 5th Earl of Seaforth, forcing the Mackenzies to surrender and hand in their weapons.

After Sherrifmuir, Mar kept his troops encamped at Perth whilst they waited for the promised military support from France to arrive, as well as the arrival of Prince James Francis Edward Stuart. Then, on 22 December 1715, the Old Pretender himself did arrive at Peterhead in a fishing boat and joined the Jacobite forces. However, his uninspiring appearance didn't do a lot to arrest the desertions from his already seriously depleted and flagging army. Meanwhile, the French forces came under attack from the Royal Navy whilst en route and failed to reach Scotland. More bad news for the Jacobites was that Argyll's reinforced and revitalised government troops were advancing north towards Perth and this had the effect of causing the Jacobites to withdraw to Montrose.

For James, the Old Pretender, the writing was on the wall. He knew the rising was over before it had really begun and he left Scotland a broken man, never to see his native land again as he returned to France on 4 February 1716, while the Jacobite army moved to Ruthven Barracks and dispersed.

The Earl of Mar and most of the other Jacobite leaders also escaped into exile to avoid the charge of high treason. However, the majority of the exiled Jacobites were able to return in 1717, when the Act of Grace resulted in George I pardoning those involved with the Jacobite risings – with the exceptions of the Earl of Mar, the Earl of Marischal and the renowned outlaw Rob Roy MacGregor, who all lost their titles and estates.

Mar went on to link up with the Old Pretender in Rome, where, despite James lavishing him with extravagant titles, he spent most of his time conspiring against the would-be king. By 1725, when James realised what was happening, Mar was no longer welcome at his court.

The defeat of the Jacobites in 1715 allowed the Whigs to exercise a vast majority in the House of Commons and this marked the start of a period known as the Whig supremacy (1715–1760), during which the Tories were excluded from any positions of influence.

The 1719 Scottish Jacobite Rebellion and the War of the Quadruple Alliance (1718–1720)

The 1713 Treaty of Utrecht had resulted in Spain losing Sicily and Sardinia. Then, in 1717, Spain attempted to regain their Italian possessions by occupying Sardinia. However, when they tried the same trick in Sicily in 1718, the Royal Navy blasted the Spanish fleet out of the water at the Battle of Cape Passaro. This was the trigger for the War of the Quadruple Alliance, which saw Spain ranged against Britain, France, the Holy Roman Empire and the Dutch Republic. The alliance was unique, in that it was the only time in the eighteenth century that Britain and France were allies, as they sought to ensure that Philip of Spain adhered to the original terms of the Treaty of Utrecht. This newfound entente cordiale may have had something to do with the fact that France at this time was no longer ruled by King Louis XIV, who died in 1715, and was ruled instead by his five-year-old great grandson, King Louis XV, under the guidance of the Duc d'Orleans, King Louis' brother.

The Jacobite Rising of 1719 was part of the War of the Quadruple Alliance and was a Spanish-backed attempt to restore the Stuart dynasty to the throne of Britain in the form of the exiled James Francis Edward Stuart (the Old Pretender). As far as Spain was concerned, it would, at the very least, divert British forces that would otherwise be involved in the main theatres of the war of the Quadruple Alliance.

In early 1719 Spain's chief statesman, Cardinal Alberoni, and the Irish-born Duke of Ormonde launched an ambitious plan, which involved a Spanish maritime invasion of Britain, the purpose of which was to ignite a Scottish and English rebellion and depose the Hanoverian monarch, George I. The plan was for Spanish troops to land in the south-west of England at the same time as a corresponding invasion of Scotland by a Swedish expeditionary force and Spanish marines.

The Swedish gripe with Britain was due to a dispute with the Hanoverians, which highlighted the complex issues caused by Britain being ruled by Britain's first Hanoverian monarch. However, the Swedish landing never took place as Charles XII of Sweden died in November 1718.

In March 1719 the Spanish invasion fleet, which constituted the main spearhead of the attack, led by James Butler, Duke of Ormonde, left Cádiz for the south-west coast of England with some 7,000 troops on board. However, the fleet was severely damaged by storms off Cape Finisterre and didn't make it to their intended destination of Cornwall.

Around the same time, the smaller diversionary force of 300 Spanish marines, commanded by George Keith, Earl of Marischal, set sail from Pasajes for the western Highlands of Scotland and reached Stornoway in the Isle of Lewis. Meanwhile, another contingent of Scottish exiles also arrived from France, including the Earl of Seaforth, William Murray, Lord George Murray, and Cameron of Lochiel.

The combined Scottish and Spanish force elected to try and implement the plan as best as possible, despite the fact that they were now on their own. Their mission was to join forces with the Scottish Jacobites and encourage a rising of the clans. They managed to muster a Scottish Jacobite force of about 1,000, which was mainly made of Mackenzie and Cameron clansmen, plus other small groups, including one led by the fabled outlaw Rob Roy Macgregor, who had also fought in the Battle of Killiecrankie in 1689 as a young man, and then at Sherrifmuir in 1715. They made their base at the MacKenzie stronghold of Eilean Donan Castle, which is on an island at the meeting point of Lochs Duich, Alsh and Long, adjacent to the Isle of Skye.[2]

The Jacobites left their stores and most of their ammunition at Eilean Donan Castle, guarded by forty Spanish marines, before pressing on to Inverness. But things went from bad to worse when, in early May, five ships of the Royal Navy arrived on the scene via Loch Alsh, having got wind of what was going on, and spent the next two days pulverising the castle. A Royal Navy raiding party then captured the stronghold and sent the prisoners away to Edinburgh, before the ships' guns destroyed it completely.

The main Jacobite force, meanwhile, continued to move inland towards Inverness, but they had now become aware that a force of pro-government Highland clansmen and Dutch soldiers led by Major General Wightman had left the garrison at Inverness to confront them.

The combatants coincided on 10 June 1719 at Glen Shiel, south-east of Loch Duich, in the north-west Highlands. The Jacobites formed a defensive position on the approach to the pass of Glen Shiel, and the government troops fanned out across both sides of the gorge once they had spotted the Jacobites.

Although the two armies were of similar numerical strength, the Hanoverian forces had superior firepower in the form of mortars, and had arrived fresh from Inverness, in direct contrast to the tortuous journey the Jacobites had undertaken.

Late in the afternoon, the government Hanoverian forces began a coehorn mortar[3] bombardment of the Jacobite position, keeping the Spanish marines pinned down while simultaneously allowing the government troops to advance. After three hours of attritional combat, the Hanoverian troops eventually managed to close the distance sufficiently to storm the Jacobite lines, forcing a retreat.

The government forces totally outgunned the Jacobites, and it was said that the copious amount of smoke from the burning heather allowed many of the Highlanders to melt away into the night. The Spanish marines were also forced to retreat, and later had to surrender.

The 1719 Jacobite Rising was over before the Old Pretender had even set foot on Scottish soil. Lord Carpenter, the government commander in Scotland, advised London that the entire 1719 rebellion had been ended by a single battle. It was also the last engagement between British and foreign troops on mainland British soil, as the Jacobites included Spanish marines. Another significant aspect of the battle was that it was the only one throughout the Jacobite risings that the Highland clansmen remained on the defensive rather than employing the legendary Highland Charge that had previously struck the fear of God into government troops.

In October 1719 a British naval expedition under Lord Cobham landed 6,000 troops in the Spanish city of Vigo in retaliation. They held the port for ten days and destroyed vast quantities of stores and equipment before leaving. The message was sent loud and clear that Britain had the capability to attack the Spanish mainland at will, whereas the Spanish would not succeed if they tried to attack Britain.

However, attempts to confiscate Highland estates in retaliation were unsuccessful. The MacKenzie clan twice rebuffed attempts to confiscate their estates at Glens Affric and Collie in 1721, and demonstrated in the process that the Highlands were ungovernable without the cooperation of the clan chiefs.

The War of the Quadruple Alliance ended with the 1720 Treaty of The Hague, which ensured that Philip of Spain returned the territory he had gained during the war.

Between 1722 and 1743, leading up to the 1745 Jacobite Rebellion, there were rumblings of discontent and some failed attempts to overthrow the Hanoverian monarchy. The first of these was the Atterbury Plot of 1722, which was a conspiracy led by and named after Francis Atterbury, Bishop of Rochester and Dean of Westminster, who had long been an opponent of Prime Minister Walpole. He was a recent convert to the Jacobite cause and his main concern as a prominent high church bishop was to see the church restored to its rightful place. He feared that the Tories would never be able to usurp the Walpole-led Whig government to do that.

The collapse of the South Sea Company in 1720 led to a financial and economic crisis and political scandal in Britain, which the Jacobites felt they could exploit. This led to Atterbury combining with an assortment of influential people such as Lord North, the Earl of Arran, General Dillon, the Earl of Mar, and the Duke of Ormonde to try and instigate a Jacobite rising.

The conspirators aimed to recruit old soldiers, along with volunteers from the Irish Brigade of the French army, to seize the Tower of London, the Bank of England, the Royal Mint and other government buildings in Westminster and the City of London. Their intention was to capture the Hanoverian royal family and assassinate other key figures, before instigating numerous risings across the country. They also planned to land men in Cornwall by ship, whilst another detachment would sail to Scotland and initiate a rising there.

The group intended to target counties where they knew they could count on support. The rising was planned to coincide with a forthcoming general election and aimed to exploit the unpopularity of the Hanoverian king, George I. It was the greatest threat to the Hanoverians between the Jacobite risings of 1719 and 1745. However, before the plan could come to fruition, the plot was discovered.

The Duc d'Orleans, Regent of France, didn't want any involvement and informed the prime minister that the Jacobites had asked him to send 3,000 men in support of the uprising, which was to take place the following month. The discovery of the plot resulted in some of its most prominent leaders being hanged for treason. Atterbury himself was said to have been betrayed by the Earl of Mar and was arrested in August. He was initially detained in the Tower of London, before being sent into exile.

There was also discontent in Scotland, which exploded into the Glasgow Riots of 1725. The root cause was the malt tax, which was a duty that had been imposed in England in order to help pay for war against France. After the 1707 union of England and Scotland, the tax was also applied in Scotland. This was not received very well by the Scots, many of whom were already not greatly enamoured with the union.

The riots began on 23 June 1725 in Hamilton and quickly spread throughout Scotland. The riots were suppressed by the army, and several protestors were killed and many others transported, before the British government eventually made concessions. The disturbances were called the Glasgow Riots as the most ferocious of them occurred in Shawfield in Glasgow, although significant outbreaks of violence also occurred in Edinburgh, Stirling, Dundee, Ayr, Elgin and Paisley.

General Wade (1673–1748) was the man appointed to quell the riots, but he is better known in Scotland for his legacy of the road building programme he implemented in the Highlands. It had become very apparent during the Jacobite Risings of 1689, 1715 and 1719 that government troops were severely hampered by the lack of roads and bridges in the Highlands. King George I appointed General Wade as commander of the government forces in Scotland, and one of his first tasks was to oversee the construction of barracks, which were built at Ruthven, Kilcumein (soon replaced by Fort Augustus), Bernera and Inversnaid. He then linked the forts with military roads, thus allowing the military greater access and therefore greater control of the Highlands.

Wade built forty bridges and 243 miles of road between 1725 and 1737. He was also ordered to produce a report in 1724 on the Jacobite fighting strength in the Highlands and came to the conclusion that there were about 22,000 men able to bear arms. Of these, 10,000 supported the government and the other 12,000 supported the Jacobites. In 1743 Wade was promoted to field marshall, and took joint control of the Anglo-Austrian army in Flanders, before being recalled to assist in quelling the 1745 Jacobite Rebellion.

George I died on a trip to his native Hanover on 11 June 1727 and a new king, George II (r. 1727–1760), came to the throne. He was born in 1683 in Hanover and was the son of George I and Sophia Dorothea. He was brought up as a German prince, and spoke English with a strong German accent, but at least he could speak the language, unlike his father. As we have seen, he also fought on the British side at the Battle of Oudenard in 1708.

George II's wife was Caroline of Ansbach (1683–1737). She was born at Ansbach on 1 March 1683 and was the third and youngest daughter of John Frederick Margrave of Brandenberg-Ansbach and his second wife, Eleonore Erdinuthe of Saxe-Eisenach.

Prince George Augustus of Hanover had been under pressure to become married and thus secure the Protestant Hanoverian line of succession. He was matched with Caroline and the pair were married at the palace chapel at Herrenhausen in Hanover on 22 August 1705. On 20 January 1707 they had their first child, Prince Frederick of Hanover, and he was quickly followed by three others – Anne, Amelia and Caroline.

When George I succeeded Queen Anne to the British throne, George Augustus and Caroline also left for England in 1714. Three years later Caroline gave birth to George William, and there was a dispute over the choice of godparents as they were chosen by George I without consulting the parents. The situation deteriorated to the extent that the couple were placed under house arrest at St James's Palace, while the children remained under the care of King George I. The pressure of this situation made Caroline ill, but eventually George I relented and allowed the couple to see their children. However, not long after this George William died. Over the next three years Caroline produced three more children, including William, who later became the Duke of Cumberland.

George Augustus was duly crowned as King George II at Westminster Abbey on 11 October 1727 after the death of George I, but Queen Caroline was considered to be the real power behind the throne. She was beautiful, intelligent, and popular with her subjects. She also turned a blind eye to George's numerous mistresses. Robert Walpole continued in the role of prime minister, a role that he had skilfully executed for a number of years, and now he had the added support of the influential Caroline.

In 1736 further riots with Jacobite connotations, known as the Porteus Riots, occurred in Edinburgh. The situation came to a head when, on 14 April 1736, a smuggler by the name of Andrew Wilson won the admiration of many of the town's folk by assisting a fellow smuggler to escape from the city's Tollbooth Prison, for which he was sentenced to death.

His execution was a highly charged affair as Wilson had a great deal of support from the Edinburgh public. A minor riot, with Jacobite overtures, erupted, which the city's guards quelled by firing into the crowd and killing and injuring a substantial number of rioters.

John Porteus, the captain of the guard, was accused of giving the order to shoot, and of participating in the shooting himself. He was brought to trial in July and sentenced to death However, he petitioned Queen Caroline, who acted as de-facto regent for her husband, King George II, and the execution was postponed.

This decision resulted in a group of armed men taking the law into their own hands on 7 September 1736, when they broke into the Tollbooth Prison and seized Porteus, before hanging him in the street.

It was said that Jacobite sympathisers of high standing were involved in the kidnap, and although a substantial reward was offered by the authorities to bring the perpetrators to justice, no one was ever convicted. The sympathies of the people and the clergy were so unequivocally on the side of the rioters that a planned fine to punish the city had to be severely reduced and was then paid to Porteus' widow instead.

Queen Caroline died at St James' Palace on 1 December 1737, after a botched operation on an umbilical hernia, leaving George absolutely devastated.

Chapter 6

The Build Up to the 1745 Jacobite Rebellion Against the Backdrop of the War of the Austrian Succession (1740–1748)

Shortly after Caroline's death, and against Walpole's better instinct, Britain became embroiled in the War of the Austrian Succession. The beginnings of Britain's involvement in the conflict can be traced to 1731, when Robert Jenkins, a captain of a British merchant ship, had his ear sliced off by Spanish coastguards when they boarded his ship during a time of peace. His severed ear was then shown to an outraged British Parliament.

Several years later opposition politicians and the British South Sea Company sought to make political capital out of the incident, believing that a victorious war would improve Britain's trading opportunities in the markets of Spanish America. A further factor was a domestic political campaign by an alliance of Tories and anti-Walpole Patriot Whigs who wanted to remove the long-serving British prime minister. Subsequent British attacks on Spanish possessions in Central America resulted in a high death rate, but most of the casualties were from disease rather than fighting. However, Walpole's opponents achieved their main aim, and as a result of the conflict Walpole did resign in February 1742, mortified to have to abandon his principle of peace. Consequently, the anti-Walpole Patriot Whigs came to power and then excluded their former Tory partners from government.

After Walpole's resignation the war became part of the wider War of the Austrian Succession, which was ostensibly to protect the right of Maria Theresa to succeed her father as ruler of the Habsburg monarchy – a succession that was disputed by France. Britain allied with Austria against France, Prussia and Spain in a struggle to prevent Bourbon France achieving worldwide dominance, which in turn was likely to impact on British commercial interests.

Meanwhile, the Tories were enraged at being excluded from government, and a group led by the Duke of Beaufort requested French assistance in restoring James, the Old Pretender, believing that was their most likely route to power. The request was declined by Cardinal Fleury Chief Minister of France as he and most other French ministers now dismissed the Jacobites as 'unreliable fantasists'. However, Fleury's successor, the Marquis D'Argenson, was not of that opinion.

The first British involvement in the War of the Austrian succession came at the Battle of Dettingen (now called Karlstein am Main) in Bavaria, which took place on 27 June 1743. It was fought between an Allied army which consisted of British, Hanoverian and Austrian troops, who were collectively known as the Pragmatic Army, against a French army commanded by the Duc de Noailles.

John Dalyrymple the 2nd Earl of Stair (the son of the 1st Earl of Stair who had ordered the Glencoe massacre), was in overall operational control. The Allied army was ostensibly commanded by George II, the last British king to lead his army into battle. He was alongside his youngest son, the Duke of Cumberland.

Under George II's orders, Dalyrymple marched his troops from the Austrian Netherlands to threaten the French in Bavaria. Dalyrymple was anxious to keep his main supply routes open along the River Main and took up a position between Aschaffenburg and Kleinostheim while awaiting the arrival of King George II. However, the French army, under the command of the Duc de Noailles, took up a postion on the upper part of the Main River, which in effect cut the supply line to the Pragmatic Army from the east and he also cut the supply route from the west by occupying Schigenstadt. The opposite bank of the river was also occupied by approximately 60,000 French troops, leaving the Pragmatic Army without supplies, hemmed in, and facing starvation.

King George II finally arrived and was left with no option but to order a retreat which began on 27 June 1743. Noailles intended to block the retreat at Dettingen and sent a detatchment of his infantry to capture Aschaffenburg, whilst his main force, led by the Duc de Gamont, moved towards the village of Dettingen.

Graumont had precise orders to keep the boggy ravine at the edge of Dettingen to his front. However, he failed to do this and had the bog behind him, changing the tactical situation as there was now no longer a bog between him and the Pragmatic Army.

The French cavalry initiated proceedings by charging at the British cavalry and infantry on the Allied left. They managed to withstand the assault and responded with some decimating volleys of artillery fire of their own.

Next, the French guards attacked the Allied centre, but were repulsed by disciplined British platoon fire, which involved platoons firing in strict rotational order to create a continuous wall of fire. The tactic had a devastating effect and resulted in a chaotic French retreat. At the same time, French attacks on the right were being fought off by British and Austrian cavalry. The combined effect was that the Allies gained the upper hand and then forced the French to flee through the bog, leaving the Allies to take the town of Dettingen.

Dalyrymple was in favour of pursuing the retreating French and exploiting the victory. However, George II resisted the temptation to do so, as the Allies were in a dishevelled state themselves after the battle and would have struggled to cross the river under fire. In fact, their position was so uncertain that they had to leave their wounded behind in order to increase their mobility.

King George II had never before enjoyed such popularity. The victory was widely celebrated in Britain and the song 'Rule Britannia' was even written to mark the occasion. However, in truth, although the battle had proved the British infantry's fighting capabilities (a training academy at Sandhurst was named Dettingen in recognition of this), the battle had a limited impact on the overall picture of the conflict, which now shifted to Flanders.

Ultimately, war became unpopular. The public perceived that Britain's participation was purely to protect George II's Hanoverian ties, a stance that was propagated by the fact that George wore a yellow Hanoverian sash rather than British military emblems at Dettingen.

The victory by the British at Dettingen rankled with Louis XV of France and he decided to collaborate with Charles Edward Stuart about the possibility of launching a Jacobite rebellion in Britain. Charles Edward Stuart (1720–1788), aka Bonnie Prince Charlie, was the grandson of James II, and the son and heir of James Francis Edward Stewart, the Old Pretender. He was born and brought up in Rome, but despite his father's three failed attempts to win the crown, was keen to launch another rising to place his father on the throne. Jacobite supporters considered him to be the son of the rightful king, and Charles himself believed that his destiny was to regain the crown for the Stuarts.

The invasion was planned for February 1744, so accordingly Charles left Rome for France in January 1744 and began assembling a force including ships and 12,000 troops at Dunkirk. Rumours began to circulate in Britain that the French were planning an invasion in conjunction with the Jacobites, and the government began to round up known Jacobite suspects. British regiments were withdrawn from Flanders to meet the threat, which was also a factor in the French inflicting a series of defeats on the British in that theatre at that time.

The French made elaborate preparations in Brest in the hope of fooling the Royal Navy that the fleet would sail from there and thus lure them away from the actual departure port of Dunkirk. However, when the dummy French squadron left Brest on 26 January 1744 the Royal Navy were not taken in by the subterfuge and did not follow them. A short while later, in March 1744, bad weather forced the actual French fleet that had left from Dunkirk back to port, causing Louis XV to cancel the intended invasion. It was a decision that turned out to be a precursor to the gradual withdrawal of support from the French as they turned their attentions more and more to the War of the Austrian Succession. They eventually won control of Flanders at the Battle of Fontenoy on 11 May 1745, in which Marshal Saxe of the French army defeated the Allied army led by the Duke of Cumberland.

The battle was fought just outside Tournai, which occupied a strategic position on the River Scheldt, and was an important trading town, so Marshall Saxe knew that when he took the town the Allies would attempt to regain it.

The Allies attempted a series of attacks on the flanks and when these were repulsed they then launched a full-scale attack on the centre. This was also repelled, and the French launched a counter-attack in the form of a cavalry charge which inflicted massive casualties on the Allies and caused their retreat. This enabled the French to quickly gain control and strengthen their advantage, taking Ghent, Oudenard, Bruges and Dendermonde, and later Ostend and Nieuwpoort, in modern-day Belgium.

After the debacle of the 1744 French Jacobite invasion, Charles visited Paris to continue to press the French authorities and present a case for an alternative invasion of Scotland, but this was to no avail. Around this time, Charles met with John Murray of Broughton, who later claimed that he counselled Charles against the idea of invasion and that he put Charles' ideas to other eminent Jacobite Scots who also voiced opposition to the idea should substantial French support not be forthcoming.

However, the French were encouraged by the major victory in the Austrian War of Succession at the Battle of Fontenoy and this led to them having a change of heart and supporting Charles' plans to a degree, in so far as they provided two ships – a sixteen-gun privateer *Du Teillay*, and *Elizabeth*, an old sixty-four gun warship captured from the British in 1704 – as well as soldiers from the French army's Irish Brigade.

So, in the spring of 1745, without the knowledge of his father, Charles started to assemble an invasion force and organised supplies and weapons. He was prepared to take the chance that once he had started the invasion, the French would surely support him to a much greater degree.

Shortly afterwards, though, the British gained a great victory in another theatre of the War of the Austrian Succession, known as King George's War in the British Colonies, at The Siege of Louisberg on 28 June 1745.

Louisberg, Canada, was a threat to the northern British colonies as it provided a base for the French navy and was also used by privateers. It was of strategic importance as it provided access to the St Lawrence River, which connected French colonies in the region with the rest of the world. An engagement took place in which a New England colonial force aided by the Royal Navy laid siege to Louisberg, which eventually ended with French capitulation on 28 June 1745.

Charles Edward Stuart was keeping a close eye on proceedings, and it was obvious that, with British troops so committed abroad, this was his only chance to launch a dramatic attempt to win back the British throne for the Stuarts.

Chapter 7

The 1745 Jacobite Invasion Force Sets Sail

On 5 July 1745, against the advice of his father and his advisors, and without French support, Charles departed from Saint Nazaire, aboard the *Du Teillay*, with his trusty companions, who became known as the Seven Men of Moidart.

The Seven Men of Moidart

The Marquess of Tullibardine William Murray

The Marquess of Tullibardine (1689–1746), William Murray, was the elder son of the 1st Duke of Atholl and the brother of Lord George Murray. He had served with the Jacobites in both 1715 and 1719, and as a result had spent the intervening years in exile in France.

By the time of the 1745 rebellion his health had deteriorated and he suffered from gout, so it was said that he didn't create a great impression when he unfurled the standard at Glenfinnan to ignite the 1745 Rebellion as he required the support of two men to complete the task.

He was captured after the Battle of Culloden and imprisoned in the Tower of London, where, due to his ill health, he died shortly afterwards.

John William O'Sullivan

John William O'Sullivan (1700–c1760) was a highly experienced Irish professional soldier who had seen extensive service in the French army. His service in Corsica meant that he was considered an expert in the kind of guerrilla warfare the Jacobites would be employing.

He was appointed the Jacobite army adjutant general and quartermaster general and was highly regarded by Charles. As a result, he had great influence in the Jacobite Council of War.

After the rebellion he returned to the French army.

Sir Thomas Sheridan

Sir Thomas Sheridan (1684–1746) had been involved in the 1715 rising and was close to Charles; he had been Charles' childhood governor. He was the son of a former chief secretary of Ireland and there were rumours that his mother was an illegitimate child of James II.

After the defeat at Culloden he escaped from Loch nan Uamh on the French privateer *Mars* (see Chapter 11), but died later that year in Rome after a period of ill health.

Sir John MacDonald

Sir John MacDonald was a French national of Irish origin, and having served in the French cavalry, was appointed by Charles as inspector-general of cavalry.

After Culloden, he surrendered at Inverness and was repatriated.

Francis Strickland

Colonel Francis Strickland (1691–1746) was an English Jacobite who had been involved in the 1715 rising. His family, who owned the Sizergh Castle Estate in Cumbria, were Roman Catholics and long-standing Jacobites.

He had gained some military experience in Europe and gravitated to the Jacobite court in Rome.

He became ill on the march to England and left at Carlisle, where he died on 1 January 1746.

George Kelly

The Rev George Kelly (1688–1762) was an Irish Nonjuring Protestant clergyman who was involved in the Atterbury Plot of 1722, for which he was arrested and imprisoned in the Tower of London before later escaping.

Charles brought him along to mastermind the propaganda part of the operation. As part of that role he went to France after the Battle of Prestonpans to rally French support for the rising and to inform the authorities of the Jacobite victory. However, he then failed to return to Scotland.

Aeneas MacDonald

Aeneas MacDonald (1715–1770) was the son of a Clanranald tacksmen, who went into banking and spent the majority of his adult life in Paris.

He was arrested after Culloden and originally sentenced to death, but in the end was sent into exile instead.

* * *

The *Du Teillay* and *Elizabeth*, departed for the Western Isles on 15 July 1745, but four days into the voyage they were intercepted by HMS *Lion*, which attacked *Elizabeth*. After a four-hour battle, both Jacobite ships had no option but to return to port, as *Elizabeth* had suffered considerable loss of men. Charles set sail again on *Du Teillay* and eventually arrived with only his seven men. He first put foot on Scottish soil on the tiny island of Eriskay, in the Outer Hebrides, on 23 July 1745. The beach he landed at is now called – Coilleag a' Phrionnsa (Gaelic for – The Cockleshell Strand of the Prince).[1] The day after he arrived on the island, Alexander MacDonald of Boisdale advised him to return home, to which Charles replied, 'I am come home.'

On 25 July Charles left Eriskay and set sail for the Scottish mainland, which he accessed via Loch nan Uamh, the sea loch that borders the Rhu Peninsula, south of Arisaig. He then moved about thirteen miles inland and arrived at the head of Loch Shiel on 19 August. The Prince and the Seven Men, his bodyguards and companions, then stayed at nearby Kinlochmoidart. Seven beach trees were later planted in a meadow at Kinlochmoidart to commemorate his companions.

In 1745 the majority of Scottish inhabitants, taking the lowlands into account, were Presbyterian and hostile to the Stuarts. The Jacobite power base of the Highlands had also changed, with fewer Highland chiefs willing to risk all for the sake of changing the king. Ultimately, the clan chiefs who supported the cause did so for a variety of reasons, including political and religious motivations, disaffection with the union with England, or because of neighbourly disputes with other clans. However, the greatest motivating factor was whether they felt any personal loyalty to the Stuarts.

Many eminent local Jacobite supporters, including MacDonald of Sleat and Norman Macleod, contacted Charles and advised him to return to France. They were aware of the potentially devastating impact of defeat and viewed that prospect as highly likely without French support. However, enough of the Scottish Jacobite nobility were persuaded to back the cause to make the rising viable in Charles' eyes. Among their number was the canny Scot, Donald Cameron of Lochiel, who only committed to the cause after weeks of debate and after Charles provided security for the full value of his estate should the rising fail. Charles was prepared to do this as Lochiel had a great deal of influence in the Highlands, and it's questionable whether the rising could have gone ahead without his backing. Another sceptic was the powerful Clan Chief Macdonald of Clanranald. But though he considered the venture risky, he eventually agreed to lend his support, sending his two sons to the raising of the standard. MacDonnell of Glengarry was another influential clan chief who was persuaded to come out for the prince. The clan chiefs in turn forced their men to come out by using bribery and threats.

On 19 August, after breakfasting at Dalelia House at the southern end of Loch Shiel, Charles arrived at the appointed rallying point of Glenfinnan, at the head of a flotilla of boats, along with fifty MacDonald Highlanders, only to be met, to his utter dismay, by a complete absence of clansmen.

Shortly afterwards, however, Jenny Cameron (see Chapter 12) rode over the hill, leading 600 from the Cameron clan, who in turn were swelled by 150 MacDonald clansmen.

In the end, the Jacobite Highland clansmen arrived in their droves to rally to the cause, having received the call from Charles via their clan chieftans that 'We do require and command that all our subjects from the age of sixteen to sixty, do upon the setting up of our royal standard immediately to it.'

The clans that were present when the Marquis of Tullibardine unfurled the Royal Stuart Standard to mark the beginning of the campaign were: MacDonald of Clanranald; MacDonald of Glencoe; MacDonnell of Glengarry; Cameron of Lochiel; Stewart of Appin.

At the ceremony, Charles promised freedom and prosperity to all his subjects. A toast was then made in brandy to 'their Stuart King and Prince and to the Rising'. Shortly afterwards, Charles sent a messenger to visit the absent clans that were reputed to be friendly to him, to join him on his way. The message encouraged the clan chiefs 'To stir them up, to rise with him, to put the crown on him', and the legend of the dashing, charismatic prince began to spread throughout the region as the twenty-five-year-old Bonnie Prince Charlie caught the imagination of the Jacobite Highland clansmen. The ignominy of his father's failure was thirty years before and Bonnie Prince Charlie was certainly a more charismatic figure.

Two days later around 1,500 clansmen left Glenfinnan and started the march southwards. They were resplendent in their flat, blue-knitted caps, which were synonymous with Highland clansmen. They attatched their clan symbol on their bonnets, along with a white cockade made from scraps of cloth. It was also decreed that at least one item of tartan must be worn.

The senior government legal officer in Scotland, Lord President Duncan Forbes, sent word to London of the rising in Scotland on 9 August 1745. The commander of the Hanoverian government forces in Scotland was John Cope, who only had 3,000 raw recruits at his disposal. However, he was ordered to crush the rebellion swiftly, which the government were supremely confident he would achieve using General Wade's network of forts and roads.

The two armies functioned in completely different ways. The Jacobite army travelled light, without baggage trains, and lived off the land where they could. This enabled them to cover the ground more swiftly than the government army. However, the Jacobites were severely hampered by a lack of heavy artilliery, which caused problems when it came to breaking down the defences of modern strongholds such as Stirling Castle and Fort William, meaning their only option was to lay siege to these fortresses. The government army, on the other hand, carried vast quantities of supplies, food and ammunition as they moved at a steady pace. The government also had the Royal Navy at its disposal, which could provide arms and supplies for collection at various coastal points, and could also blockade ports, preventing the arrival of French ships attempting to get supplies to the Jacobites.

Chapter 8

The Early Exchanges of 'The 45' and the Battle of Prestonpans

The Highbridge Skirmish marked the first action of 'the 45' and took place on 16 August 1745 at Highbridge, Lochaber, at a bridge over the River Spean, which was part of General Wade's military road.

Two Redcoat companies of the Second Battalion of the Royal Scots Regiment, under the command of the notorious Captain Scott (later Lieutenant Colonel Scott), were making their way from Fort Augustus to reinforce the government garrison at Fort William. As they attempted to cross Highbridge, they encountered eleven men from the Jacobite Clan MacDonald of Keppoch. It is said that Clan MacDonald managed to give the impression that they were a much larger force by leaping and skipping about and constantly moving whilst playing the bagpipes, as well as by extending their tartan plaids between each other. It seemed to work; believing they were up against a vastly superior force, Captain Scott sent two redcoats over to the Jacobites to discuss possible surrender terms. However, the soldiers were given no quarter and were duly taken prisoner by the clansmen. Captain Scott then ordered the rest of the two battalions to retreat, but in doing so they were later surrounded by other groups of Jacobites and forced to surrender.

A host of incredible stories were emanating from the Highlands and the authorities were becoming increasingly alarmed as Bonnie Prince Charlie moved southwards to take Perth on 4 September 1745. He entered the city to triumphal acclaim and pronounced his father the rightful king. Once he was in the Fair City, he tarried a while to gain some much-needed finance, by means of some heavy taxes, and he also took the opportunity to gather many more recruits.

During this period in early September, Prince Charles also stayed at Blair Castle for several days with his immediate band of followers.

The Early Exchanges of 'The 45' and the Battle of Prestonpans 113

During that stay, the eminent Jacobite figure of Lord George Murray was persuaded to come out once again. He was the sixth and youngest son of John Murray, 1st Duke of Atholl, and was in his early fifties by the time of the forty-five rising. He had received a pardon in 1725 for his participation in the 1715 and 1719 risings, and as a result was able to return to Scotland from exile and take the oath of allegiance to George II, which subsequently allowed him to be appointed by John Cope as the Deputy Sherriff of Perthshire. He was initially sceptical of Bonnie Prince Charlie's chances of success and had resisted the temptation to become involved. But as the Jacobites entered Perth, his Jacobite leanings got the better of him and he decided to pledge himself once again to the cause. Unlike Charles, he was an experienced soldier and was therefore appointed to a role of senior command, taking over from the Irishman O Sullivan due to his greater understanding of Highland affairs and customs.

Charles continued his all-conquering progress to Edinburgh and on 15 September 1745 was royally entertained in the ancestral Stewart Palace of Linlithgow, just fifteen miles from the capital, and in doing so became the last Stewart royalty to visit the palace.

Meanwhile, General Cope left his cavalry at Stirling under the command of Thomas Fowke and set off with his infantry for the Corrieyairack Pass to catch up with Charles. The Corrieyairack Pass is a twenty-two-mile route, descending from the Spey valley in a series of precipitous twists and turns between Laggan and Fort Augustus on Loch Ness. The pass was built to link Fort Augustus and Speyside for military purposes by General Wade in 1731, and leads through the wild Monadhilath Mountains, climbing to 2,500ft in places. It once formed the main access route between the western Highlands and the Lowlands. Today, it has been reduced to little more than a track.

As Cope approached the pass, he was informed that it was crawling with Jacobites. As a result, he thought it prudent, after consulting with his officers, to withdraw from the area. However, this left Edinburgh exposed and the Jacobites advanced on it, making use of the new military road intended for use by the British Army. As Charles closed in on the capital city, Cope marched his troops to Aberdeen, circumnavigating the Corrieyairack Pass, where they were loaded onto ships before sailing to Edinburgh. This meant that as Charles camped two miles outside of the Edinburgh city walls, Cope's infantry were still disembarking and joining up with Fowkes' cavalry at the port of Dunbar, thirty miles away.

Intelligence that the Jacobites were coming had previously been passed on to the Provost of Edinburgh, but the reports were ignored and consequently the city was in a state of panic and unreadiness as Charles and his army arrived outside the gates and ordered the Edinburgh City Council to surrender. In an attempt to stall proceedings until Cope arrived, the council sent several deputations to have talks with the prince. Meanwhile, 800 Jacobite Highlanders under Cameron of Lochiel eagerly waited outside Netherbrow Port for the order to take the city by force. In the end, they merely waited until the council's latest deputation made their way by coach back into the city, then, as the gates were opened, the Highlanders rushed in and brought the city under their control. Shortly afterwards, on 17 September 1745, Charles rode in triumph through the Cannongate and proclaimed his father, James, King of Scotland and Great Britain, and himself as regent. Edinburgh Castle, though, still remained in government hands.

The very next day Charles rode triumphantly through the city and 20,000 people lined the streets to watch as he entered Holyrood House, the majestic royal palace at the foot of the Royal Mile. Here, he bided his time while entertaining all manner of Jacobite nobility and hosting numerous balls. Meanwhile, a Jacobite recruiting programme also took place in Edinburgh, while 2,500 Jacobite troops awaited their next orders.

As Cope made his way from Dunbar, news reached him that the Jacobites had already taken the capital and were preparing to challenge his army. He assumed the Jacobites would confront him from the west, and, on the morning of 20 September 1745, he amassed his army at Prestonpans, a small fishing village to the east of Edinburgh, near Musselburgh. However, the Jacobites under Lord George Murray had instead assembled to the south of Cope's position. When Cope became aware of this, he adjusted accordingly and moved position so that his rear was covered by marshy ground. Lord George Murray was undeterred by this manoeuvre. He had intelligence of a way through the marsh, which enabled his men to silently traverse it during the night, and at about 5am he took up a position facing the left flank of the government forces.

When Cope belatedly became aware of the Jacobite presence, early on the morning of 21 September 1745, his men were still turning around when they encountered the Highland Charge coming at them at full speed. The power, ferocity and high velocity of the charge caused the British dragoon regiments positioned on either flank of Cope's infantry to abandon their posts, which left the inexperienced infantry troops dangerously exposed and surrounded on three sides. They broke ranks in sheer terror and fled the field. As a result, the Hanoverian forces were routed within fifteen minutes and hundreds of government troops were killed or wounded, and another 1,500 taken prisoner.

The Battle of Prestonpans came to be immortalised in Jacobite Scottish folklore as a symbol of resistance to British rule, and Cope, Fowkes and another commander, Lascelles, were summoned to a court martial to explain the defeat. They were exonerated as the court came to the conclusion that the commanding officers had done all they could reasonably do, and the one thing they couldn't control was the shameful behaviour of the private soldiers when faced with the Highland Charge.

After returning to Edinburgh in triumph, the prince continued to enjoy the high life at Holyrood House, where he hosted his famous balls and charmed all the Jacobite ladies. He remained there for a further six weeks while he received more recruits from the north and more weapons and money from France. He also raised further finance for the campaign by collecting taxes and by selling off goods seized from Leith Custom House.

To strengthen his support in Scotland, Charles also published two declarations, on 9 and 10 October 1745. The first dissolved the 'pretended' union and the second refused to acknowledge the Act of Settlement, whereby Protestant succession to the throne was secured. He also issued instructions for the *Caledonian Mercury* to publish minutes of the 1695 parliamentary enquiry into the Glencoe massacre, which was widely considered to have been a whitewash.

After Prestonpans, clan chiefs with pro-Jacobite leanings were more inclined to support the prince, as it was beginning to look like the campaign may yet not end in ignominious failure. However, yet more continued to wait to see what happened or simply remained loyal to the government.

At a council of war in Edinburgh in October, it was decision time for the Jacobites. Should they head for London, or consolidate their gains in Scotland? Charles was strongly in favour of marching on London, and argued that an invasion of England was crucial for attracting French backing, and for ensuring an independent Scotland by defeating the Hanoverians. He was supported in this view by the Irish exiles.

Charles assured his fellow rebels that he had been in touch with English supporters, who were ready to join the uprising on their arrival from Scotland. He also assured them that a French landing in England was imminent. However, the senior Scots, led by Lord George Murray, disagreed. Their aims only extended as far as the restoration of the Stuarts to the Scottish throne, the reinstatement of an independent Scottish Parliament and the cessation of the union with England. They also argued that it would be foolish to leave Scotland unsecured.

There were some rumblings of discontent among the Scots on the Jacobite council, and a few concerns were being raised that Charles was too autocratic and relied too much on his Irish advisors. However, Charles persuaded the council to agree to invade England on the provision that the promised English and French support was forthcoming.

On 4 November 1745 the Jacobite rebels left Edinburgh and marched southwards for England. As they did so, government forces retook the city and the central Lowlands.

Chapter 9

The Jacobite Foray into England and the Subsequent Retreat back into the Highlands

The government had become alarmed by the reverse at Prestonpans, and it was apparent that a greater number of troops needed to get to the Scottish border with England as quickly as possible in order to quash the Jacobite threat as they advanced south. To this end it was decided to employ two separate forces.

Field Marshall Wade was ordered to move to Newcastle with a force of 11,000, and a further 12,000 men under Sir John Ligonier were ordered to march to Chester to counter the Jacobite force moving into England from the north-west. However, Ligonier became ill at Lichfield and was replaced by George II's son, the Duke of Cumberland, who now became the commander in chief of government forces in Scotland. He, like most of the troops now under his command, had been recalled from Flanders.

A game of cat and mouse now commenced between Cumberland and the Young Pretender, and it was also around this time, in September 1745, that Duncan Forbes, Lord Culloden, was given the task of raising clan-based Highland militias loyal to the king. Colonel John Campbell, Lord Loudoun, was placed in overall command of them and one of their first assignments was to reinforce Stirling Castle. They also played a vital role in preventing further Jacobite recruitment and enforcing the law of the government in the Highlands, as well as taking part in several skirmishes against the Jacobites.

On the route southwards Bonnie Prince Charlie made a social call on a distant cousin and staunch supporter, the Earl of Traquair (also named Charles Stuart), who lived at Traquair House, thirty miles south of Edinburgh in the town of Innerleithen. As Charles left, the earl wished him luck and promised that he wouldn't open the gates of Traquair House until the Stuart dynasty was restored to the throne.

Traquair is Scotland's oldest inhabited house, and the gates remain locked to this day, with visitors and residents alike having to use the side entrance.

Whilst the main body of the Jacobite army continued to move southwards, skirmishes were still taking place further north, and in November 1745 the Jacobites took control of Montrose Harbour in north-east Scotland. In response, HMS *Hazzard*, a sixteen-gun Royal Naval sloop, arrived in the harbour and brought the town back under government control by virtue of her guns dominating the Montrose Basin.

However, the Jacobite captain, David Ferrier, refused to take this lying down and managed to secure Inchbraoch, a part of the shore of the harbour. Then, when a French vessel landed with supplies of cash, weapons and troops, it moored out of reach of HMS *Hazzard's* guns, enabling her own cannons to be manhandled onto the shore. The cannons were then brought to bear on HMS *Hazzard*, forcing her to surrender. The Jacobites then sailed HMS *Hazzard* to France, where they renamed her *Le Prince Charles* (see Chapter 10).

On 8 November 1745 Bonnie Prince Charlie crossed the border into England, accompanied by 8,000 Jacobite Highlanders. Traditionally, Scottish forays into England had tended to be via Berwick upon Tweed, but Murray opted for a route via Carlisle and the north-west of England, as this had been the area that was most strongly Jacobite in 1715. This proved to be a good option, as the Jacobite rebels didn't encounter any opposition and were subsequently able to cross the border into England unchecked. The fact that the Jacobites had also taken the town of Montrose and other Scottish east coast harbours around this time facilitated the landing of French weapons and supplies, which in turn gave the Jacobites a further fillip and seemed to validate Charles' claims of French support for the invasion.

On 9 November 1745 the rebels arrived at the border fortress town of Carlisle. Since the 1707 Union of England and Scotland, the defences were not as functional as they once had been, and the garrison was now only manned by eighty elderly veterans. Despite the fact that the rebels didn't have siege artillery and lacked the necessary time or equipment to starve the garrison into submission, the castle capitulated on 15 November 1745 when word was received that Wade's makeshift relief force on its way from Newcastle had been delayed by snow.

During this period Charles stayed at Highmoor House in Carlisle and convened another council of war to discuss their next moves. Four options were discussed: 1.) return to Scotland; 2.) march against Wade; 3.) remain in Carlisle in the hope that English Jacobites would rise; 4.) march towards London.

Lord George Murray continued to advocate a return to Scotland, fearing that as they went deeper into England, they would become more and more hemmed in. But again, the prince had the final word and the advance continued.

Retaining a small garrison at Carlisle, the Jacobites continued south to Preston on 26 November 1745, then Manchester on 29 November. It was in Manchester that the Jacobites received a timely boost when they linked up with a sizeable group of English Jacobites that had been formed as the Manchester Regiment under the command of Francis Towneley, a Lancashire Catholic who had seen service in the French army and whose brother, Richard, only just escaped execution for his involvement in the 1715 rising. However, Preston, a previous bastion of Jacobite support, only managed to provide a grand total of three recruits.

The same discussions among the Jacobites of whether to consolidate their gains or press onto London took place at Carlisle, Preston, and Manchester. Charles was adamant they should press on, whereas others felt they had already gone too far. Again, at the prince's instigation, it was agreed to keep moving south after he assured them that Sir Watkin Williams-Wynn and his Welsh Jacobites would join the rebellion. Sir Watkin Williams-Wynn was the main Welsh Jacobite. He was a Denbighshire landowner and Tory Member of Parliament, and prior to the 1745 rebellion had met with several prominent Jacobites and had promised support – if the prince brought a French army.

The London-based Tory politician the Duke of Beaufort was also offering support and was preparing to capture the strategic port of Bristol. He was also agitating for a body of troops to be landed near London.

As the advance into England progressed at breakneck speed, panic began to take hold in London. There now seemed to be very little standing in the way of the Jacobites' march on the capital as they continued to move southwards. The actors at Drury Lane even added a new song to the end of their performances; it was called *God Save the King*. Meanwhile, George II had his bags packed and was ready to flee England for Hanover.

Many people don't realise that there is more than one verse of *God Save the King/Queen*. One little-known verse goes thus: *Lord grant that Marshall Wade/May by thy mighty aid/Victory bring/May he sedition hush/ And like a torrent rush/Rebellious Scots to crush/God Save the King.* This may explain why the Scots prefer *Flower of Scotland* at sporting events.

The invasion route had been carefully selected to include areas where there was likely to be a strong Jacobite groundswell of support. But though big crowds continued to turn out to watch the rebels march past, the anticipated English support was not actually materialising, meaning the rebels were now facing a real risk of being cut off as they went further south.

On 4 December 1745, having reached Derby in double-quick time, there were no further reinforcements waiting for them and still no sign of the promised French landing, so they halted at Swarkstone Bridge and another council of war was convened with between 15–20 senior commanders attending.

The Scottish generals came to the conclusion that to move beyond Derby would see them move further from reinforcements and into the jaws of defeat. The only sensible option for the Jacobites, as far as they were concerned, seemed to be to retreat and regroup north of the border and wait for support to arrive from France.

The Scots generals cited that intelligence had been received that, to the south, the Duke of Cumberland had posted his men in a defensive position around Northampton and that Wade's troops were moving southwards from Newcastle-upon-Tyne. Further factors were that there was believed to be a third force ready to defend London, making it seem doubtful that the Hanoverian government would actually fold, even if the Jacobites did make it all the way to the capital. Another factor was the failure of a French invasion of southern England to actually materialise. However, there was some positive news in that French supplies had arrived at Montrose, along with pay and troops from the Royal Ecossaise and the Irish Brigade, plus a further 10,000 troops were apparently on their way to Scotland.

Lord George Murray estimated that the combined number of government troops totalled 18,000, which was a vastly superior force compared to the 8,000 Jacobite Highlanders they were pitted against. He also continued to assert that they had gone as far as possible and believed it would be madness to continue and risk being cut off.

As the heated discussion continued, Charles was forced to admit that he had not actually heard from the English Jacobites since leaving Manchester, which meant he had lied as he had previously claimed otherwise. As a result, his relationship with the commanding Scots, and in particular Lord George Murray, was now broken beyond repair.

Murray was adamant that, in the circumstances, they should retreat back across the border, where, in his opinion, they could fight in Scotland for years and force the Crown to agree terms as British troops were greatly needed for warfare on the Continent. Murray's opinion prevailed and after much wrangling the Jacobite army turned back towards Scotland on 5 December 1745. A dispirited Charles is said to have said afterwards, 'In future I shall summon no councils, since I am accountable to nobody for my actions but to God and my father. Therefore, I shall no longer ask for or accept advice.'

It seemed that the level of English support the rebellion would attract had been grossly overestimated, and dislike of the Hanoverians had been wrongly interpreted as support for the Stuarts.

As the swiftly moving Jacobite army withdrew from England, they managed generally to evade the pursuing government forces. They initially stayed at the town of Ashbourne, Derbyshire, before moving on to Leek in Staffordshire the following day. However, there was insufficient room in Leek for the entire army to be accommodated, so they split into two factions and moved through the towns of Macclesfield and Stockport, before coming together as one on the road to Manchester, which they entered as one unit. They left Manchester on 10 December 1745 and moved onto Wigan, before staying in Preston on the 12th.

Around this time, despite the recent victory at Fontenoy, the French were struggling to finance the war of the Austrian Succession. They only had the finances available to either retake Louisberg or support the Jacobite rising in Britain. So, although they had initially assembled a force to support the Jacobites, they switched their priority to Louisberg once they learnt that the Jacobites were in retreat from Derby.

Charles' intention was to make a stand at Lancaster, and to that end James Drummond, the 3rd Duke of Perth, had been despatched to muster reinforcements from Scotland, while the prince and the remainder of the army entered Lancaster on 13 December 1745.

However, Lord George Murray received information that Field Marshall Wade's men were closing in and had arrived in Preston shortly after the Jacobites had left. This information prompted Charles to order a move on to Kendall instead, where he could rendezvous with the Duke of Perth and his party of reinforcements.

Whilst making his way to Kendall, the Duke of Perth passed through Penrith and was attacked by a superior force of government horse and foot, from which he retreated, before being attacked again in Kendall by a mob, which he dispersed by firing into.

Shortly afterwards, a troop under the command of Lord George Murray reached the village of Clifton, from where he ordered the troop's artillery and heavy baggage forward to Penrith under an armed guard. En route, the baggage and artillery train came across some English light horse, which they attacked taking prisoners, from whom they managed to establish that the Duke of Cumberland himself, with a body of 4,000 horse, was only about a mile behind. Accordingly on 18 December 1745 Lord George Murray placed his men at strategic points at Clifton Moor in readiness.

When Cumberland's red-coated dragoons arrived in the vicinity, they immediately dismounted at the foot of the moor and opened fired on the Jacobites. In response, Lord George Murray ordered the MacPhersons and Stewarts, who were situated to the left of the enemy, to advance, and for the MacDonalds and MacDonnells to do the same from the right.

The Macphersons on the left soon came under heavy fire, which was the cue for Murray to draw his sword, giving the signal for the clansmen to withdraw their swords and charge. The government dragoons retreated at the fearsome sight of the Highland Charge, whereupon they were fired at by the Jacobite MacDonnell of Glengarry Regiment.

The Jacobite and the government troops then set upon each other in the dark, but after approximately thirty minutes Lord George ordered his troops to fall back onto the road to Penrith and join the rest of the Jacobite army. Cumberland then launched a final attack at about 6pm, but by then most of the Jacobites had withdrawn.

Some make a claim, particularly those from Cumbria, that this was the last battle on English soil. However, as this was more of a skirmish than a full-scale, set-piece battle, Sedgemoor is more correctly considered to be the last battle.

Twelve Jacobites and fourteen of the duke's men were killed. The English dead were given a proper burial in Clifton churchyard, whereas the Scottish Jacobites were just buried under an oak tree, known locally as the 'Rebel Tree', which is now identified by a plaque.

On 20 December 1745 the Jacobite rebels crossed the border back into Scotland, but they still maintained a garrison of 400 in Carlisle Castle, in case they should return to England.

Cumberland's men duly arrived at Carlisle on 22 December and subjected the Jacobite inhabitants of the garrison to an artillery bombardment, before finally forcing their capitulation on 30 December 1745. The majority of the garrison were from the Jacobite Manchester Regiment and the officers were singled out for transfer to London and subsequent execution for treason. The remaining soldiers were locked up in dungeons, either in Carlisle or Lancaster, for several days before meeting their fates of either death or transportation. Today, within the dungeon at Carlisle Castle, an unusually shaped stone can be seen. The story goes that its strange shape is due to erosion caused by the Jacobite prisoners licking the moisture from it to prevent themselves from dying of thirst.

Whilst the main body of the Jacobite army were retreating from England, other factions were still causing problems for the Hanoverian forces north of the border. In the north-east of Scotland Lord Lewis Gordon was made responsible for the recruitment of more Jacobites and had managed to muster a large regiment of three battalions, while the government commander in chief of the north, John Campbell, 4th Earl of Loudoun, sent Norman Macleod of Clan MacLeod from Inverness with 500 men of the Independent Highland Company to combat the Jacobites in that region.

Meanwhile, in the north-west of Scotland, the first siege of Fort Augustus took place. The fort was built in 1729 by General Wade and was named after William Augustus, Duke of Cumberland. It was situated in a strategic position at the south-west end of Loch Ness, and was liberated by a force of 600 men from the Independent Highland Companies.

Norman Macleod advanced to Inverurie, sixteen miles north-west of Aberdeen, with his men of the Independent Highland Company, and on learning of MacLeod's advance, Gordon and his Jacobites sought to go on the offensive, leaving their base at Aberdeen on 23 December 1745 with 1,100 men and five cannons. They crossed the River Don and took the road to Fintray along the left bank of the river, while also sending a detachment on an alternative route as a decoy.

At about 4pm the Jacobite Irish Brigade crossed the river just south of Inverurie, and as they navigated the ford, they were engaged by Macleod's men, resulting in the rebels taking heavy casualties, before pressing on and attacking the government forces in the south-west of the town. Gordon and his Jacobites then crossed the River Ury and attacked the town around the church, taking the defending MacLeods unawares and causing them to make a fighting retreat to Elgin.

It was certainly becoming apparent that although they were in retreat, the Jacobite army were far from a spent force. They had been reinforced by troops from Aberdeenshire and Banffshire and had been supplemented by the Royal Ecossaise and the Irish Brigade, meaning that Charles' force now numbered approximately 9,000. Also, money and weapons supplied from France still continued to come through the Jacobite-controlled ports around Aberdeen, despite the Royal Navy's attempts to prevent it. These factors, allied to the victory at Inverurie – which now meant the Jacobites controlled the north-east of Scotland – gave them a morale boost and the confidence to attempt to take Glasgow and Stirling Castle, which they felt would provide a strong base and a port for a possible later invasion of England. However, a cloud on the horizon was that Charles was still waiting for news from his brother, Henry, of the planned French landing in south-west England, which now seemed increasingly unlikely.

Meanwhile, the Highland Independent Companies still continued to recruit heavily in the north and were also gaining numerous recruits from the western Lowlands and Argyll. The government was still concerned that the Jacobites could attack London, so Cumberland was recalled to the capital to organise defensive forces there, whilst Henry Hawley took over as commander in chief of Scotland.

On Boxing Day 1745 the Jacobites entered Glasgow, where they raised taxes and forced the city to supply them with provisions, before heading to Stirling Castle[1], which, throughout history, has been the scene of numerous sieges due to its strategic position on the River Forth as the gateway to the Highlands.

The Jacobite Foray into England and the Subsequent Retreat 125

The Jacobites had passed by the castle in September 1745, en route to Edinburgh, but on that occasion had neither the siege equipment nor necessary time to capture it. However, on the return journey to the Highlands they had French-supplied artillery and siege equipment consisting of two 18lb heavy cannons.

The castle and the town, as was common in those days, were separate entities. The town was only designed to hold out for a few days, whereas the castle was a different story; it was an extremely strong fortress enhanced by natural defences and the garrison within consisted of 650 troops commanded by William Blakeney.

The Jacobites took the town, but the siege of the castle made little progress and was abandoned when a government relief force of around 7,000 men under the command of Henry Hawley arrived from Edinburgh. The Jacobites were forced to break off from the siege and confront Hawley's force, who they duly encountered at Falkirk Muir on 17 January 1746.

The Jacobite army under the command of Lord George Murray set up with the Highland clansmen in the front line and the Lowland infantry in the second line, in such a way that the government dragoons would be obliged to attack uphill. The battle started in atrocious conditions, failing light and a heavy snowstorm, when the government Hanoverian dragoons initiated proceedings by charging uphill at the Jacobite right flank. As they did so they encountered Jacobite musket fire, which slowed the momentum of the attack considerably, enabling the Highlanders to draw their dirks (long-bladed dagger), which they plunged into the soft underbellies of the horses as the dragoons approached, before then turning the dirks on their riders as they fell.

In the terrible weather and general confusion, the Jacobite Highlanders then went on the charge down the hill, tearing into and routing Hawley's left flank, an event preserved for posterity and celebrated in the Scottish folk song *The Hielandmen Cam Doon The Hill*. A cavalry back-up for the Highland Charge was then provided by the two French Celtic regiments, the Ecossais Royales and the Irish Brigade, who acquitted themselves well and were pivotal in helping to ensure a Jacobite victory.

The Ecossais Royales, who could be identified by their blue coats, were also known as the Jacobite Royal Scots and were a French regiment consisting mainly of Scottish Jacobite exiles, commanded by Lord John

Drummond. The other French Celtic regiment, the Irish Brigade, or the Irish Piquets as the French called them, were originally led by Justin McCarthy Mountcashel. They maintained the tradition started by Patrick Sarsfield's Wild Geese in 1691 of Irish regiments fighting for France (rather confusingly, bearing in mind the attire of government troops, they wore a red coat).

The battle of Falkirk Muir was characterised by poor leadership on both sides, and in the ensuing chaos and terrible weather the Jacobites failed to follow up on the retreating government troops, mainly because the ill-disciplined Highlanders were more concerned with looting the baggage train. This had the effect of letting Hawley's troops off the hook and allowed them to retreat to Edinburgh in good order. Cumberland saw the reverse as a little embarrassing and took action against those he considered responsible, but he didn't really consider the battle as a major defeat.

By now, Cumberland was back in Scotland, and two weeks after the Battle of Falkirk Muir, news reached the Jacobites of his arrival in Edinburgh, on 30 January 1746. Charles wanted to bring Cumberland to battle, but was talked out of it by Lord George Murray and his fellow Scots, who thought that due to the depletion of their own ranks, through desertions and sickness, they would be better to retire to the Highlands and renew the campaign in the spring, as was the usual way with Highland warfare.

On 1 February 1746 the Jacobite army started the long haul back to Inverness from the Lowlands. One division was commanded jointly by Lord George Murray and Lord John Drummond and consisted of the Lowland regiments and the Celtic French regiments of the Irish Brigade and the Ecossais Royale. They took a route via Perth and Aberdeen. Meanwhile, Bonnie Prince Charlie commanded the other division, which consisted of the clan regiments, and they took the more direct but more demanding route over the Drumochter Pass.

It was during this period that the campaign entered a new phase of attrition, in which both sides divided their resources and participated in minor skirmishes rather than pitched battles. The Jacobites prioritised the capture of government-held garrisons, particularly those in the Great Glen, which stretches for sixty-two miles from Inverness in a straight line to Fort William, and included Fort George in Inverness, Fort Augustus and Fort William. These forts were constructed after the Jacobite rising of 1715, but had fallen into a state of disrepair by 1745, when they were hastily reinforced.

At the beginning of February 1746, John Campbell, 4th Earl of Loudoun, had gathered his command of nearly 2,000 men, mostly drawn from the Independent Highland Companies at Inverness. He was intending to seek battle with Prince Charles as his force approached Inverness, but was ordered by Duncan Forbes to withdraw due to the believed superiority of numbers of the prince's force; a belief that was due in part to the earlier deception of Colonel Anne at Moy Hall (see Chapter 12).

Campbell's men made their way over the Cromarty Firth, then the Dornoch Firth and into Sutherland. However, this now meant that Major Grant and his two Independent Highland Companies within Fort George in Inverness were now very much at the mercy of the Jacobite force of Prince Charles' division of 3,000 men in the area.

The Irish Jacobite general John O Sullivan undertook a reconnaissance mission on 19 February 1746 and was able to establish that one of the bastions of the fort had unstable foundations, which he felt could be exploited. The Jacobites pummelled that area with the single cannon they had, causing Major Grant to surrender on 21 February 1746, fearing that the ramparts of the castle would be destroyed beneath him. However, Cumberland considered that Major Grant had surrendered too easily, and he was court martialled and dismissed from the army. Bonnie Prince Charlie's army later demolished the castle to prevent it falling into enemy hands. The ruins remained until 1834, when the present Inverness Castle was built.

Another government-held fortification that the Jacobites prized was Ruthven Barracks, one of the military barracks constructed by General Wade in the wake of the Jacobite Rising of 1715. They were built between 1719 and 1721 on the site of a castle that had once belonged to Alexander Stewart, the infamous 'Wolf of Badenoch'[2]. The original barracks had been burnt down in 1689 by John Graham of Claverhouse, Viscount 'Bonnie' Dundee.

Ruthven Barracks in Badenoch, close to the military road near Kingusie, commanded Strathspey and held a strategically important position with regard to controlling access to the Cairngorns – it was the main thoroughfare between the Lowlands and Inverness. The barracks also controlled the river crossing and the military roads to Inverness, Perth and Fort Augustus, and as such were at the hub of troop movements throughout the Highlands. The strategic importance of the barracks made it inevitable that they would see some action at some stage during the campaign.

In the first action, on 29 August 1745, when the Jacobites were heading south, government forces within Ruthven – which consisted of Sergeant Molloy and just fourteen men – managed to defeat 200 Jacobites with the loss of just one man. However, in February 1746, as the Jacobites returned north, Gordon of Glenbucket and 300 Highlanders, with artillery and siege busting equipment, overwhelmed the now-promoted Lieutenant Molloy and he and his men were forced to surrender.

On 21 February 1746 a Jacobite contingent of the Irish Brigade from the French army, under Colonel Walter Stapleton, along with 1,500 Cameron and MacDonald clansmen, arrived at Fort Augustus to commence the second siege, which took place from 22 February to 1 March 1746. The British government defenders within the garrison consisted of two companies commanded by Major Hugh Wentworth, with another company stationed in Kiliwhimen Barracks, to the south of the fort.

The outlying company in the barracks was quickly overrun by the Irish Brigade, who then placed a battery of cannons there to rain fire upon the fort and force them to surrender. Wentworth, like Major Grant at Fort George, was considered to have capitulated too easily by Cumberland, and like Major Grant, was subsequently court martialled and dismissed from the army.

The site of the old fort is now occupied by a Benedictine Abbey and Roman Catholic boys' school, and all that remains of the former fort are the bastions projecting from the corners of the building.

Afterwards, the Jacobites continued onto Fort William, which was the last remaining stronghold in the Great Glen still under government control.

Chapter 10

Culloden

The Duke of Cumberland, with the best available troops and artillery, continued to take the coastal route north so that resupply could take place by sea. As he moved northwards he strategically left troops in various locations to secure those areas. He entered Aberdeen on 27 February 1746, where he rested his army for the winter. However, this time was not wasted, as he took the opportunity to drill his troops in new tactics to counter the notorious Highland Charge.

Another factor, which was to prove crucial, was that the government troops had now been issued with bayonets which were fitted around the muzzle of the musket for the first time, meaning that the bayonet now didn't have to be removed to shoot and vice versa, unlike the previous plug bayonets. General Mackay had suggested such an idea after his shocking experience at Killiecrankie in 1689.

Meanwhile, the Jacobites based themselves in Inverness, and in March 1746 Lord George Murray left with a detatchment of about a 1,000 men to try and reclaim his family's estate of Blair Castle, which was of vital strategic importance, just north of the pass of Killiecrankie. It had temporarily been left unattended by the Jacobites and was subsequently captured by government forces led by Colonel Sir Andrew Agnew, who had garrisoned it with 500 of his Scots Fusiliers.

On the morning of 17 March 1746 the Jacobites captured Blair Castle's fortified outposts, from where they were in range to open fire on the castle. Lord George Murray was joined by his cousin Charlotte (see Chapter 12), who congratulated the men on their achievements so far (many of the men were from the Atholl Brigade, which had been predominantly raised by Charlotte).

Lord George Murray summoned Andrew Agnew to surrender, which he refused to do, prompting Charlotte to fire the first cannon shots of the siege in indignant anger. Lord George then had the unenviable task of ordering further cannon fire upon his family home (which earned the distinction of being the last British castle to be besieged). By 1 April 1746 the inhabitants of the castle were close to starvation, but Lord George Murray and his men had to abandon the siege, as they had been summoned by the prince to join the main Jacobite force at Inverness.

On 4 March 1746 advanced elements of the Jacobite force arrived outside the strategically important Fort William and blockaded Loch Linnie at the Corran Narrows to prevent supplies reaching the fortress from the water. However, Alexander Campbell, the garrison commander, quickly responded and despatched three boats with seventy men aboard to confront the Jacobites at the Narrows. They took the Jacobites by surprise and had the better of the skirmish, and also destroyed property and livestock in the area to deny supplies to the Jacobites. Meanwhile, the Jacobites were reinforced by additional units from Fort Augustus who also brought heavy siege artillery with them.

Fort William was a more modern fort with more formidable fortifications than Fort Augustus and Fort George, and also had the advantage that the head of Loch Linnie provided cover as well as allowing resupply from the sea. As a result, the besiegers were able to make very little impact, and when Cumberland and his army marched out of Aberdeen in early April, the besiegers were recalled to Inverness by Bonnie Prince Charlie and the siege was abandoned, meaning that Fort William was the only one of the three Great Glen forts that had managed to hold out against the Jacobites. However, very little remains of the old fort today.

On 20 March 1746 a large Jacobite force commanded by James Drummond, 3rd Duke of Perth, advanced towards the government position of Dornoch in the north-east Highlands, which was a strategic position as it controlled the route over the Dornoch Firth. The Jacobites approached from the east and were aided by thick fog. They were also aided by the fact that Lord Loundoun, commanding the government troops, was anticipating an attack from the west as he had assumed the Royal Navy would be covering the east, despite being given information to the contrary. The government troops were, therefore, taken by surprise when vast numbers of Jacobite soldiers arrived at Meilkle Ferry, having crossed from the other side of the Dornoch Firth at Tain. The forty guards at Meilkle Ferry, realising they were seriously outnumbered, withdrew without getting involved in combat. They raised the alarm for

Lord Loundoun's regiment, who hastened to the ferry only to find that 1,500 Jacobites had already landed, and so they also retired without firing a shot.

A few days later, on the night of 25–26 March 1746, a French ship by the name of *Le Prince Charles* (see Chapter 9) managed to slip into the Kyle of Tongue laden with supplies, weapons, ammunition and chests containing gold, bound for Prince Charles and his Jacobites.

The Jacobites managed to successfully get the cargo ashore and move it away, despite the attentions of the British frigate HMS *Sheerness*. However, the following day Captain George MacKay, son of the chief of the Clan MacKay, intercepted the Jacobite convoy at Drumnacoub, and after a short skirmish, captured it and prevented valuable supplies and men reaching the main body of the Jacobite army. The situation then rapidly went from bad to worse for the Jacobites as they also lost John Murray of Broughton, a key man responsible for organising supplies and logistics.

Following the Skirmish of Tongue, where money and urgent supplies destined for the Jacobites had been seized by government forces under Captain MacKay, Bonnie Prince Charlie despatched a formidable unit of Jacobites, under George MacKenzie, 3rd Earl of Cromarty, to retrieve the valuable cargo, which was now at Dunrobin Castle in Sutherland. They took the castle by storm on 15 April 1746 and were able to retrieve the supplies, while the incumbent 17th Earl of Sutherland was fortunate to narrowly escape their clutches.

The Earl of Cromarty and his Jacobite force then received orders to rejoin the prince and the bulk of the Jacobite army at Inverness. But as they made their way back, they casually left a gap in the column between the officers on horseback and the infantry in the vanguard. Men from Clan Sutherland, under the command of Captain MacKay, tracked them from the hills above and then swooped down on them near Golspie, exploiting the gap between officers and men. The majority of the Jacobite officers were captured and many of the men were either killed or drowned trying to swim across Loch Fleet.

Cromarty fled into Dunrobin Castle, but McKay and his men forced their way in and captured him, putting him on a ship bound for London, where he was convicted of high treason along with his fellow captured

Jacobite officers (see Chapter 12). Cromarty was later pardoned, whilst the others were executed.

These events were to have profound implications further down the line at Culloden. The loss of such a vast quantity of money and supplies was a serious setback for the Jacobites, as was the fact that Charles was denied some of his best men and much-needed reinforcements.

Meanwhile, on 8 April 1746 Cumberland and the main body of his Redcoats pressed on. His men were well rested and in good spirits as they crossed the River Spey unopposed and headed towards Inverness. In direct contrast, the Jacobite command structure was now at loggerheads, and the men were tired, dispirited and hungry, having marched through the appalling winter weather and then been involved in various skirmishes.

Charles was in dire straits: a desperate situation called for desperate measures. He had the idea of printing counterfeit money in the absence of real money, and he knew just the man to turn to.

That man was Robbie Strange, a twenty-five-year-old engraver and printer. He wasn't exactly a dyed-in-the-wool Jacobite, but his girlfriend, Bella Lumsden, most certainly was and she told him when he proposed to her that joining the Jacobite army was a condition of her acceptance of his hand in marriage. Consequently, Robbie joined Lord Elcho's Lifeguards, with whom he fought at Prestonpans, Falkirk and, finally, Culloden.

As well as being an excellent plate engraver, he also had other artistic talents which were soon recognised, resulting in him being asked to design and make commemorative fans for the ladies attending balls at Holyrood House. He was also commissioned to engrave a portrait of Charles while he was at Edinburgh Castle. However, despite Robbie's diligent work in counterfeiting notes, Cumberland was fast approaching, so the printing plates had to be shelved as preparations were made for imminent battle instead.

Cumberland's well-trained and disciplined army continued in good shape and in good spirits as they advanced towards Inverness and closed in on the Jacobite army for what would surely be the decisive battle of the campaign. They camped near Inverness, at Nairn, on 14 April 1746, and Cumberland himself stayed in a house on the High Street, which is now marked with a plaque for posterity.

Meanwhile, the Royal Navy continued to prevent Jacobite supplies getting through, meaning that the Jacobites were desperately short of food and money to pay the men. Also, many disparate groups of Jacobite troops, who had been involved in various minor skirmishes, were still a long way from base camp. Charles sent word for them to join him urgently, but for many it was unlikely they would make it back on time.

The situation was grim: the troops Charles did have were exhausted, cold, and hungry; his army bereft of money or supplies. However, there was still time to pull back from the abyss and many senior commanders believed that was just what they should do. They advocated withdrawing to regroup, but the prince was determined to make a stand. And because of the lack of food, the consensus among the Jacobite command structure was that confronting Cumberland in battle was the only option.

On learning that Cumberland's army was rapidly approaching Inverness, the prince and his associates billeted themselves inside Culloden House. Meanwhile, the remaining rank and file clansmen made themselves as comfortable as possible in the grounds while they prepared for the impending battle.

The Jacobites now needed to find a site of their choosing where they could take on Cumberland's men in a bid to prevent them reaching Inverness. To that end, Lord George Murray rode to the east and identified a position close to Dolcross Castle. But Charles, taking advice from his Irish advisors, dismissed this suggestion. Instead, General John O' Sullivan scouted Culloden Moor, part of the desolate, windswept Drumossie Moor, just to the west of Culloden House, which he believed would prove unsuitable for Cumberland's cavalry and heavy artilliery. Murray objected, stating that it was suitable for horse but totally unfavourable for the Highland Charge as it was too boggy underfoot. His objections were waived aside.

The Jacobite ration of food was now down to three dried biscuits a day, and they only had sufficient to last a further three days. So, on the dawn of 15 April 1746, the dishevelled and hungry Jacobite troops trudged onto the forbidding moor to do battle. The 6,000 men that were available waited for the enemy to put in an appearance. However, it transpired that Charles' cousin Cumberland was still in Nairn, celebrating his twenty-fifth birthday with his men, who had all been issued a tot of spirit for the occasion.

On hearing this news, Charles took the decision that rather than fight a pitched battle in their weakened condition, they should try a final desperate roll of the dice and initiate a surprise night attack to catch the revellers unprepared. To his absolute dismay, Lord George Murray was detailed to lead the attack, which required a thirteen-mile night march to Nairn.

To make the attack feasible, they had to reach Nairn before first light, at 2am, a task that must have appeared very daunting to the half-starved and exhausted troops as they set off under the cover of darkness. Many went AWOL in search of food, while others simply collapsed on the march. Speed was critical to the success of the mission, but general fatigue and the demanding nature of the terrain conspired to slow the march down to a crawl, and by 2am they were still two miles from their destination and had to turn back. The plan had the potential to be a master stroke, if the troops were in a suitable condition to carry it out, but as that wasn't the case, it was a huge and costly mistake.

No sooner had the now even-more exhausted Jacobite troops returned to Culloden House and laid down their weary heads to get some much-needed sleep, they were awoken by the skirl of the pipes to wearily trudge back onto the boggy, barren moor, as Cumberland's troops had just appeared over the horizon.

Contrary to popular belief, the battle of Culloden didn't pitch Scotland against England. Throughout all of the Jacobite campaigns, both armies comprised of English, Scottish, Irish and Welsh soldiers, and a little-appreciated fact is that the government army throughout the entire 1745/46 campaign, and at Culloden, contained more Scots and more Highlanders than the Jacobites. In effect, Culloden was the culmination of a bloody civil war in Scotland, which, in many instances, divided families and pitched clan against clan. The British government army also contained soldiers from Hanover, whereas the Jacobites had two French-based Celtic regiments, the Royal Ecossais and the Irish Piquets or Irish Brigade.

The Jacobites formed up on the moor, but in doing so an unseemly and bitter argument ensued as to who should take the fabled right wing, a position buried deep in the pshyche of Highland folklore and held with distinction since 1314 at Bannockburn, and throughout all of the Jacobite campaigns, by Clan MacDonald. However, on this day, Lord George Murray and his Atholl men – a conglomerate of Stewarts, Murrays, Robertsons, Menzies and MacGregors – insisted on taking this position and the MacDonalds had to move aside. Lined up beside them were Cameron of Lochiel's regiment, who were alongside the Appin Regiment, which consisted mostly of Stewarts and Maclarens. Next to them were Lord John Drummond's brigade, consisting of Lovat's regiment (Frasers) and Lady Mackintosh's Clan Chattan, comprising mainly Mackintoshes and Macbeans. Then there was Monaltrie's regiment of Farquharsons, which was a regiment of assorted MacLeans and Maclachlans, and then the Chisholm regiment. The 3rd Duke of Perth, James Drummond, commanded the three Clan MacDonald regiments, consisting of Clanranalds, Keppoch's and Glengarrys, who, much to their chagrin, had the ignominy of taking the left wing.

A hundred yards behind them, the second line formed up, with Colonel John Roy Stewart's brigade in the centre and the rest of the line consisting of the Duke of Perth's regiment, Glenbuchat's regiment, Kilmarnock's footguards, Lord Ogilvy's regiment and Lord Lewis Gordon's regiment. The flanks of the second line were covered by the cavalry of the Irish Brigade and the Royal Ecossais. At Murray's insistence, the Jacobite formation, unlike the previous day, had now moved to an area that was enclosed on the right and left flanks by the stone walls of the Culwhiniac enclosure to provide greater protection.

The Jacobites were still getting organised when Cumberland's Redcoats came onto the moor, facing the Jacobites about 650 yards away. After six months of cat and mouse, the two armies finally faced each other on 16 April 1746, for what everyone knew would be the final and decisive confrontation of the series.

The pipers roused the men and stirred the blood in the Highlander's veins for one last stand. This was the signal for the Jacobite artillery to pour fire onto the government lines, utilising what few cannons they had remaining – after the majority of them had been jettisoned on the long retreat back to the Highlands. However the government army was far better equipped and had far more heavy artillery, and responded with a fearsome barrage that decimated the already outnumbered Jacobite ranks and quietened their guns.

The Jacobite clans standing in the front line with the wind and sleet in their faces were becoming seriously unnerved as they were pounded with mortars and cannon shot. They were spooked and twitchy to get on the charge. However, Charles continued to hold them back as he was waiting for Cumberland to attack before he countered. Cumberland, though, refused to be drawn and Charles, realising that the Jacobites were unable to match the government's fire power, finally ordered his front line to go. The charge was initiated with its customary ferociousness, but soon descended into utter chaos.

As the charge got underway, the flanking enclosure walls on either side hindered it initially, but that soon became the least of the Jacobites' worries. The Redcoats utilised a new tactic of volley fire, initiated specifically to counter the Highland Charge, and which had been practised ad infinitum in Aberdeen[1]. This involved a continuous process of the front line firing a volley of musket fire then reloading, whilst the second line behind them moved forward to fire a further volley, before they reloaded and the third line then moved forward to fire as the system continued rotating, creating a continuous wall of fire. As the Jacobite charge drew nearer to the government front line, the Redcoats switched to canister shot, which was a deadly concoction of cans full of musket balls or grapeshot. It increased the effectiveness of the fire over a shorter range and was effective at making a serious dent in the massed wall of onrushing Highlanders.

The centre of the Jacobite line was initially in the lead, and there has been some suggestion that this section charged too early, before the order was given to do so. However, the marshy ground in that area and the conditions underfoot caused the centre and the left hand side to slow down, whereas the right flank was able to move at greater speed, meaning that the clansmen were forced to bunch on that side, increasing the distance the advancing hordes had to cover and lengthening their exposure to the artillery fire. Thus, the penetrative effect and the shock impact of the attack, which relied on speed and ferocity, was greatly diminished and only concentrated on one section of the Redcoats' line. The bunching also prevented the clansmen following on behind from getting at the enemy. Another problem was that those arriving later were not able to discharge their own muskets for fear of firing at their own men, which further diluted the impact.

Despite the fact that they were dropping like flies, the Jacobite clansmen continued to rapidly charge forward, hammering through the driving sleet, smoke and gunfire. They threw caution to the wind and gave it everything they had. However, many were killed by the massed volleys of musket fire before they even made it to the government lines.

A testament to the immense bravery of the charging Highlanders was the fact that such a large number of them did smash into the government troop's left wing with a sudden impact, and although the charge was not as potent as usual, it caused a violent shockwave within the Redcoat ranks. The lines buckled in several places and initially gave ground, but ultimately held firm as the government forces were ready for them with their bayonets and more new tactics.

Now the battle reached its height. An horrific period of ferocious combat ensued, in which historians believe that around 700 Jacobites were slain in just a few minutes of desperate hand-to-hand fighting. Those weeks of drill in Nairn and Aberdeen paid off for the Redcoats as they got stuck in with their bayonets and managed to execute their drills with complete faith in their comrades, superb discipline and nerves of steel. Each man was required to ignore the fearsome Highlander immediately in front of him and instead bayonet the enemy on his immediate right, targeting the side not protected by his targe (round shield) and where he was vulnerable to a bayonet thrust to the floating rib as he lifted his broadsword to strike. As a further insurance, a second line of government troops behind the first were detailed to plug the gaps and move round to cover any breaches of the line and bring down those clansmen that did break through.

Lord George Murray then ordered the Jacobite second line of the two Celtic French regiments and Kilmarnock's footguards to come up and perform their usual role of supporting the Highland Charge. On this occasion, however, they were unable to effectively back up the charge as they had to cover the threat posed by the Hanoverian dragoons who were performing an outflanking manoeuvre. Withering government fire was also a factor in keeping the Jacobite supporting regiments pegged back.

Another problem was that the enclosure walls had now became even more of a liability, and Lord George Murray's worst nightmare came true when government troops in the form of the Campbell Argyll Militia tore down a section of the wall and created a gap, allowing their cavalry to get through and put down numerous volleys of musket fire into the Jacobite rear, and into the retreating Jacobites.

Meanwhile, the MacDonalds on the left flank of the Jacobite charge, which had encountered the worst conditions underfoot, lagged a long way behind and arrived too late to support their comrades in the hand-to-hand fighting.

Cumberland's tactics and the boggy ground had combined to inflict a heavy price. The charge had been successfully nullified, forcing the clansmen to fall back and allowing the government cavalry regiments to continue to work their way round and outflank the Jacobites, causing the retreat to quickly become a rout. The Jacobites were now in total disarray. Abject defeat was staring them in the face and those still remaining fled into the hills. Charles also made a hasty exit at this point. The result was the total annihilation of the Jacobite Highland hordes in less than an hour. This was the first and only time that the Highland Charge had failed, and it was never to be seen again.

Many Jacobite Highlanders were cut down as they fled and it is said that many were also slain as they lay wounded on the battlefield as government troops commenced a battlefield clearing operation, which apparently involved bayoneting anybody still living and relieving corpses of their valuables.

After Culloden 5–6,000 Jacobites still remained at large, and over the next few days about 3,000 survivors made their way to Ruthven Barracks and reported for duty in the hope that Bonnie Prince Charlie would raise his standard again. However, on 20 April 1746, Charles, who was already on the run, sent word for them to disperse and return home, with the promise to resume the fight if French support ever materialised. His final words via the message to his men were, 'Let every man seek their own safety in the best way he can.' The Jacobites then set fire to the barracks out of anger and frustration, but also to prevent them falling into government hands.

Approximately 1,000 Jacobites died in the dreadful massacre on the battlefield at Culloden, but Cumberland was determined to exact further revenge and put paid to any further Stuart Jacobite rebellions. Indeed, there was still a continued Jacobite threat, and the belief on both sides of the divide that another rising was looming. To avoid this, around a quarter of the British Army's overall strength remained in Scotland as government troops sought to contain the Jacobite threat. Cumberland ordered that no quarter was to be given and that escapees should be hunted down like vermin, resulting in around another 2,000 being killed in the aftermath of the massacre.

The orgy of indiscriminate slaughter continued for a long time after Culloden. Many atrocities and brutal reprisals were committed by British soldiers on innocent civilians. Cattle were confiscated and Nonjuring Episcopalian or Catholic churches or meeting houses were burned down. Many of these actions were carried out on behalf of the government by the Independent Highland Companies of militia, made up of clans loyal to the government, and also by the Campbell Argyll Militia. They were given 'letters of fire and sword', which meant they could legally eliminate their traditional feudal clan enemies. They set about their task with relish and were well rewarded for doing so.

Thousands were arrested, and treated harshly, and many died of their battle wounds before their trials. Those that did survive were executed or transported, or were sent to English gaols to serve lengthy prison sentences of hard labour.

In Inverness, which was the nearest town to the battle, the old Tollbooth was used as a prison. Now the steeple is all that remains of the building. However, the Tollbooth was too small to hold all of the prisoners, so the government sought other options. Prison ships were moored nearby and churches were transformed into gaols. Some were imprisoned in the parish church of St Mary (now the Old High Church of Inverness), where numerous executions were carried out in the churchyard.

In June a number of Jacobites surrendered at Fort William after the British government had promised them immunity from prosecution, only for the infamous Captain Scott, the governor of the fort, to have them all drowned in a salmon net. However, soldiers from French regiments were treated more humanely as prisoners of war. They were given proper treatment for their wounds and tended to be exchanged for British prisoners rather than executed.

Many Jacobites continued to fight on rather than face the dire consequences of surrender and continued to engage in low level disruption or in the assassination of unpopular government officers or sympathisers. Some enlisted in the Irish Brigade or French Scottish brigades such as the Royal Ecossais.

In April 1746, Henry Masterman, a crown clerk to the Court of King's Bench, was given the task of interviewing and documenting the evidence against Jacobite prisoners in order to find sufficient evidence to charge them; a duty he had also performed after the 1715 rising. The trials were to be conducted in England rather than Scotland as most of the accused were now languishing in English gaols. Masterman and his clerk, Richard Wright, were dispatched to gaols in Carlisle, Lancaster, Chester, York, Lincoln and London, in a process lasting two months.

Chapter 11

The Prince on the Run

Cumberland was anxious to put this Scottish diversion behind him and return to the main theatre of the War of the Austrian Succession in Flanders. However, he continued to be frustrated by his failure to capture the prince, who was still at large roaming the Highlands and Islands and evading the enormous manhunt for him, despite the £30,000 (£15 million in today's money) price tag on his head.

For the next three months, he continually outwitted Cumberland's troops, causing the romantic legend to grow. He spent ten weeks island-hopping in the Hebrides. When he wasn't at sea, he was sleeping anywhere he could find shelter, or just in the open fields. The exposure and privation were beginning to make him ill, but it is said that he remained good humoured despite the trials he faced, and this endeared him to the clansmen, who remained loyal and risked life and limb for their prince.

On 28 April 1746 the prince made it to the shores of Loch nan Uamh, close to where he had first arrived on the mainland at the beginning of the campaign. He was under the impression that a French ship would be waiting for him to whisk him away. However, on his arrival, French ships were conspicuous by their absence, so instead Charles and his companions decided it would be prudent to make a crossing to Stornoway, on the island of Lewis and Harris in the Outer Hebrides, believing that they would have a better chance of escaping from there. However, the weather intervened and ferocious storms meant they only got as far as Benbecula, a small island lying between North and South Uist in the Outer Hebrides. Ironically, two days after the Prince had left, two French privateers, *La Mars* and *La Bellone*, did belatedly arrive in Loch nan Uamh and anchored with the intention of providing transport for Jacobite noblemen.

On 2 May 1746 both French ships had collected some Jacobite escapees and were still at anchor, when HMS *Greyhound*, HMS *Terror* and HMS *Baltimore* arrived in the vicinity. HMS *Greyhound* closed the distance and fired a broadside at *La Mars*, causing many casualties and fatalities. HMS *Greyhound* then turned her attention to *La Bellone* and unleashed another savage broadside which broke *La Bellone's* mast. *La Bellone* then responded with two broadsides of her own which forced HMS *Greyhound* back and allowed *La Mars* to sail away. HMS *Terror* moved in to prevent her escape, but as she did so she was shot up by a broadside from *La Mars*. *La Bellone* then continued to engage the British ships whilst *La Mars* made a break for it.

The outcome of the skirmish was that both French ships managed to get away. However, there was an outbreak of fever on board *La Bellone* on the voyage to France, and James Drummond, 3rd Duke of Perth, was among those who died.

A short while later, Charles arrived back on the mainland and moved into the area of Morar, Arisaig and Moidart, where he could feel relatively safe in Jacobite Clanranald country. Whilst in this area, he spent some time as a guest of Angus and Catriona MacDonald (née Catriona Graham) at Borrowdale House. Catriona was originally from Corriecarklet on the shores of Loch Katrine and three of their sons had fought for the Jacobites, the oldest of which had been killed at Culloden.

Not long afterwards, the prince and his companions thought it best to get on the move again. They borrowed a rowing boat from the MacDonald's and also a kilt from Lady Borrowdale to help the prince blend in more readily with the natives. They headed for the Outer Hebrides, but were caught in a terrible storm en route. They somehow managed to reach Benbecula, where they were able to hide for a few days while recovering from the ordeal of the journey.

They then made their way by sea to Scalpay, off Harris, where the prince was helped ashore and subsequently hosted by Donald Campbell, a tacksman of MacLeod of Dunveggan. Campbell was not a Jacobite, but nevertheless was an advocate of the Highland code of hospitality. He also furnished the prince with a change of clothes, as his original attire was now wringing wet.

On departure, the prince left Lady Borrowdale's tartan kilt at the house, two fragments of which have survived for posterity. One is in the West Highland Museum, in Fort William, and the other is among a collection of Stuart relics at Stonyhurst College in Lancashire. Peter MacDonald, a historic tartan expert and handloom weaver of Crieff, was able to reconstruct the original tartan pattern from the strands, and research carried out at Stonyhurst College by Tom Massey Lynch has authenticated the recreated tartan as an accurate portrayal of the original. It is the only tartan which had been proven to have been worn by a member of Scotland's Royal Stuart dynasty.

Around this time, on 8 May 1746, a group of Jacobites regrouped at Marlaggan, on the shores of Loch Arkaig, to try and keep the Jacobite fight alive. However, they melted away when word came to them that their leader was in the Outer Hebrides.

The prince made another eventful boat trip, which has forever been immortalised in *The Skye Boat Song*, a ballad that features the words: 'Carry the lad that's born to be king, over the sea to Skye'. The song captures the romanticism of Bonnie Prince Charlie's Highland travels and in particular an episode when he was spirited away in a small boat by Flora Macdonald from Benbecula to Port Kilbride on the Isle of Skye, as he continued to evade government troops.

Although Flora was not a Jacobite supporter, she ended up becoming the most famous Jacobite heroine of them all, as she was sympathetic to the prince's plight and felt that she couldn't betray him. She was born in Milton, South Uist, and when her father, Ranald Macdonald of Milton, died in 1723, soon after Flora's birth, her mother, Marion, remarried another man from the same Sleat of MacDonald Clan by the name of Hugh MacDonald. Hugh was a captain in MacDonald of Sleat's Highland Independent Company, which had been active in South Uist searching for the prince. However, Flora's mother was an ardent Jacobite supporter.

The prince and his companions arrived on South Uist, and Felix O' Neil, one of the prince's staff who had escaped with him from Culloden, casually made contact with Flora on 18 June 1746. He enquired if government troops were due to pass through at any point and then sounded her out as to her willingness to assist the prince to escape to Skye, as he had heard she was going there to visit her mother. Flora was reluctant at first, fearing that her stepfather would be punished if they were caught, but she didn't wish to betray the prince either, so agreed to help. The fact that her father was associated with the government army was obviously helpful to the fugitives, as Flora would have some awareness of military movements and would also be able to procure the necessary travel passes that the army had introduced to aid them in their hunt for the prince.

The first part of the escape was to visit a friend of her mother's, ardent Jacobite supporter and local Jacobite coordinator, Lady Clanranald (see Chapter 12), at her home at Nunton House on the island of Benbecula and inform her of their intentions. Flora made the journey with Neil MacEachin, her man servant, and they were both arrested for not having a pass.

Flora refused to cooperate unless she could first speak to her stepfather. The request was granted, but she was held overnight until he could come the following morning, Sunday, 29 June 1746, when he issued the relevant passes to Flora and Neil as well as to Betty Burke, Flora's Irish maid. Flora then continued on her way to Benbecula to visit Lady Clanranald.

Meanwhile, Neil MacEachin took Charles and his companions in a boat across the water to Benbecula, where they found a ramshackle little hut to hide – in a place called Rarnish – out of the way of prying eyes. However, the terrible weather forced the prince and Neil MacEachin to leave their hut and keep on the move, and they headed to the hill of Buabhai, from where they kept a watch for Flora.

The next day, Flora, Lady Clanranald, Flora's brother and sister-in-law, and Lady Clanranald's seven-year-old daughter met with the prince's party in a bothy and partook of a meal. However, the meal was interrupted by a shepherd lad who worked for Lady Clanranald. He informed the assembled company that General John Campbell had arrived in the area with a party of 1,500 troops. He also stated that the French were looking for the prince to rescue him, and that John Campbell was aware of this and had posted a frigate at either end of the Minch to prevent them entering.

Meanwhile, the notorious Captain Ferguson had been searching Nunton House, even having the audacity to spend the night in Lady Clanranald's bed in her absence. Additional contingents of redcoats, under the equally notorious Captain Scott, were also in the area making a systematic sweep of the islands.

On hearing this news, Lady Clanranald hurried back to Nunton House. When the soldiers asked where she had been, she told them she had been visiting a sick child and they accepted that explanation. However, Felix O' Neil was not so lucky. He was captured and tortured under the orders of Ferguson. He was put on a rack and whipped by Ferguson's hangman, but still refused to reveal the whereabouts of the prince, before eventually being sent to Edinburgh Castle as a prisoner.

A pass had been allocated for Flora's Irish maid, Betty Burke, and the intention was for the fugitives to take advantage of this by disguising the prince as Betty. Flora and Lady Clanranald found a suitable outfit for the prince to wear, including shoes, stockings, garters and a dress.

They had to wait for nightfall before they could attempt to cross the Minch, and the three 'ladies' found shelter by the lochside as they waited for sufficient darkness. They then left Benbecula on 27 June 1746. During the journey, Charles is said to have put his hands protectively over Flora's face as she slept, to shield her in case the sailors accidentally trod on her as they attended to the sails.

In the early hours of the morning, just as dawn was breaking, they arrived in Skye at the mouth of Loch Dunvegan in MacLeod (government supporters) territory. As they neared the shore, soldiers opened fire on them, so they sailed further along the coast to Port Kilbride on the most northern tip of the island, to a place now known as Prince Charles' Point. According to legend, the prince and Flora fell in love during this escape.

Just above the hill from Prince Charles' Point was a house called Monkstadt (which is still there), where Lady MacDonald, a fanatical Jacobite, lived. Her husband, Alexander MacDonald of Sleat, was a member of the Hanoverian army and was away looking for the very fugitive who was now hiding a short distance from his house. Flora had left him by the shore while she checked the lay of the land.

Flora knocked on the door of Monkstadt, but, to her dismay, was ushered into the dining room by Lieutenant Alexander Macleod, who was in charge of the government troops in the north of Skye, and was closely questioned about the prince's whereabouts. She managed to deftly answer his questions and avoided raising any suspicion, so he duly left the house. However, Lady MacDonald was concerned for the safety of the prince as the area was teeming with redcoats. Consequently, the prince only stayed a couple of nights before moving off with Flora to the smaller island of Raasay, to the east of Skye, where the owner, Malcolm MacLeod, was a Jacobite.

In order to sail to Raasay they had to first leave Monkstadt for Old Kingsburgh House, which was Lady MacDonald's father's house, nine miles to the south. They set sail again and successfully landed at a spot named ever since as Rudha Phrionnsa (Prince's Point), from where they made their way over the hills to safety at Kingsburgh. Alan MacDonald, who Flora was to later marry, was the son of the house, although he was away at Fort William serving with the government at the time.

Prince Charles then retired his alter ego of Betty Burke and dressed in the garb of a Highland clansman instead. The prince and his companions then made their way to Portree harbour, on the east side of Skye, where Bonnie Prince Charlie bade farewell to Flora at MacNab's Inn (now the Royal Hotel) and boarded a boat to take him to Raasay. Flora was never to see Charles again, despite his promises to the contrary.

As she made her way back home, Flora was arrested for her part in the escape and imprisoned aboard the frigate *Bridgewater*, just offshore from Leith, then at Dunstaffnage Castle, Oban, before being transported on the ship HMS *Furnace* to the Tower of London (see Chapter 12).

After several more excursions between the Highlands and islands, Charles returned to the mainland. He made his way to the Great Glen, which he reached on 9 August 1746. Eventually, he was able to link up with the chief of Clan MacPhearson of Cluny, who he stayed with near Ben Alder while he continued to wait for news of those elusive French ships. The ships finally arrived in early September 1746, when *L'Heureux* and the *Le Prince de Conti* sailed into Loch nan Uamh, having been diverted from their original port of call at Loch Boisdale in South Uist.

Later, as the prince made his way to the area, he hid in a cave in Glenmoriston, where he stayed for three weeks with his companions. During that time one of his bodyguards, Robert Mackenzie, was killed in the nearby town of Invermoriston, on the west bank of Loch Ness, by English troops, who believed him to be the prince. Mackenzie bore a striking resemblance to the prince and shouted as he was dying, 'You have murdered your prince!' The soldiers, in their eagerness to get their hands on the £30,000 reward, were happy to believe him and abandoned the search. By the time the English soldiers' mistake was realised, the prince had arrived in France. A cairn near Ceannacroc Bridge marks the spot where Robert Mackenzie was killed.

Another cairn, known as Prince Charlie's Cairn, which is not far from where he originally arrived on the Scottish mainland on the shores of Loch nan Uamh, marks the spot from which he left for France on 20 September 1746 aboard the French frigate *L'Heureux*.

After five months of daring adventure as a fugitive evading capture from the Hanoverian forces in the western Highlands and Islands, the prince had finally escaped.

Chapter 12

Women of the Jacobite Rebellions

During the Jacobite risings of the seventeenth and eighteenth centuries, women were not expected to be involved in actual warfare on the battlefield. Many women, though, did get involved in certain aspects of the conflict, often showing great heroism and ingenuity. Wives on both sides of the conflict often accompanied their men folk whilst on the march. However, on the government side there was a rule that if a man was killed in battle, his wife either had to leave the entourage or marry someone else the next day.

Corrag the witch of Glencoe
It is said that a witch by the name of Corrag lived in Glencoe at the time of the massacre. She predicted there would be a massacre on 13 February 1692 and she had informed anyone who would listen – which was precisely no one. She had the courage of her own convictions, though, and on that date didn't hang around in the village, instead spending the night on the freezing mountains.

The next morning, she returned to the village and was not unduly surprised that the massacre had taken place. She immediately went to see Clan Chief Maclain, only to find he had been shot by the redcoats. In disgust at the appalling sight, she took his broadsword and threw it in the water of Loch Leven. As she threw it, she shouted, 'So long as this sword lays undisturbed by man, no man from this glen will die by the sword again.'

The MacDonalds of Glencoe were at Culloden and no one died from the glen that day. Similarly, no MacDonalds from Glencoe died in subsequent British military campaigns up until 1916. However, in June of that year a dredger was clearing Loch Leven to allow bigger ships to pass through it as part of the First World War effort. The captain of the dredger then came into the local pub to show off a sword he had found at the bottom of the loch. He was taken aback, though, by the locals who were familiar with the story and recoiled in horror at the sight of the broadsword.

The next morning, 1 July 1916, was the first day of the Battle of the Somme. The death toll from the first day of the battle was horrendous and included seven MacDonald's from Glencoe.

Lady Nithsdale Winifred Maxwell

When the 5th Earl of Nithsdale, William Maxwell, was captured at the Battle of Preston in 1715, he was sent to the Tower of London along with other Jacobite officers and duly sentenced to death for treason.

On hearing of this, his wife, Lady Nithsdale (1680–1749), set off for London from her home at Terregles, Dumfries, determined to do what she could to prevent this. She made the majority of the arduous journey in the bitter February weather on horseback, apart from a section between Newcastle and York, where she was able to take a coach.

Upon arrival in London, she petitioned King George I to release her husband, which he immediately refused to do. In desperation, she threw herself at his feet and begged for his freedom, but still to no avail. With little other option available to her, she resorted to plan B, which was to plan an escape. However, time was tight; her husband's execution was due to take place the next day.

Together with her maid and two other Jacobite ladies, she successfully executed a plan which involved her husband wearing some of the maid's clothes and slipping past the not-very-attentive guards.

Afterwards, the conspirators laid low for a few days in London, before making good their getaway to Rome, where they lived in the court of James, the Old Pretender.

Maria Clementina Sobieska

At the age of thirty-one, James Edward Stuart's advisors introduced him to a Polish princess, Maria Clementina Sobieska (1702–1735), with a view to marriage. She was discovered by Charles Wogan, who had been specifically tasked with scouring the European courts to find a good match. She certainly had the right Jacobite credentials – her godfather was the Pope and she was the granddaughter of the Polish King John Sobieska. She was also very beautiful and only sixteen.

King George I was uneasy about the situation. He feared, astutely, that the union would produce Jacobite claimants to the throne, and indeed, inevitably, that proved to be true, as she became the mother of Charles Edward Stuart and Cardinal Henry Benedict. Consequently, as a preventative measure, George I issued an appeal to the Holy Roman Emperor, Charles VI, to have her kidnapped as she crossed his lands en route from Silesia to Rome, where she was due to be married. Charles VI had no hesitation in acquiescing to George I's request and having her subsequently imprisoned in Innsbruck Castle, despite the fact that he was Maria's cousin.

Wogan was now given the job of securing her release, which he successfully managed, it is believed, with the aid of some Jacobite cavaliers, one of whom was reputed to be the father of Clementine Walkinshaw, who was later to become Bonnie Prince Charlie's mistress.

Maria Clementina was then secreted away to Bologna where she was married by proxy to James, who was in Spain at the time. A more conventional wedding ceremony later took place on 1 September 1719 in the Chapel of the Episcopal Palace of Montefiasiore, Italy, in the Cathedral of Santa Margherita. Pope Clement XI recognised them as the King and Queen of Great Britain and invited them to live in Rome.

On 3 December 1720 their first son, Prince Charles Edward (later to become Bonnie Prince Charlie), was born in Rome. However, the marriage was rapidly going downhill. Maria had made a great friend in the governess of her son, but James dismissed her for being disrespectful. Maria on the other hand did not like James' favourite, John Hay of Cromlix, and suspected her husband of having an affair with his wife.

Maria left James and went to live in the convent of St Cecilia in Rome in 1726. They were reconciled in January 1728, but thereafter lived more or less separate lives.

Maria's health deteriorated and she died, at the age of thirty-two, in January 1735. She was given a state burial in St Peter's Basilica in Rome by order of Pope Clement XII.

Rachel Chiesley, Lady Grange
Rachel Cheisley (1679–1745) was the daughter of John Cheisley of Dalry and the wife of the Honourable James Erskine of Grange. He was also the younger brother of the Earl of Mar, the main instigator of the 1715 Rebellion.

Rachel's father was executed for murder after he shot Sir George Lockhart, who had ruled against him in a divorce case brought by his wife. Rachel was about ten years old at the time.

Her husband was a prosperous lawyer, and, on the surface, they appeared to be happily married. However, Lady Grange was known for her temper and the marriage eventually descended into acrimony, to the extent that by 1730 they were living in separate adjoining houses in Edinburgh.

Marital bliss was also not helped by the fact that she was a supporter of the Hanoverian government, whereas her husband was an enthusiastic Jacobite. She was convinced that her husband had been unfaithful, and it has been portrayed that her behaviour became increasingly erratic and abusive towards her husband and children.

In 1731 she sent a letter to the authorities accusing her husband of being involved in plotting a Jacobite rebellion. There may well have been some truth in this as he frequently met with Jacobite sympathisers, and his brother was the prominent Jacobite, the Earl of Mar.

Shortly after this, Lady Grange was abducted and kept in a house near Torwood for a short period before being moved to Perthshire. Her abductors were Highlanders who seemed to be working for Lord Lovatt, a friend and frequent visitor to the house of Lord Grange.

After this, she was moved through the Great Glen to Glenfinnan, and then by boat to Castle Tioram in Loch Moidart, where she was incarcerated in a tower room. Meanwhile back in Edinburgh, Lord Grange claimed that his wife had died after an illness and a sham funeral took place which involved a coffin filled with stones. However, rumours began to surface that she was alive and being kept as a prisoner, so her captors then moved her to the Monach Isles, thirteen miles west of North Uist in the Outer Hebrides, where she was kept in solitary confinement for two years. The prisoner was then moved again, this time to the island of Hirta in the St Kilda group of islands – forty miles to the west of North Uist and part of the most western islands of the Outer Hebrides in the most remote location in Britain – where she was kept for several wretched years.

Eventually she was moved again, this time to Waternish in Skye, where she was put to work spinning wool, having been taught the art. This gave her a faint glimmer of hope as she came to the realisation that the wool was being sent for sale in Inverness, and she managed to send a note, secreted within the bales, addressed to one of her friends.

Her friend informed the government of Lady Grange's predicament, but all requests to send a ship to retrieve her were blocked by the government, who were in turn being influenced by Lord Grange and his cronies. Unfortunately, this sad tale doesn't get any better as she died a few years later, still in captivity, at the age of sixty-one.

History portrays her as an awful vindictive woman, but eighteenth-century attitudes to women may have been such that her character wasn't reported kindly for posterity. However, her children were in their twenties by the time she was abducted and they made no attempt to inform the authorities or rescue her, which, though unforgivable, possibly speaks volumes about her character.

Lady Mar (Previously Lady Frances Pierrpont)
The Honourable James Erskine of Grange, the younger brother of the Earl of Mar, also made an attempt to take custody of his brother's wife after the Earl of Mar's death (see also Lady Grange).

After the 1715 rising, the Earl of Mar was exiled to Italy. He was adamant, however, that his second wife, Frances, knew nothing of his plans and the authorities took no action against her and allowed her to join him.

However, exile did not agree with her. Due to the duplicity of her husband, other Jacobite exiles suspected her of being a government spy, and this traumatic experience led her to experience mental health issues that left her severely incapacitated.

Upon her husband's death, Lady Mar (1690–1761) returned to England and a battle for custody ensued between her famous sister, Lady Mary Wortly Montagu, a writer and poet, and the Honourable James Erskine of Grange.

Grange had purchased his brother's confiscated estates and was anxious to take custody of Lady Mar and take her and her daughter to Scotland as a means of avoiding the substantial rent he was paying her. However, the entourage was stopped en route by an officer of the law with a judicial warrant ordering that her ladyship be returned to London, where she was to be cared for by her sister.

Clementina Walkinshaw
Clementina Walkinshaw (1720–1802) was the mistress of Bonnie Prince Charlie. She was the youngest of ten daughters of John Walkinshaw of

Barrowhill and his wife, Katherine Paterson. Clementina's father had become a wealthy Glasgow merchant after founding the textile village of Calton, and he owned the area of Barrowfields and Camalchie.

She first met the prince when she was twenty-five years old and living at her uncle Sir Hugh Paterson's residence at Bannockburn House near Stirling. Charles came to stay with Sir Hugh shortly after the Battle of Falkirk Muir and while the Siege of Stirling Castle was still in progress.

Clementina nursed Charles back to health from a heavy cold, much to the exasperation of Lord George Murray, who was annoyed that the campaign was being held up for a mere cold. The two became lovers during this period, but had to part after only a month as Charles had to abandon the siege of Stirling Castle and march for Inverness. However, they were reunited in 1752, when Charles helped her out of financial trouble, and she subsequently joined him on his wanderings around Europe and became his mistress for eight years.

In 1753 their daughter, Charlotte Stuart, was born in Liege. However, the relationship began to disintegrate amid claims by Clementina that Charles had become violently abusive towards her, and in 1760 she left him, taking her young daughter with her.

Katherine Paterson, Lady Barrowfield (Clementina Walkinshaw's Mother)
Clementina Walkinshaw's mother was Katherine Paterson, Lady Barowfield (1683–1780). She was Episcopalian in faith and a Jacobite supporter. Her husband, John Walkinshaw, was captured after the Battle of Sherrifmuir in the 1715 rising and was imprisoned in Stirling Castle. Fearing for his life, Katherine managed to gain admittance to the castle for a visit, during which she swapped clothing with her husband and thus enabled him to evade the guards and escape. Meanwhile, she remained in the prison cell and faced the wrath of the furious guards. Eventually they released her and she was ultimately able to rejoin her husband, who had by now gone into exile in France.

In 1717 he was pardoned by the British government and the couple were able to return to Glasgow.

The Ladies of Dalelia

It is said that the ladies living at Dalelia House, on the southern end of Loch Shiel, where Charles had taken shelter before making his way to the rallying of the clans ceremony at Glenfinnan, had sewn the Stuart

Royal Standard, which was unfurled by the Marquess of Tullibardine (see Chapter 7).

Anne Campbell
Anne Campbell (1690–1761) was married to the influential Jacobite Sir Donald Cameron, 19th Chief of Clan Cameron. However, he was not sleeping with the enemy, as she, like her mother, Isabel, were from a Jacobite branch of the Campbell clan, which was believed to have been led by the son of Campbell of Glenlyon, of Glencoe massacre infamy.

Jenny Cameron of Glendessary
Jenny Cameron (1698–1772) was the eldest daughter of Hugh Cameron, the Chief of Clan Cameron of Glendessary, a cadet branch of Clan Cameron of Lochiel. She led the clan out for the Jacobite rising of 1745, on behalf of her brother who was ill (see Chapter 7).

Her reputation was slaughtered by the press of the day, who immediately labelled her as the prince's mistress and as a wanton woman. They reported that she arrived at Glenfinnan for the rallying of the clans dressed in the striking attire of a green riding dress and a tartan doublet, as she brandished a sword at the head of 600 clansmen and a herd of cattle. The papers also claimed that she had been sexually active from the age of eleven, had numerous children, including one with a Franciscan monk, and had, apparently, caused her sister-in-law to die of shock when she was caught cavorting in bed with her brother. Also, as far as the press were concerned, she was renowned for fighting duels and had spent time on the battlefields of Flanders dressed as a man as she accompanied her lover, Irish soldier Lieutenant Colonel O'Neil, who died during that campaign. There was also a damaging biography titled *The Reputed Mistress of the Deputy Pretender*. Recent historians discredit these accounts, and it is believed that, in fact, this caricature was the work of a government smear campaign to harm her reputation, which had been prompted by the knowledge that she had raised clansmen to participate in the uprising and was a zealous Jacobite.

It is also believed that anti-Jacobite satirical publications, including the *True Patriot* and the *Jacobite Journal*, received government funding. These publications were produced by Mary Cooper and Henry Fielding, who were also heavily involved in the production of a scathingly titled musical, *Harlequin Incendiary of Columbine Cameron,* performed at Drury Lane, and which was equally instrumental in the destruction of Jenny Cameron's reputation.

It is believed that most of these rumours were maliciously started by Archibald Arbuthnot, a Whig minister who was an enemy of the Camerons. The public certainly believed the hype and Jenny Cameron became notorious. However, it is also believed that she was a favourite of the prince and spent time at his court.

She was present at the Battle of Prestonpans and at the Battle of Falkirk, where she was taken prisoner and imprisoned in Edinburgh Castle in February 1746, but later released. However, it is thought by some that the Jenny Cameron who was arrested and sent to Edinburgh Castle was, in fact, not the same one that led the clansmen to Glenfinnan, but instead an Edinburgh milliner of the same name, who had gone to care for a wounded relative at the Siege of Stirling. Cumberland certainly believed his prisoner was the notorious Jenny Cameron and urged the Duke of Newcastle to interrogate her. However, it is not thought that she faced a brutal interrogation, and she was released after nine months.

A lady called Jenny Cameron – whether it was the same lady that led her clan out at Glenfinnan is unclear – returned to her milliner's business, which very much benefitted from an increase of trade as people came from far and wide to hear about her dalliances with the prince. In fact, trade was such that the lady in question thought it prudent to neither confirm nor deny the rumours.

After the rising she lived in East Kilbride, but continued to be monitored suspiciously by the government until as late as 1753. She lived in the mansion of Blacklaw, which she renamed Mount Cameron, and that is where she died and was buried in 1773; despite her wish to be buried in the grounds of her family estate in Glendessary.

It was said that those passing her actual burial place in East Kilbride may have sometimes seen a bright light hovering over her grave. This was presumed to allude to the fact that Jenny's spirit was restless and unhappy that she was not laid to rest in her Highland homeland. It has also been said locally that since a new estate in the vicinity of her grave has been given some names that relate to the Highlands – Glen Garry, Glen Moy, Mount Cameron Drive and a Glendessary – that her spirit has become a lot less restless, and the bright hovering light can no longer be seen.

Margaret Murray of Broughton

Sir John Murray of Broughton held a prominent position in the Jacobite hierarchy as the prince's secretary. His wife, Margaret Murray, née Ferguson, was beautiful and spirited, and was known for riding with her sword unsheathed. She also had direct involvement in the seizing of horses and money for the Jacobite army.

She rode alongside her husband as the Jacobite army triumphally entered Edinburgh. As she rode, she wore an outfit designed to replicate that of her husband's regiment, the Jacobite Hussars, replete with fur hat adorned with the Jacobite white cockade. She also carried her trademark unsheathed sword and brandished a pistol. She then positioned herself at the market cross outside St Giles Cathedral and got involved in the recruitment of men to the cause. After this she accompanied her husband throughout most of the campaign.

Effie

On the route southwards Bonnie Prince Charlie stopped overnight at Strathallan's lodgings in Millrow, Dunblane, and Effie, a maid within the establishment, was given the job of polishing the prince's boots. She came into his room to collect them, but instead of taking them away, she undertook the task in his room while he slept, gazing wistfully at him.

Prince Charles awoke during the night to find an embarrassed Effie staring at him. He beckoned her towards him, but Effie, overcome with self consciousness, simply kissed the boot that she was still polishing. Charles exclaimed, 'What is wrong lass, are you scared of me,' to which, Effie replied, 'Och, no, that's not it at all. I am scared to my heart for you. You are going against the English and there are ten of them to every one of your own men. I fear for you my prince.' 'You need not worry my dear,' the prince said, 'once I have gone into England, there are many there who will come forward to support my father's cause.'

A year later, as the Jacobites retreated north from Derby, the prince stayed in Dunblane again. This time, the Duke of Cumberland's army was in hot pusuit, and a few days later the duke himself also stayed in Dunblane. In the morning, two local men who had been caught pilfering from the army baggage train were brought before Cumberland. He ordered the miscreants to be hanged and then continued with his breakfast, as if nothing untoward had happened.

After completing his breakfast, he mounted his horse and continued on his way with his officers. As he passed Strathallan's lodgings, a pot of burning oil missed him by inches but connected with his horse, causing the startled beast to rear and send Cumberland sprawling onto the ground. An officer who had spotted a female figure disappearing from the window shouted to the others to surround the building. As the soldiers kicked in the doors of the lodgings, Effie scrambled into a drain leading to the Allan Water and made her escape into the surrounding countryside. Meanwhile, the troops continued to wreck adjacent dwellings as they searched for her.

After a short while, Cumberland called them off as he had made a solemn promise to Lord Drummond, the local clan chief and staunch government supporter, that he would not destroy the town of Dunblane.

Rosemary Dacre

Rosemary Dacre came into the world at Dalston, near Carlisle, in November 1745, just as Donald MacDonald of Kinlochmoidart of the Jacobite army arrived on the scene to try and secure some provisions for his men.

As he approached the house, a servant begged him not to do anything that would distress the mother and the newborn baby. On seeing the baby, MacDonald of Kinlochmoidart gently pinned a Jacobite white cockade to her shawl and gave his word that they would be safe.

Seventy-seven years later, in 1822, when George IV visited Edinburgh, where Rosemary Dacre was now living having married Sir John Clerk of Penicuik, he was shown the very same white cockade.

Mrs Skyring

When the 1745 Jacobites crossed the border, English Jacobites were not exactly queuing up to join the ranks, despite the Jacobite army being met by enthusiastic crowds lining the route.

The prince encountered such a gathering on the banks of the River Mersey when he rode out of Manchester to meet the aristocracy of Cheshire, and one particularly enthusiastic Jacobite among the crowd was an old lady called Mrs Skyring. She had sent half of her annual income to the deposed King James II in exile, and when Prince Charles arrived on Britain's shores, she sold numerous valuables in order to be able to hand over a large sum of money when she met him. As she handed the money over, she kissed his hand and professed that she felt she could now die at peace with herself.

She did die a few days later and it is said that it was the Jacobite decision to turn back at Derby that brought on her death.

The Whitehaven Three – Ann Leroyd, Jane Mathewson and Margaret Strachan

Rebel prisoners that had been captured at Carlisle and at the Skirmish of Clifton Moor arrived in Whitehaven during December 1745. Among them were three women, Anne Leroyd, Jane Mathewson and Margaret Strachan. They had been captured alongside their menfolk, who were eventually marched off to trial in August 1746.

The clerk processing the prisoners wrote, 'As far as the women are concerned, I don't find any evidence of any fault done by them but accompanying them.' Accordingly, the women were left behind in Whitehaven House of Correction, to be released in the due process of time.

However, rather than spend longer in custody than necessary, the women took matters into their own hands by tunnelling out.

Elizabeth Clavering and Margaret Simpson

Two women, Elizabeth Clavering and Margaret Simpson, had accompanied their men, Edmund Clavering and George Hamilton respectively, on the long Jacobite trek down south in 1745. They were all captured somewhere between Carlisle and Penrith and detained in York Castle, charged with levying war and high treason. The two men were duly hanged.

Elizabeth was born Elizabeth Grant. She was a seamstress from Banff in north-east Scotland, and her husband, Edmund, was a member of the Northumbrian gentry.

Margaret Simpson, on the other hand, married George Hamilton in prison, which caused considerable consternation when the authorities became aware of this. She was released in early 1747, whilst Elizabeth was transported to the Caribbean a few months later along with 149 other prisoners. The transport ship the *Veteran* was almost at her destination of Antigua in the West indies, when she was attacked and captured by a French privateer called the *Daimant*.

The Duke of Newcastle, who was responsible for all prisoners, lobbied the governor of the Leeward Islands for the return of the human cargo, but the reply came back that all prisoners were already in France.

Lady Anne Kilmarnock
An intangible factor at the Battle of Falkirk Muir, on 17 January 1746, was the role played by Lady Anne Kilmarnock, who laid on a sumptuous meal for General Hawley with the express intention of delaying him from rejoining his troops as events unfolded on Falkirk Muir.

Her husband, William Boyd, 4th Earl of Kilmarnock, came from a family that were supporters of the government and he had never previously shown any inclination towards the Jacobites, or had any Jacobite involvement, so it was a surprise to many that he joined the Jacobite army in 1745. It was said that his main reason for doing so was pressure from Lady Anne, along with her mother, the Countess of Linlithgow. The decision proved costly, as he was captured at Culloden and dragged, bareheaded, from the battlefield to meet his fate, having lost his hat. His son stepped from the Hanoverian ranks and embraced his father, before giving him his own hat. This poignant moment was all too brief, as he was subsequently stripped of his estates before being executed at Tower Hill in London.

Lady (Colonel) Anne Mackintosh
Anne Macintosh (1723–1787) was born Anne Farquharson, daughter of the enthusiastic Jacobite John Farquharson of Invercauld House near Breamar. John Farquharson was the Chief of Clan Farquharson and had fought for the Jacobites in 1715. He later received a pardon for his participation in the fifteen, and didn't take part in the forty-five. However, his daughter was very much a chip off the old block and was involved in the forty-five right up to her neck.

Four years prior to the rising of the forty-five, she married Angus, who was twenty years her senior and Chief of Clan Mackintosh from the Inverness area and who were generally loyal to the Stewart cause. Her husband, though, was not a Jacobite supporter; he was a captain in the British Black Watch regiment.

When Bonnie Prince Charlie arrived in Scotland, Anne, despite her husband, became very proactive in raising 600 clansmen to fight with the Clan Chattan regiment for the Jacobite cause, and was inclined to issue threats to ensure their participation.

In the absence of her husband, who was away with the army, command of the Mackintosh Clan passed to MacGillivray of Dunmaglas of Clan MacGillivray. Meanwhile, Anne's husband was captured by the Jacobites as he fought on the losing Hanoverian side at Prestonpans. Anne's clansmen subsequently saw action at the Battle of Falkirk Muir on 17 January 1746, where MacGillivray is credited with making a major contribution to the Jacobite victory.

As Charles made his way back to Inverness, he arrived at Moy Hall, at Tomatin, to the south of the town, on 16 February 1746, as a guest of Lady Anne, while he and his entourage waited for the rest of his army to catch up. Inverness was still held by the government, and Lord Loudoun, the commanding officer there, got wind of the VIP guest and a detatchment was organised to capture him. However, a Jacobite sympathiser in Inverness, the chief suspect being Lady Drummuir (see below), had also become aware of the government plans for a raid on Moy Hall and sent a messenger to warn Lady Anne.

On hearing the news that Loudoun was heading towards them with a force of 1,500 men, Lady Anne quickly organised two scouts to give advance warning of their approach. She also organised a further five of her servants to lay in wait further along the road. Meanwhile, the prince, who was kept in the dark of proceedings lest he attempted a full-scale attack on Loundoun's men with potentially disastrous consequences, was despatched with his baggage to Loch Moy.

The Clan Macleod redcoats duly arrived on the scene with a piper in the vanguard. As they approached, one of the men concealed by the roadside opened fire, killing the piper. His Jacobite companions then called to imaginary clansmen, giving the order to charge. Fearing that they were about to face the terrifying Highland Charge, the Hanoverians fled from their imaginary foes, and, in the belief that the area was crawling with Jacobite clansmen, Loudoun ordered a retreat.

Anne's subterfuge had conquered an army and saved the prince. Charles didn't escape the incident completely unscathed, though, as he became ill with pneumonia as a result of hiding out by the loch and had to retire to bed during the critical forthcoming weeks.[1]

Although Anne did not accompany the regiment herself and never led them into battle, the outrageous success of this engagement earned her the moniker of Colonel Anne. Later, upon her husband's release from Jacobite imprisonment, he was handed over to the custody of his wife, and when they met she greeted him with the immortal words, 'Your servant Captain', to which he replied, 'Your servant Colonel'.

After Culloden, Lady Anne was quickly arrested. The redcoats looted Moy Hall and then mounted her on a horse to make the journey to Inverness, where she was held prisoner for six weeks. Due to her status as a lady, she was allowed to receive visitors, many of whom were in awe of this woman who had defied both her husband and the government. She was then taken to London, but was eventually released back into her husband's custody, as he had once been into hers. Apparently they were able to let bygones be bygones and lived the rest of their life happily together, until Angus died in 1770. They had no children and Anne moved to Leith, where she died in 1787.

Lady Jean Drummond, Duchess of Perth

The Duchess of Perth, Lady Jean Drummond (c.1683–1773), was the daughter of a committed Jacobite, the Duke of Gordon, and was married to the 2nd Duke of Perth, Lord James Drummond, who had been heavily involved in both the 1689 and 1715 risings.

James Drummond had accompanied James II to Ireland in 1689 and had also led the cavalry at the Battle of Sherrifmuir. At the end of the 1715 rising he had fled to exile in France, where he died in 1720.

For a time after her husband's death, the Duchess of Perth lived with her mother in Edinburgh, but then resided at Drummond Castle in Crieff, Perthshire, after her mother's death.

In February 1746 both Lady Drummond and her friend Lady Strathallan were arrested at Drummond Castle and imprisoned in Edinburgh Castle for drinking the prince's health. The two ladies were then released in November 1746.

Lady Drummond died in 1773, at Stobhall, Perthshire, having lived to approximately ninety years old.

Margaret Nairne, 2nd Lady Nairne

Lady Nairne (1669–1747) was the only daughter of the 1st Lord Nairne and was seventy-seven years of age at the time of the Battle of Culloden. She had been a great Jacobite supporter during the 1715 uprising and had ordered and threatened her Highland levies into battle. Also, much to the chagrin of her brother-in-law, John Murray, the Duke of Atholl, who was a committed government supporter, she encouraged her husband, William Murray, to join the Jacobites, as well as their two sons Lord George Murray, and William Murray, the Marquess of Tullibardine, who both took part in the 1715 and 1745 risings.

Both her husband and eldest son, William, were captured at the Battle of Preston in 1715 and sent to the Tower of London, having been charged with high treason. Lady Nairne made the journey south to petition George I personally and was successful in securing their release. In the forty-five, she still brought her overbearing personality to bear by ensuring that her family and clansmen supported the prince.

One of Lady Nairne's daughters was Charlotte Robinson, Lady Lude, who was very much in the same mould as her mother; the other was Lady Strathallan. Her great-granddaughter, Carolina Oliphant, would have made her very proud as she became a renowned pro-Jacobite songwriter and wrote many songs relating to the Highlands and the Jacobite risings.

Charlotte Robertson of Lude (Lady Lude)

Charlotte Robertson of Lude was a daughter of Lady Nairne. She was in her thirties and a widow with a nine-year-old son when the forty-five rising started.

Along with her mother, she was notorious for the threatening and bullying tactics she employed to raise clansmen to fight for the prince. Men from her estate were threatened with the burning of their houses if they didn't comply, and in many cases these threats were carried out. Most of these men subsequently deserted en route to Edinburgh, only to receive yet more threats to force them to rejoin.

Her cousin was William, the Marquess of Tullibardine, and as the Jacobites headed south, he offered to entertain the prince at Blair Castle, which was part of his family's Atholl estate. Charlotte, who was quite overcome at the prospect of meeting the prince, organised a ball in his honour to raise funds for the cause.

As the Jacobites retreated to the Highlands in January 1746, Lady Lude received a taste of her own medicine as government forces plundered many of the grand estates, including hers, while she was still in residence. Later in the campaign, she was involved in the Siege of Blair Castle with her cousin Lord George Murray (see Chapter 10).

After the failure of the rebellion, Charlotte was arrested for her activities, but didn't lose her estates because the heir, her son, was yet to come of age. Ironically, she was imprisoned briefly at Blair Castle and both her and her mother, Lady Nairne, were recommended for prosecution. However, family connections prevailed after Lady Nairne wrote to her Hanoverian nephew James, Duke of Atholl.

It was a different story though for Charlotte's sister, Lady Strathallan, who was not treated with anywhere near the same leniency.

Lady Strathallan

Lady Strathallan was Lady Nairne's other daughter, and sister of Lady Lude. She was arrested in February 1746, along with Lady Drummond, for the heinous crime of being seen drinking to the prince's health, an offence that saw her imprisoned in Edinburgh Castle for almost a year.

Bella Lumsden (also known as Isabella Lumsden and later as Lady Strange)

Following the defeat at Culloden, Robbie Strange, the counterfeit money printer (see Chapter 10) went into hiding in the Highlands and evaded capture for many months. Eventually, pining for his sweetheart, Bella Lumsden, he decided to take a risk and returned to his beloved Bella in Edinburgh, where he spent most of his time hiding in the attic making ladies fans.

One day, the redcoats, acting on a tip off, paid Bella's residence a visit. They found her quietly working at her spinning wheel. They hunted high and low but came away empty handed. When they had knocked at the door, Bella had quickly beckoned Robbie to hide under her dress, which was long and hooped and extremely wide at the bottom.

After that perilous escape, Robbie and Bella fled to the Continent and the pair became married. Many years later, they were able to return to Britain and settle in London, where Robbie went on to become a pioneer of the technique of line engraving and was even knighted for his achievements.

Lady Drummuir (Katherine Duff)

Lady Drummuir (c1669–1758) was the widow of Alexander Duff of Drummuir who became the Provost of Inverness and who, during the 1715 rising, had claimed that city for the Jacobites.

She was known for her good works and would often hand out coppers to the poor on her way to church. She also founded the Trades Hall wing of Bow Court, which she gifted for use by the trades. The inscription on the plaque at Bow Court reads: 'Katherine Duff, Lady Drummuire, gifted the six incorp Trades and Masons of Inverness the ground on which this building stands in 1729'. The six crafts were hammermen, wrights, tailors, skinners, weavers and shoemakers. There is also a coat of arms dated 1729, which includes a motto that reads 'Kind Heart be True and You Shall Never Rue'.

Just around the corner from Bow Street in Inverness is 45 Church Street, where Lady Drummuir lived. However, the house was demolished in 1843. All that remains now are basement cellars and what were stables. Prince Charles stayed at her house as he made his way to Culloden, then Cumberland stayed there after the battle. She is reputed to have said of the experiences, 'I have had two king's bairns living with me in my time and may never wish another.'

Lady Drummuir was also considered to be the chief suspect who sent the warning message to Colonel Anne Macintosh that government troops were on their way to capture Bonnie Prince Charlie (see Lady (Colonel) Anne Macintosh).

Lady MacDonald of Monkstadt

Lady MacDonald of Monkstadt assisted the prince when he went 'over the sea to Skye' with Flora MacDonald (see Chapter 11). She was said to have been beautiful, and her and her husband, Alexander MacDonald, were very kind to their tenants and consequently very popular.

She lived with her family at Monkstadt House on Skye, which, in 1732, became the seat of the Clan Donald. It is now a hotel.

Isabel Haldane, Lady Ardsheal

Isabel Haldene of Lanrick (1718–1782) was the daughter of John Haldane of Lanrick and the wife of Charles Stewart of Ardsheal, the 5th clan chief of the Stewarts of Appin.

Charles, who was renowned as a strongman and brilliant swordsman, was against getting involved in the Jacobite rising, believing it was doomed to failure. However, Isabel was a fervent Jacobite and she shamed Charles into action by threatening to lead the Stewarts of Appin herself if her husband wasn't man enough to do so. She is reputed to have handed Charles her apron and said, 'If you are not willing to be commander of the Appin, stay at home and take care of the house, and I will go and command them myself.'

After that rebuke, Charles duly led his men out. They went right through the campaign and acquitted themselves with honour at Culloden by being one of the few clans that managed to break the first line of redcoats, a feat that resulted in an appalling casualty list.

Charles himself managed to escape unscathed from the carnage and after the battle hid in the hills for several days before fleeing to France. In his absence his estates were confiscated, and he was sentenced to death.

Isabel was heavily pregnant and at home in Ardsheal on the night of 15 December 1746, when government troops, under the command of the infamous, and now promoted, Colonel Caroline Frederick Scott arrived, searching for Ardsheal. Scott had been involved in the defence of Fort William and then later in the search for Bonnie Prince Charlie. He was notorious for committing atrocities in reprisal for the rising.

He demonstrated his cruel streak in his treatment of Isabel. His unit occupied her family home and then returned to confiscate cattle and food before throwing her and her children out, ransacking the house and then burning it down.

Isabel then travelled to relatives in Stirling, where she gave birth to a daughter, Anne. Three days later, she left her children with her family in Stirling and travelled to France, where she joined her husband in exile, staying until his death in 1757.

She came to England in 1779 to receive treatment for dropsy and is buried in the graveyard of the Church of All Saints, Northampton.

The Prophecy of a Wise Woman from the Stewarts of Appin Clan
Before the battle of Culloden it was said that a wise woman (or witch) of the Stewarts of Appin clan prophesised that nine Donalds would fall bearing the blue banner.

The Stewarts of Appin found themselves on the right flank of the front line and were in the section that was able to make good progress during the Highland Charge.

The first to fall was Donald Carmichael, who was carrying the standard as he died in a hail of bullets. The standard was then taken on by seven more men named Donald, who were either mown down by gunfire or bayoneted. However, the ninth man named Donald, Donald Livingstone, otherwise known as Domhall Molach (Hairy Donald), detached the standard from its staff and wrapped it around his body. He was struck by a musket ball but had a miraculous escape as the folded silk is reputed to have saved him by deflecting the bullet from his heart.

He duly returned the bullet-ridden standard to his clan chief and went on to live to the age of eighty-eight.

Lady Findlater
To further add to the carnage of Culloden, Lady Findlater and some other women arrived on the scene immediately after the battle in a horsedrawn coach and proceeded to administer a good horse-whipping to wounded and dying Jacobites in revenge for the pillaging of her house earlier in the campaign.

Anne Leith
Anne Leith was a widow from Aberdeenshire who was living in Inverness at the time of the Battle of Culloden. On hearing of the Jacobite defeat, and in stark contrast to Lady Findlater's behaviour, she went up on to the moor with her maid servant, Eppy, and a female friend, Mrs Stoner, armed with bandages and medical supplies to see what she could do to help the wounded and dying. In doing so, the ladies took a considerable risk as they could have been beaten or raped by redcoats, who had been given licence by the Duke of Cumberland to carry out whatever atrocities they wanted on the 'Highland vermin', as he described them.

In the following weeks, she visited Jacobite prisoners in Inverness and tried to make them as comfortable as possible. She also badgered her influential relatives on the government side to provide better treatment for the prisoners, demanding that they be treated correctly as prisoners of war, and continued to do so until they were shipped off to England.

Eventually the infamous Captain Eyre got to hear of her antics and had her arrested. However, she was released after only a brief period of incarceration.

Anne McKay

Anne McKay suffered terribly at the hands of her captors. It is unlikely that a Jacobite lady of higher breeding would have been treated as badly.

Robert Nairn, deputy paymaster of the Duke of Perth's regiment, and Ranald MacDonald of Belfinlay, found themselves incarcerated in a damp cellar in a back alley of Inverness, with a redcoat sentry guarding them. They had been injured at the Battle of Culloden and had subsequently been evicted from the field hospital at Leanarch Cottage on the battlefield when it was discovered they were Jacobites.

A near neighbour in the alley was Anne Mckay. She was born Anne MacLeod on the Isle of Skye and had moved to Inverness to await news of her husband, whom she subsequently discovered had been killed at the Siege of Carlisle in November 1745.

Anne acted with compassion and brought the prisoners food and dressed their wounds when she was able. The wounds were of such a serious nature that both were incapacitated for some time. Indeed, MacDonald had a gangrenous leg, which resulted in his death while in the cellar, aged just twenty.

Meanwhile, Robert Nairn was informed that he was to be transferred to London to stand trial there. When he was eventually fit enough to attempt an escape, a plan was hatched by some local Jacobite ladies, in which it was agreed that the undertaking of the plan, and therefore all the risk, would be solely the responsibility of Anne McKay. She duly played her part by supplying Nairn with some alternative clothing, then distracted the sentry by using her feminine wiles to take him into a back close while Nairn bolted for it.

The poor sentry was severely punished by Colonel Leighton, the officer in charge, for his indiscretion in leaving the prisoner unattended, and received a lashing with the cat o' nine tails. Colonel Leighton then turned his attention to Anne McKay, threatening to incarcerate her in the Bridge Hole if she didn't give the name of a suspected accomplice, who he believed was Lady Anne Mackintosh, a renowned thorn in the government side. The Bridge Hole was a notorious, coffin-shaped cell at the foot of Ness Bridge. It only had room for one prisoner, with barely any room to move a muscle.

Anne McKay was not forthcoming with any informantion and was duly imprisoned in the Bridge Hole, where she was forced to stand for three days and nights. Despite this considerable discomfort, she still refused to betray her co-conspirator. In desperation, Leighton tried to trick her by sending an Irish lady to her, who offered her whisky to drink to the health of Prince Charlie. Anne refused the offer, stating that, 'We are McLeods and we support the government.'

Still Anne failed to cooperate, so Leighton threatened to have her whipped through the town. However, at this point, some prominent Inverness ladies, including, it is believed, her possible co-conspirator, Lady Anne Mackintosh, petitioned Provost Fraser and their influence led to Anne being released. She learned upon her release that government soldiers had beaten her seventeen-year-old son to death.

Flora MacDonald after her release from the Tower of London
By 1747 the tide of public opinion had turned against further Jacobite punishments. The 1747 Act of Indemnity pardoned any remaining prisoners including Flora MacDonald (see Chapter 11). She was subsequently released from the Tower of London in 1750.

She returned to Skye, where she married Allan Macdonald of Kinsburgh. They had five sons and two daughters, but the family later found themselves in debt, so in 1774 they emigrated to North Carolina. Shortly after their arrival in the States, trouble was brewing in the form of the American Revolution and Alan took the side of the British, joining a regiment of Royal Highland emigrants with whom he served until his capture at the Battle of Moor's Creek.

Flora was forced into hiding while the American Rebels destroyed the family plantation and she lost everything. In 1779 Flora returned to Kingsburgh, on Skye, and Alan eventually followed her when he was released.

A few years after her release from the tower, it is claimed that she met the Duke of Cumberland at a dance, where they had a convivial conversation, during which she told him that she had acted in kindness as she felt sorry for the state the prince was in, and that she would have done the same for him if he had been in Charlie's position.

She died in 1790 and is buried on Skye, in the grounds of Kilmuir Church, not too far away from where Charles landed on the island. The grave is marked by a Celtic cross and some say she was wrapped in the prince's bed sheet. There is also a statue dedicated to her situated outside Inverness Castle.

Lady Ogilvy
Lady Margaret Johnstone Ogilvy (1724–1757) was the daughter of Sir James Johnston of Westerhall in Dumfrieshire and Barbara Murray. She and her husband, David Ogilvy, 6th Earle of Airlie, were both committed Jacobites.

When the Jacobites marched into Edinburgh, Lady Ogilvy was by her husband's side. But when it came to the long, arduous march into England, women were specifically banned from accompanying their husbands. This rule was widely flouted, which is hardly surprising as David Ogilvy, who had issued the order, ignored the rules himself and allowed Lady Ogilvy to accompany him southwards, as well as on the long, demoralising trip back from Derby. She was even present on the fringes of the Falkirk battlefield holding her husband's spare horse.

Lady Ogilvy was not at Culloden. Instead, her and several other women waited anxiously for news in Inverness. After the battle, David Ogilvy escaped and eventually made it into exile. However, his wife was arrested in Inverness and imprisoned in Edinburgh Castle.

She was allowed visitors and her visiting female Jacobite friends hatched a plan in which they persuaded the washer woman who visited the cells to swap clothes with Lady Ogilvy. She walked past the guards disguised as the washer women and made it out of the prison. She then made her way to North Berwick, where she boarded a Dutch ship bound for the Continent along with some other Jacobites.

However, the ship was unable to reach the port due to high winds, so she returned to Edinburgh, where she boarded a coach bound for London disguised as a young gentleman. She was nearly rearrested, though, as she was mistaken for the prince himself. Her fellow passenger, who was an Edinburgh merchant by the name of Archibald Hart, helped her out by telling her Hanoverian accusers that she was, in fact, a well-bred lady, but was in disguise as she was trying to avoid gambling debts. She then made good her escape to the Continent and was reunited with her husband in Versailles.

Lady Ogilvy then became pregnant and was anxious that her child should be born in Scotland. She risked her freedom and made her way back to give birth to her son, Angus, before returning to France.

Her husband rose to the rank of general in the French army and was known as *Le Bel Ecossais* (The Handsome Scotsman).

Eventually they both received pardons and were able to return to their homeland, where they had a new mansion built to replace the original Airlie Castle, which had previously been confiscated by George II.

Lady Ogilvy died at the age of thirty-three in 1757, whilst her husband died forty-six years later, in 1803, at the age of seventy-nine.

Peggy Stuart

Peggy Stuart of Lanrick, near Dourne, along with her sisters, frequently harboured Jacobite menfolk on the run.

On one occasion they were hiding two Culloden escapees when an English officer arrived at the door. The two fugitives quickly hid, while the attractive Peggy opened the door and managed to distract the officer using her feminine charm.

She requested that as there was no man in the house would the officer be so courteous as to leave his men outside and search the home by himself. This was an offer the officer was only too pleased to accept.

Peggy held the candle low on the pretence that it was to enable the officer to see the stairs more easily. Then, when she came to the place where the two men were hiding under some coats, she managed to distract him by pretending to stumble and then dropping the candle as she simultaneously, deliberately put it out. The gallant officer helped her to a chair to recover from her stumble and by the time a new candle was in position the men had made their exit through a window.

Elizabeth Eyre

Francis Farquharson of Monaltrie on Deeside was a cousin of Colonel Anne Mackintosh. He was captured at Culloden and sent to the Tower of London and sentenced to death. It is said that he was being led out to Tower Hill for his execution when a lady arrived on the scene willing to pay a large ransom to save him. This was accepted and he was sent into exile instead.

It is believed that the lady in question was Margaret Eyre, from a staunchly Catholic and pro-Jacobite family, the Eyres of Hassop in Derbyshire. Francis married Margaret shortly afterwards and they subsequently moved to Berkhamstead in England, where Francis studied new agricultural practices.

After twenty years, he was allowed to return to Scotland and the pair settled in Aberdeenshire, where Francis was able to successfully apply the farming methods he had developed.

Lady Teresa Traquair

Bonnie Prince Charlies's cousin and namesake, Charles Stuart, the 5th Earl of Traquair (see Chapter 9) was imprisoned in the Tower of London for his involvement in the forty-five uprising. His wife, Lady Teresa Traquair, an English heiress born Teresa Conyers, was concerned about her husband's health and naturally anxious to see him while he was in the Tower. She reasoned that the only way she could see him was to share his confinement, so she sought permission from the Duke of Newcastle, governor of prisons, to do just that.

Her husband denied all charges against him and in the end his case was never brought to trial, resulting in the release of both husband and wife in January 1748.

Lady Amelia Murray

Lady Amelia Murray was the daughter and heiress of James Murray of Strowan and Glencarse. She was married to Lord George Murray in 1728 after he had returned to Scotland, having been pardoned for his involvement in the 1715 and 1719 rebellions. They had three sons, one of whom became Sir John Murray, 3rd Duke of Atholl, and two daughters.

Lord George Murray went into exile in the Netherlands after the Battle of Culloden for eight years, while Lady Amelia and her children remained at Blair Castle. They stayed in touch by letter and the correspondence came to light many years later and has been kept for posterity within the archives of Blair Castle. The couple frequently professed their love for each other but were very careful not to reveal their true identities and used a series of code names as subterfuge.

Once the political situation had eased a little, Lady Amelia moved out to the Netherlands to be near him, but tragically their time together was severely limited as Lord George Murray died shortly afterwards.

Lady Anne Stewart of Burray

The Laird of Burray in Orkney, James Stewart, fought at the Battle of Culloden. However, upon his return, the authorities were alerted by the son of a man Stewart was accused of murdering in 1725. Several of their clan tenants also claimed they had been forced to participate in the rebellion and he and his wife, Anne, were both arrested on suspicion of treason in August 1746.

They were sent by ship to London. James became ill on the journey and on arrival in London was transferred to Southwark prison, where he died, on 24 August 1746. Meanwhile, Anne languished on the prison ship, the *Royal Sovereign*. After some agitation by well-placed relatives, she was eventually transferred to the care of Mr Money's house in Derby Court, Southwark, London.

Mr Money and his wife were what were then known as Messengers. They were given an allowance by the authorities to take in prisoners that the authorities didn't really know what to do with as a kind of halfway house between prison and release. Lady Clanranald and Ann Mackinnon were also in this establishment at the same time.

Lady Anne Stewart was freed during the general amnesty in July 1747 and went to live in Leith.

Christian Hakeney

John Doig, a twenty-four-year-old weaver and crofter from Carseburn near Forfar was a reluctant Jacobite who had been forced into service against his will and deserted as soon as the opportunity presented itself.

After the defeat at Culloden, he thought it prudent to surrender rather than wait to be captured and duly presented himself to John Kerr, who, as a clergyman, was required by a directive issued by the Duke of Cumberland to accept surrender from the rank-and-file Jacobites. Unfortunately, Kerr failed to provide Doig with any paperwork, and when the redcoats came calling he was unable to offer any proof that he had voluntarily surrendered. He was summarily arrested and imprisoned in Inverness.

His wife, Christian Hakeney, wasn't going to take that lying down and went to see the officer in charge. She was powerless to stop him being shipped to London, but she was advised that, in all probability, he would be released, if she could produce the correct paperwork that should have been issued at the time.

Not only did she visit John Kerr and procure the correct certificate, but she also went to see the Sheriff of Forfar and got him to provide a letter stating that he had been forced out against his will.

She also wrote a letter, begging for the release of her husband who was now seriously ill in Tilbury Gaol. She then made her way to London and delivered the documents in person to the house of John Maule, one of the government's lawyers, who studied the documents and duly authorised the release of the prisoner.

Sophia Forbes

Charles Cumine didn't have any particular Jacobite affiliations, but was persuaded by his wife's uncle, prominent Jacobite Lord Pitsligo, to come out for the prince. However, after joining up, he soon realised he had made a terrible mistake, which became even more apparent when he was arrested after Culloden and shipped to gaol in London.

However, like John Doig, he was fortunate to have a very resourceful wife, who was also prepared to make the journey to London to secure her husband's release. She was a supporter of the Hanoverian government and she managed to get herself an audience with George II, during which she explained to His Highness that she didn't think it was fair that she and her children, as loyal subjects, should be reduced to poverty because of the foolish actions of her husband. Luckily, the king could see her point of view and ordered Charles' release and restored the family's estates.

Lady Bruce

Lady Bruce (1696–1791) was an elderly Jacobite supporter who lived in the Citadel area of Leith, which was then an area inhabited by the gentry. She welcomed anybody with Jacobite connections, including Lady Stewart, and, on another occasion, Flora MacDonald, who visited during the brief time she was living in Leith as she made her way back to Skye after her imprisonment. She had also visited Flora while the latter was imprisoned on HMS *Bridgewater* in Leith.

Another frequent visitor and resident of Leith was Robert Forbes, a Nonjuring bishop of the Scottish Episcopal Church, who had previously been imprisoned in Stirling and Edinburgh Castles for being suspected of intending to join the rebellion. His main claim to fame was that he wrote a major works about the forty-five uprising entitled *The Lyon in Mourning*.

Lady Ann Mackinnon

Another resident at Derby Court was Lady Ann MacKinnon, who was given the worst room in the establishment due to her perilous financial position.

In July 1746 her husband, the MacKinnon clan chief, had helped the prince to travel from Skye to the mainland. A momentous trip, as, according to legend, it was when the prince passed on his secret recipe for Drambuie, which has since been passed down through the MacKinnon family.[2]

Shortly after the prince had arrived on the mainland and bade his farewells, Anne and her husband were arrested. The old laird was incarcerated in Southwark Gaol. No evidence could be found against Anne, and she was sent to the Moneys, where she spent a year. Her husband was released after a further two-and-a-half years, having also spent the latter part of his sentence with the Moneys.

After they had both served their time, they lived together in Edinburgh.

Lady Clanranald

Lady Clanranald, the lady who had been instrumental in the prince's escape with Flora MacDonald (see Chapter 11), was also imprisoned at the Moneys.

Apparently, the experience affected her mental health, and an order was signed to send her to Bedlam.[3] However, Mrs Money refused to allow it, insisting that the lady's husband be informed first. This, in effect, saved her, as he also refused to allow it.

Lady Isabella Cromarty

Lady Isabella Cromarty was born in 1705 as Isabella Gordon, daughter of Sir William Gordon of Inver Gordon.

Lady Cromarty's husband, George Mackenzie, 3rd Earl of Cromarty, and their son, John, had previously fought alongside their clansmen at the Battle of Falkirk Muir, but were then captured at Dunrobin Castle by men from Clan Sutherland under the command of Ensign Mackay (see Chapter 10).

At the son's trial, on 20 December 1746, he was given an unconditional pardon as he pleaded his youth and his father's influence. His father, however, didn't fare so well and his pleas for mercy went unheeded and he was sent to the Tower.

Isabella made the journey to Kensington Palace, London, to plead with His Majesty on behalf of her husband. She waited at the entrance of the palace for the king to pass through and when he did, she begged on her knees and handed the king a petition for his release.

She also requested permission from the governor of the Tower to see her husband, which was initially refused. However, she then went above him and petitioned the governor of prisons, the Duke of Newcastle, who granted the request for her and her three daughters to visit. In due course, the king considered the petition and decided the earl could leave the Tower and reside at a messenger's house, where he remained a prisoner for several years while Isabella shared his imprisonment there with him.

He was eventually released, on condition that he did not venture further north than the River Trent in Nottinghamshire, so never returned to Scotland. His titles and estates were also forfeited, meaning that they lived the rest of their days in poverty.

Lady Anne Primrose

Lady Anne Primrose, née Drelincourt (1709–1775), was the widow of Hugh, Third Viscount of Primrose, who was a lieutenant-colonel in the Enniskillen Dragoons, before his death in 1741. She was the daughter of the Reverend Peter Drelincourt, Dean of Armagh, and his wife, Mary Maurice, daughter of the Dean of Londonderry/Derry.

She lived in London and put up Flora MacDonald in her house near the Strand when Flora was first released from the Tower of London.

When Charles made a clandestine visit to London in 1751, in an attempt to reignite the cause, he visited Lady Primrose, with a view to raising funds and support. On this same trip, he was also inducted into the Juror Church, believing that the only way forward to becoming King of Great Britain was to become a Protestant.

Some say there was a second child between Clementina Walkinshaw and Bonnie Prince Charlie, supposedly born in 1752 in the Duchy of Bouillon. The boy was said to have been brought to London and brought up under the care of Lady Primrose.

Elizabeth Stirling

Elizabeth Stirling was married to Alexander Murray, the 4th Earl of Elibank, the man behind the failed Elibank Plot (see Chapter 14).

She once rebuked an Edinburgh ministerial official when he referred to her as Betty, responding, 'It should be Mistress Betty or Miss Betty, certainly not bare Betty.' Of course, forever afterwards she was then known as 'Bare Betty'.

The Finsthwaite Princess

In the churchyard of St Peter's Church, in the village of Finsthwaite, near Newby Bridge, in the Lake District, lies a grave with an unpretentious headstone, marking the death, at the age of twenty-four, on 16 May 1771, of one Clementina Johannes Sobiesky Douglas (1746–1771). The tombstone also contains the cryptic message 'Behold thy king cometh'.

It is thought by many that this is the grave of a child conceived by Clementina Walkinshaw and Bonnie Prince Charlie when they first met. The names are significant as Charles' mother was named Maria Clementina Sobieska and was the granddaughter of King Johannes of Poland. Douglas was an alias known to have been used by the prince.

There could be other explanations, such as that she was the child of a Jacobite supporter who favoured those names. Whatever the truth of the situation, Jacobite supporters often visit the grave and adorn it with white cockades on significant Jacobite anniversaries.

Louise of Stolberg

Princess Louise Maximillienne Caroline Emannuele of Stolberg-Gedern (1752–1824) was born in Mons in the Austrian Netherlands (now Belgium) and was the oldest daughter of Prince Gustav Adolf of Stolberg-Gedern and his wife, Princess Elisabeth of Hornes, the younger daughter of Maximilienne, Prince of Hornes. At the age of seven, she was sent to a convent school in Mons after her father was killed at the battle of Leuthen (1757).

At the age of twenty, an arrangement was made for Louise to marry Charles Edward Stuart, which involved negotiations between well-placed members of Louise's family and King Louise XV of France, who, like his father, was keen to continue to propagate the Stuart line of ascension. Charles was thirty-one years older than his new bride and the couple had not met previously when the marriage took place by proxy on 28 March 1772 in Paris. The first time they did actually meet was at a renewing of the vows ceremony in Marcereta, Italy, on 14 April 1772.

Initially, they lived happily together in Rome, and then in 1774, they moved to Florence, where they used the titles of the Count and Countess of Albany. They failed to conceive a child and Charles, frustrated at being denied the throne, was becoming an abusive drunkard. Meanwhile, Louise embarked on a prolonged affair with an Italian poet, Count Vittorio Alfieri.

Eventually, in December 1780, Louise left Charles and took refuge in a convent, before being invited to stay at the the Palazzo della Cancelleria, the home of her brother-in-law, Cardinal Henry Stuart, the Duke of York (the title was not officially recognised as it was given to him by his father, the Old Pretender). He stood by Louise and supported her financially. However, her affair with Alfieri continued and when Henry got wind of this and realised it had been going on while she was married, he cut her off completely.

From then on, they made no secret of their relationship and lived together. Her financial situation also improved considerably on Charles' death, in 1788. They lived initially in Paris, where Louise established a famous salon, which was renowned as a place to receive a gathering of elegant people and famous writers and artists.

The couple were lucky to flee Paris just before they were about to be arrested by the Republican authorities of the French Revolution in 1792. They then moved to Florence, where Louise opened another salon in 1793, and they continued to live together until Alfieri died in 1803.

In later life, Louise continued to live in Florence with a new companion, an artist by the name of Francois Xavier Fabre.

In 1809, while Britain was at war with France, Napoleon summoned her to Paris to try and establish if there was a male Stuart heir to potentially accede to the throne of Britain in a further Jacobite Rebellion.

Louise died in 1824 and is buried in the Basilica di Santa Croce in Florence, where Alfieri is also buried.

Charlotte Stuart

Charlotte Stuart (1753–1789) was the daughter of Bonnie Prince Charlie and Clementina Walkinshaw. The couple had a relationship for eight years and Charlotte was born on 29 October 1753 in Liege.

Charles was a violent and abusive alcoholic during most of that period and angry public arguments were very much a feature of their relationship, leading to Clementina leaving Charles and taking Charlotte with her in 1760 while they were in Basel.

Charles refused to support either of them and Clementina was reduced to appealing to Charles' brother Henry for financial support. He provided them with an allowance but in return made Clementina sign a statement that the pair had never been married. Charlotte then received her education in various French convents.

In 1772 the fifty-one-year-old prince married Louise of Stolberg, who was only a year older than Charlotte.

Charlotte fell in love with Ferdinand Maximillien Meriadec de Rohan of Bordeaux and Cambrai, but in European Catholic law at the time she required permission from Charles to marry, which he refused to give as she was illegitimate, according to the statement that Clementina had signed. Despite Charles' refusal, she continued to live with Ferdinand as her protector and they had three children. These children, Charles Stuart's only grandchildren, have only become the subject of Jacobite lineage interest since their discovery in the twentieth century. There were two daughters, Marie Victoire and Charlotte, and finally a son, Charles Edward.

In 1783, after Charles had become gravely ill, he finally accepted Charlotte's pleas for reconciliation and changed his will to make her his heir, bestowing on her the Jacobite title of the Duchess of Albany. He also signed an act of legitimisation, recognising her as his natural daughter. This was contested by Henry Stuart but overruled by Louis XV of France.

Carolina Oliphant – Lady Nairne

Carolina Oliphant (1766–1845) was the great-granddaughter of the Jacobite battleaxe, Lady Nairne, who was renowned for converting her family to Jacobitism and sending them out for the prince, as well as intimidating her clan tenants to do the same.

After Culloden, the Oliphants had their estates seized and were accused of high treason. They fled to France, where they remained in exile for nineteen years. It was during this period that Carolina's parents were married in Versailles in 1755, before they were eventually given permission to return to Scotland and buy back their Gask estate.

Carolina, who became a famous songwriter and poetess, was born two years after their return to Scotland. Many of her Jacobite-orientated folk songs such as 'Will Ye No Come Back Again', 'Charlie is my Darling', and 'The Rowan Tree', are still popular today.

Chapter 13

The Pacification of the Highlands

After Culloden, Jacobite estates were confiscated and George II also took steps to pacify the Highlands by introducing the Disarming Act of 1746, whereby it was prohibited for Highlanders to carry weapons. For instance, one weapon that was proscribed was the dirk, which the majority of Highland clansmen carried as a personal weapon in lieu of the more expensive sword. The dirk was a long dagger, which was usually hung from a wide leather belt with an ornate buckle, known as a dirk belt. Another banned weapon was a smaller knife known as a sgian dubh which was worn in the top of the sock when wearing a kilt with only the upper portion of the hilt visible. It was used for eating with as well as for fighting and throwing. It was worn on the same side as the dominant hand.

However, George II went one step further than previous weaponry-banning orders and outlawed the wearing of tartan regalia. Bagpipes were also considered an instrument of war and were similarly banned. The act decreed that 'Only His Majesty's Forces shall wear the clothes commonly called Highland clothes'. The act also stated that 'Any person wearing them shall be imprisoned for six months and if convicted of a second offence shall be transported to any of His Majesty's plantations for seven years.' Indeed, one of the roles of the British Army in Scotland at that time was to prevent tartan being worn.

The colours of the tartans were originally derived from Highland plants, such as heather, gorse and fern, which could be used to dye coarse fabric in different forms. The variations in patterns with stripes of different colours originally signified badges of rank, then of districts, and then finally identified different clans.

The wearing of tartan, or plaid as it was mainly referred to at the time, generally indicated that someone was a Jacobite, and as a result of the ban, which was in place for thirty-six years after Culloden, a large number of traditional tartan setts or patterns were lost. However, from the latter part of the eighteenth century Scottish regiments became a valued part of the British Army, with their traditional tartan regalia and proud warrior traditions, which meant that tartans continued to be made for these Scottish regiments.

Also banned was the 'Great Plaid', which was a large piece of tartan cloth wrapped around the body and gathered at the waist. It also had the advantage that it doubled up as a blanket when on active military service. The great plaid was replaced by the kilt over time. Some say the kilt was invented by the English manager of an eighteenth-century ironworks in Glengarry, because, when the cumbersome plaid was removed in order to work, not much was left to the imagination. Others believe that the plaid gradually evolved into the kilt in the Scottish regiments of the British Army.

Ladies were not immune from the ban on wearing Highland regalia. On 20 December 1746 Lord Albermarle, the commander in chief in Scotland, ordered his troops to scour Edinburgh and bring in for interrogation any ladies who were dressed in tartan or wearing other items of clothing associated with the Jacobites. They soon located Jean Rollo, dressed in tartan and various other Highland accoutrements, and brought her to Lord Albermarle as requested. However, by the time she had forcibly argued her case, his lordship wished they hadn't done so, and she was swiftly released.

She was not alone in her attitude. Many of the more obdurate Jacobite Highlanders refused to obey the rules regarding Highland dress. One such person was Duncan Robertson of Auchleeks, who also was reputed to have had the distinction of being the last Highlander remaining on the battlefield at Culloden.

Another part of the act was that Irish and Scottish recruitment for continental armies was made illegal. Highland dance was also banned as the original purpose of it was to test the agility and stamina of Highland warriors; it was only adopted by women when the men folk were away.

The outlawing of Highland culture didn't just apply to Jacobites; it was seen as an act of treachery by the many Highlanders who had remained loyal to the king. Even so, in 1747 a further measure was taken by the introduction of the Heritable Jurisdictions Act, which was intended to dismantle the clan structure, to make them less warrior-orientated and in so doing end the feudal powers exercised by the clan chieftains over their clansmen. They were prohibited from raising private armies and were also stripped of their legal powers to administer justice (which was, in effect, the power of life and death, or 'pit and gallows' as it was known).

In 1782 there was a repeal of the act against Highland dress, which meant that tartan patterns could now be worn by civilians as well as the military. Accordingly, the clan traditions began to reappear, and they were also revived by the later Hanoverian monarchs, especially George IV and Queen Victoria, partly due to the popularity of Sir Walter Scott's novels and his romanticised version of the Highlands.

As a result, many of today's tartans date only from the nineteenth century, and now each of Scotland's 500 clans has a tartan they can call their own and anyone with that clan surname is entitled to wear it. For those of Scottish descent but with no clan tartan, they are officially permitted to wear Black Watch, Hunting Stewart, Jacobite, or Caledonia tartans. At least, that is the official line from the Scottish Tartan Register, although, in reality, of course, anyone can wear whatever tartan they want.

The Jacobites refused to go away all together and Jacobite clubs and societies continued to meet in secret, despite the risk of being arrested for treason. An element of these meetings was that they would toast the king over the water, often with glasses decorated with Jacobite symbols and mottoes, and women would also wear jewellery similarly adorned. The meetings tended to feature traditional Highland Gaelic music and song, much of it in praise of the Young Pretender.

The toasting of the Young Pretender was sometimes done in obtuse ways, particularly if they were unsure of the company they were in. For instance, they may toast the king over the water, by passing their glass over a finger bowl of water, or sometimes over a tray or special cylinder, which, if held to a mirror, was a portrait of the prince.

Members of these associations also tended to wear a white ribbon or white cockade on special Jacobite celebrations such as the birthday of Bonnie Prince Charlie. These traditions were also still being kept alive by Jacobite Scots who had emigrated abroad, as well as by many in Ireland.

Chapter 14

Further Nails in the Jacobite Coffin

After defeating the Jacobites, Cumberland was initially hailed as a hero in England. However, his halo soon became tarnished when people heard of the atrocities committed in his name in the aftermath of Culloden, and instead he became known as the 'Butcher'. He left Scotland in July 1746, then in the decades after Culloden, unresolved issues between Britain and France from the War of the Austrian Succession still continued to fester and resulted in a global conflict for world supremacy between Britain and France, known as the Seven Years War (1756–1763). During this conflict Cumberland suffered an ignominious military reverse, on 26 July 1757 at Hastenbeck near Hamelin, whilst attempting to defend Hanover from French invasion. Following the battle, Cumberland and his troops were forced back to the town of Stade on the North Sea coast of Lower Saxony, Germany, where he was hemmed in and forced to surrender.

The surrender terms were drafted at the Convention of Klosterzeven, on 8 September 1757, and duly signed by Cumberland, who had been given the authority to do so by George II. However, his father was far from happy with the resultant treaty, which saw Hanover occupied by French forces, and on his return to London, George II is reported as saying, 'There is my son, who has ruined me and disgraced himself.' In response, Cumberland resigned from the army and later died of a stroke in 1765, aged forty-four. In fact, Culloden was the only victory he achieved throughout his military career.

Meanwhile, Cumberland's erstwhile nemesis, Charles, wasn't faring much better. He still had designs on the British throne and continued to try and gain French support for another rising. However, The Treaty of Aix La Chapelle, which signified the end of the War of the Austrian Succession (1740–1748), was signed on 18 October 1748, and meant that France was no longer at war with Britain. The treaty also confirmed the right of succession of the House of Hanover both in Great Britain and in Hanover. As a result, France was forced to withdraw Charles Edward Stuart's claim to the British throne and was also forced to expel him. Initially, Charles refused to leave of his own accord, and even ordered a medal to be struck in defiance of the treaty, the *Amore et Spes* (Love and Hope medal). However, he was eventually deported to Avignon, which, at the time, was a Papal territory and not part of France. It only became a part of France after the French Revolution (1789–1799).

In 1747 an olive branch was extended to the Jacobites, when the War Office declared that, for military service, they would accept any man who was fit and no questions would be asked relating to his background or former life. This allowed many former Jacobites to serve in the British Army during the Seven Years War, thereby increasing the available manpower and also slowly beginning the process of Jacobite reintegration into British society. Many former Jacobite Scots served in the British Army with distinction during this conflict, particularly in India. Meanwhile, former Jacobite Highlanders, raised by Simon Fraser of Lovat, son of the disgraced Lord Lovat who was executed for treason after Culloden, fought with honour in Canada.

The Seven Years War in turn led to the American Revolutionary conflict between 1775 and 1781, in which former Jacobite clan regiments again covered themselves in glory; Simon Fraser once more raised a regiment, as did the Macphearsons of Cluny and the MacKenzies of Cromartie. There was even a regiment of Royal Highland Emigrants, of which Alan MacDonald, Flora MacDonald's husband, was a member (see Chapter 12).

The British were eventually defeated at Yorktown, Virginia, in 1781, but the former Jacobite chiefs had redeemed themselves, and their efforts didn't go unrewarded by the Crown. In 1782 the Disarming Act of 1746 was repealed and many of the former ancestral Jacobite estates were also returned in 1784. Meanwhile, many rank and file Highland soldiers were able to purchase land in Canada or elsewhere. Defeat in America had allowed redemption for previous Jacobite sins and the British nation was now able to move forward together.

However, James II had two grandsons: one was Bonnie Prince Charlie; the other was the less well-known Henry Benedict Stuart, Cardinal York (1725–1807), younger brother of the 'Young Pretender and the last Stuart in the male line. Henry did make a tentative claim to the throne, but, by then, Jacobite supporters were thin on the ground, and unlike his father, James Francis Edward Stuart, and his brother, Charles Edward Stuart, Henry made no attempt to seize the throne. He was ordained as a Catholic priest in 1748, and this was seen as the end of the line for the Jacobite cause as it would have been impossible for Charles to have been King of Britain with such an overt connection to the Catholic Church. Charles never forgave Henry for this.

Elibank Plot November 1752

In 1751–1752 Alexander Murray, the 4th Earl of Elibank, hatched a Jacobite plot that involved an assault on St James's Palace and the kidnap of George II and other royals. It was to coincide with a rising in the Highlands instigated by Swedish troops, and a simultaneous rising in London.

Bonnie Prince Charlie, who would be staying at Lady Primrose's house in London (see Chapter 12), would then come to the fore as King George II and his family were sent away by boat to exile in France.

The preparations had already involved the prince arriving incognito in London in November 1751 and having discussions with various leading Jacobites, including Dr William King of Oxford University, and Dr Archie Cameron, with a view to raising funds and support in an attempt to reignite the cause.

The Elibank Plot, as it became known, was discovered, but Dr Archie Cameron was the only protagonist found and arrested. He was made an example of and became the last martyr to die for the Jacobite cause when he was sentenced to hang at Tyburn in 1753. Some say that Dr Archibald Cameron's widow was, in fact, the real Jenny Cameron of Glenfinan fame and subsequent government propaganda notoriety (see Chapter 12).

Charles continued to make attempts to renew the Jacobite cause. In 1759 he had a meeting with France's chief minister to discuss an invasion, but it was not taken seriously as he was by now an incoherent drunk. This marked the end of any remaining faint Jacobite hopes in Britain.

The Old Pretender, James Francis Edward Stuart, died in Rome on 1 January 1766. Despite Henry's attempts to persuade him, Pope

Clement XIII refused to recognise Bonnie Prince Charlie as Charles III in the same way that he had recognised his father as Charles II.

As a further deterrent to Jacobite risings, a formidable new garrison was built near Ardesier on the edge of the Moray Firth in 1769, which became the new Fort George. The previous one in Inverness having been destroyed by the Jacobites and eventually replaced by Inverness Castle.

Charles's descent into drunken oblivion

As Charles' health deteriorated, Charlotte left her children with her mother in Paris and became her father's carer, having first secured financial support from Charles for her mother, Clementina. The pair moved to Rome, and Charles' health deteriorated further. He became even more of a shambling drunk, frequently repeating the line, 'I should have died with my men at Culloden.' He died of a stroke on 31 January 1788, a disenchanted and disillusioned man, deserted by his wife and followers, but cared for in his ailing years by his illegitimate daughter, Charlotte (see Chapter 12).

After Charles' death, Charlotte moved to Bologna. Her own health wasn't good; she suffered from a rare liver complaint that was prevalent among the Stuarts and died at the age of thirty-six, only two years after her father.

When Charles died, Henry Benedict believed he was now Henry IX, the rightful heir to the British throne, and he changed his coat of arms to include a crown in recognition of his royal status. He died in Rome, on 13 July 1807, having been a cardinal for sixty years. He was buried in St Peter's Basilica in the Vatican, alongside his mother and father, and Charles' body was also moved there.

Chapter 15

The Highland Clearances 1750–1880

After the Heritable Jurisdictions Act of 1747, the Highland chiefs had been reduced to simply being landlords to the clansmen, who had now become crofters rather than warriors. Many chiefs found this new way of life unsatisfactory, particularly as they couldn't get a lot out of their crofting tenants in terms of rent. The land wasn't particularly fertile, and the crofters merely eked out a living by subsistence farming and fishing as they lacked the means to buy livestock.

It soon became apparent to the lairds that a new breed of sheep, the cheviot, which was hardy enough to withstand the hard Highland winters and provided good quality meat and wool, was a far more viable prospect for making the estate pay than clansmen. However, to accommodate the sheep vast areas of the poor upland pasture were required, and the valleys where the crofters tended to live were also needed so that the sheep could be brought down for the winter. The clansmen had suddenly become expendable, and the chiefs wasted no time in evicting them.

For the clansmen, it was incomprehensible that their chiefs had betrayed them in this way. To add insult to injury, they were driven onto the poor coastal lands, or had their homes burnt down and were forced to leave on emigration ships – referred to as 'coffin ships' – where they suffered atrocious conditions, overcrowding and disease. It wasn't until the 1880's, after protesting crofters fought back with demonstrations, that the Crofter's Act was passed, providing security of tenure.

The Highlands were virtually emptied of people and the vast exodus to North America is the reason for the many Scottish place names to be found in that part of the world, not to mention the many Scottish customs such as pipe bands, etc.[1]

The name of Lady Sutherland (1765–1839) will live forever in notoriety for her involvement in the Highland Clearances. Sutherland has never fully recovered and is the most sparsely populated county in Britain.

Elizabeth Sutherland Leveson-Gower, Duchess of Sutherland, was born at Leven Lodge near Edinburgh. Both her parents, William Sutherland, 18th Earl of Sutherland, and his wife, Mary, died of fever when Elizabeth was only one year old. As the only surviving child she therefore inherited her father's estates and titles. She was educated in Edinburgh and London, before she married an Englishman, George Granville Leveson-Gower, Viscount Trentham, at St Marylebone Church in London. Her husband thus became the Duke of Sutherland and she became the Countess of Sutherland.

Her husband had made a start in clearing the crofters from the estate but hadn't made a great deal of progress before Lady Sutherland – who is said to have dominated her husband and sons – took over in 1807. Her first action was to sack the estate's factor, David Campbell, for his lack of progress and instead appoint Patrick Sellar and his sidekick, William Young, who had previously intimated that they could achieve rapid results.

The first clearances were conducted by these two in 1812, and they managed to perform the task without any undue animosity. However, further clearances in 1813 were met with an angry response from tenants, resulting in the army having to restore order. Subsequent clearances in 1814 proved even more problematic, especially when tenants got wind of the fact that Sellar himself was to buy one of the new sheep farms, and that he was set to make a fortune as a result. The situation deteriorated even further when an elderly tenant was left in a croft that was burnt down, resulting in Sellar being charged with murder and arson. At the trial, Sellar found himself abandoned by his employees at the Sutherland estate, but it didn't make any difference as he was summarily acquitted by a jury of wealthy landowners who were sympathetic to his aims.

After this debacle, Lady Sutherland, who was becoming increasingly irritated by critical newspaper reports, removed Sellar and Young from their posts and appointed Francis Suther and James Loch to oversee the clearances instead. Her ladyship's irritation was then increased when the estate had to provide relief to her tenants during a famine in 1816 and 1817. During this period, tenants were encouraged to emigrate, though no one as yet was forced to.

The clearances intensified in 1819, to such a degree that it became known as the 'year of the burnings'. People's dwellings were burnt down and they were forcibly evicted and forced to emigrate on the coffin ships.

Hostility and resistance to the clearances increased, reaching their peak during this period. By 1821, however, the estate had finally been cleared.

Marjorie MacDonnell is another name notoriously connected with the Highland Clearances. She was the widow of Duncan MacDonnell of Glengarry and was cut from similar cloth to Lady Sutherland. In 1782 she arranged to sell some land in the vicinity of Loch Garry and Loch Quoich for sheep farming. A premium price was agreed on condition that the area was cleared of existing crofters. She then heartlessly orchestrated the burning of 500 of her people's dwellings, whilst a ship stood by to take the evictees to the Americas. Those who refused to go were left without shelter to die in the hills.

The majority of the displaced Clan MacDonell of Glengarry settled in County Ontario, in a settlement that already had the name of Glengarry due to earlier waves of emigrants who had previously been displaced by the Clearances.

During the 1745 rising the land of the Morven Peninsula was owned by the pro-government Duke of Argyll. However, the majority of his tenants were Camerons or MacLeans, both clans that supported the Jacobites. In the aftermath of Culloden, the area suffered terribly, when two Royal Navy warships arrived off its shores to give the area a pounding in retribution for the inhabitant's part in the rising. Then, in the 1820s, a middle-aged Edinburgh spinster, Christina Stewart, who had made a lot of money through supplying hats to London high society, bought the land as an investment. She intended to let the land for the highly profitable activity of sheep farming, for which she could charge premium rents.

In 1824 her agents arrived to brutally tear down the tenants' houses and set fire to them in order to evict them and force them to emigrate. She never actually visited Morven; to her it was merely an investment. She had no interest or concern whatsoever for the families who had lived there for generations. She died in 1829, but her legacy of cruelty is still remembered in Morven.

Chapter 16

The Last Vestiges of Jacobitism

By the nineteenth century, Jacobitsm was more of a romantic sentiment than a political force, though there was a brief period known as the Neo-Jacobite Revival between 1886 and 1914 when serious attempts were made to restore the Stuart dynasty. The instigator was the British peer, Bertrum Ashburnham, who was also a leader of the Spanish Carlist movement and a supporter of Irish Home Rule.

In 1886 Ashburnham founded the Order of the White Rose. He was later joined by Melville Henry Massue, along with other Scottish and Irish Nationalists. They planned to put Princess Maria Theresa of Austria-Este on the throne. She was the niece of the childless Francis V, Duke of Modena, who had died childless in 1875, making Princess Maria Theresa the next claimant to the Jacobite throne.

Maria Theresa was a descendant of the Electress Sophia of Hanover, who was the granddaughter of James I (see Chapter 4). However, Maria Theresa was not interested in asserting her Jacobite claim and the plan wasn't acted upon.

Around this time another group with Jacobite leanings, the Anglo Catholic Oxford Movement, which was ran by Hurrell Froude and James Yeowell, sprang up. They were also keen to revive the Stuart dynasty and they revered King Charles I as a martyr. Then in 1891, Vivian Erskine and Melville Henry Massue formed the Legitimist Jacobite League of Great Britain and Ireland which replaced The Order of the White Rose.

The Legitimist Jacobite League of Great Britain and Ireland was a more militant organisation and they staged several protests centred on statues of leading historical Jacobite figures. They also received support from some MPs and a number of Scottish Nationalists were also drawn to the cause (one could say that Scottish Nationalism has its roots in Jacobitism and opposition to the Union).

By the time of the First World War in 1914, the heiress to the Jacobite claim was the elderly Queen of Bavaria, whose son and heir apparent was engaged in war against the British, and, therefore, not the ideal option to succeed to the throne.

The Jacobite cause is now represented by the Royal Stuart Society, which attracts those who live in hope that one day the Stuart royal dynasty will return to the throne.

The Current Stuart Heir

The direct legitimate male line of the Royal House of Stuart ended in 1807 with the death of Henry IX, the Cardinal Duke of York. However, there is still a surviving Stuart heir, Franz, Duke of Bavaria, the head of the Wittelsbach dynasty, the Royal house of Bavaria, who is a descendant of the House of Stuart, but it is not a title that he pursues.

The descent stems from Henrietta Anne (1644–1670), daughter of King Charles I, and her husband, Philippe, Duke of Orleans, and was inherited by their heirs. Marriages of the subsequent heirs then saw it pass to the House of Modena-Este and later to the House of Wittelsbach (Bavaria), with whom it rests today.

Franz was born into a fervently anti-Nazi family in 1933, in Munich. They moved to Hungary to escape the Nazis but were eventually arrested when Germany invaded the country in 1944. Franz was eleven at the time and spent the remainder of the Second World War in concentration camps. After the war, he became a collector of modern art and now lives at the Nymphenburg Palace in Munich and Berg Castle.

Chapter 17

The Legacy of the Jacobite Williamite War of 1689–1691 as a Major Factor in the Sectarian Division of Northern Ireland and the Troubles of 1968–1998

The complicated religious sectarianism that ignited in Northern Ireland during 'The Troubles' has its roots in the Williamite Wars, and much of the bitterness stems from the fact that during the Williamite Wars in Ireland the Protestants had to fight for their very survival, unlike in England, where William of Orange gained control in a coup d'état, without having to resort to violence. However, as we have previously seen, the background influences of religious intolerance go back even further.

Ill feeling persisted in the north of Ireland on both sides after the Williamite Wars. Then, in 1801, Ireland became part of a new United Kingdom of Great Britain and Ireland, in which Catholics were not granted full rights until Catholic Emancipation in 1829. Eventually, Ireland won the Home Rule Act of 1914, which was then suspended due to the outbreak of the First World War.

In 1916 a fanatical band of Irish Republicans, frustrated at the lack of progress of the implementation of the Home Rule Act, and the fact that, in their view, the act didn't go far enough, mounted an armed insurrection in Dublin in an action known as the Easter Rising or Easter Rebellion. The rebels were poorly armed and outnumbered and only managed to resist the British for six days, before the revolt was quelled and its leaders subsequently executed. Ireland was then placed under martial law and many of those involved were sent to internment camps or prisons in mainland Britain.

The Easter Rising brought republicanism back to the fore of Irish politics and acted as the catalyst, which eventually led to Ireland extracting itself from the Union, whereupon the British, the Ulster Loyalists and the Irish Nationalists reached an uneasy compromise that Southern Ireland would become an independent country called the Republic of Ireland. The six counties of Ulster would have their own separate Parliament and remain part of the United Kingdom, as was the wish of the Protestant majority there. This was opposed by the Nationalist minority in Northern Ireland and by many in Ireland. The subsequent history of Northern Ireland has been dogged by the division along sectarian lines of Nationalists or Republicans (Catholics) against Unionists or Loyalists (Protestants).

These divisions erupted in the late 1960s into the Troubles, resulting in the deployment of the British Army to restore order. This was initially welcomed by the Catholic community, but subsequently resulted in an escalation of violence, which continued until peace was finally achieved with the Good Friday Agreement in 1998.

The Easter Rising of 1916 is celebrated in Republican areas throughout Northern Ireland, and in the Republic of Ireland. It is basically a parade, but was provocative during The Troubles as it often involved paramilitary style uniforms.

On the other side of the sectarian divide, the Protestant/Loyalist section of the community still vigorously celebrate the longest siege to occur in the British Isles, the Siege of Londonderry/Derry, and commemorations have taken place ever since the inaugural occasion took place with a thanksgiving service in St Columb's Cathedral on 8 August 1689.

The first large-scale parades took place in 1789 and have been a regular occurrence ever since, under the auspices of the Apprentice Boys Association. There are two parades: the Shutting of the Gates Parade, which is on the first Saturday in December; and the Relief of Londonderry/Derry Parade, which is on the second Saturday in August. They mark the beginning and end of the siege respectively.

The other main Protestant parade celebrates the Protestant victory at the Battle of the Boyne, and the various parades throughout Northern Ireland are organised under the patronage of the Orange Order, which is named after King William of Orange. Orange Order lodges can be found throughout Northern Ireland, Scotland, England, Wales and the Republic of Ireland, as well as throughout the British Commonwealth and the United States. The order was founded at Loughall, County Amargh, in 1795 and is a Masonic style fraternity sworn to maintain the

Protestant ascendancy and Protestant civil and religious liberties. Critics of the organisation accuse the order of being sectarian, triumphalist and supremacist.

As a strictly Protestant organisation, the order does not accept non-Protestants as members unless they convert and adhere to the principle of Orangeism, nor does it accept Protestants married to Catholics. Bowler hats are also worn on parades. Some say that this is as a symbol of authority and Protestant ascendancy as, in days gone past, bowler hats would have been worn by foremen on the building sites and in the shipyards. The order is also politically a Unionist/Loyalist organisation and is committed to maintaining the integrity of the British Union. It campaigned against Scottish Independence in 2014.

The symbolic importance of the Battle of the Boyne has resulted in it becoming an integral part of the folklore of the Protestant Orange Order. Commemorative parades have been held since 1791, on 12 July, or the 'Glorious Twelfth' as it is known in Orange Order parlance.

The strange thing is that the Battle of Aughrim was the battle that was originally the focus of Protestant Orange Order celebrations. Aughrim was a powerful symbol of disaster for the Irish Catholics as it marked the final nail in the coffin in the Williamite Wars, but somehow the Boyne, which was the battle that turned the tide of the war in the Protestant's favour, ended up superseding Aughrim in the commemorative parade stakes. Some say the Boyne gained more emphasis as the Jacobite troops hadn't fought as well as at Aughrim and therefore the Boyne was a greater disgrace. Aughrim does still get a mention though in the Loyalist marching song *The Sash my Father Wore*.

On and around the twelfth, thousands of participants and spectators witness large parades involving Ulster Loyalist marching bands. Streets are bedecked with red, white and blue, and immense bonfires are lit. However, the Catholic side of the divide are far from impressed with these activities, and though many marches pass off without incident, those that pass near or through Catholic and Irish Nationalist neighbourhoods are seen as confrontational. Protestant Loyalist's insist it is their right to march through these areas, but those on the other side of the divide disagree and the subsequent stand-offs, can lead to violence. This element was particularly apparent during the Troubles, but it has always been a feature.

The parade begins at the Orange Hall and then passes through the town or city. The bands carry banners depicting various scenes of Orange heroes; the most popular being that of King William of Orange crossing the River Boyne during the battle. Common marching songs include *The Sash my Father Wore* and *Derry's Walls*, but sometimes more contentious and deliberately provocative songs such as *Billy Boys*[1] may also be played, all to the incessant beat of the Lambeg drum. The procession usually ends at a suitable park, where speeches by clergymen, civic dignitaries and senior members of the Orange Order are heard. A church service also takes place and sometimes band prizes will be awarded.

Each Lodge is responsible for organising its own parade. In rural areas the parade venue may rotate around the various towns in the locality, usually chosen to avoid confrontation with Catholic neighbourhoods, though occasionally the 'right to march' through Catholic areas is asserted.

The descent of Northern Ireland into the Troubles

When the new state of Northern Ireland was created in 1921 Unionists continued to maintain control and various measures were introduced to ensure that they always had a sizeable majority. One such measure was the abolition of Proportional Representation in 1929 in favour of the first past the post system. Electoral boundaries were also redrawn, in a process known as gerrymandering, and the Catholic minority were becoming increasingly disaffected, resulting in Catholic activists such as John Hume and Bernadette Devlin forming the Northern Ireland Civil Rights Association (NICRA) in 1967.

A particularly highly charged event occurred on 5 October 1968 in Londonderry/Derry, where NICRA marched to protest about discrimination and gerrymandering. The march was banned by the Minister of Home Affairs, William Craig, and NICRA were set to withdraw. However, the Derry Housing Action Committee (DHAC) said they would go ahead anyway, forcing NICRA to agree or lose face.

After this incident, tensions between both sides of the sectarian divide continued to rise and in 1969 the annual Loyalist parades were a veritable powder keg. A stand-off between Protestants and Catholics occurred when the Relief of Londonderry/Derry Parade passed close to the Catholic Bogside area, and the marchers were confronted by angry

Nationalist youths who had erected barricades to stop the march. The Royal Ulster Constabulary (RUC) attempted to force the Nationalists back into the Catholic Bogside, and then the incendiary situation ignited into what became known as the Battle of the Bogside.

The RUC found themselves as the whipping boys in the middle of the Loyalist marchers and the Nationalist youths, as they attempted to restore order with baton charges whilst being pelted by petrol bombs. Eventually the police resorted to using tear gas, the first time it had been used in either Ireland or Britain. Riots and widespread violence then broke out in Republican areas of West Belfast and elsewhere in Northern Ireland as an act of solidarity with Londonderry/Derry. Rioting continued from 12–14 August and it got to a stage where the RUC were unable to enter these areas, resulting in the deployment of the British Army, in what is widely regarded as the start of The Troubles.

The Troubles

When the Troubles (1969–1998) erupted in Northern Ireland, Catholics saw the introduction of the British Army as their saviour from Protestant excesses. The same, albeit in reverse, was true of the Protestant community. However, the Irish Republican Army's (IRA) aim after the Battle of the Bogside in 1969 was to usurp the army and install themselves as the defenders of the Nationalists.

They waged a guerrilla campaign against the British Army from 1970 to 1997 and managed to provoke reactions that soured the relationship between the Nationalists/Catholics and the British Army. In doing so, they successfully turned most of the Nationalist Catholic population against the army, especially during 1972 when the British government responded to the rapidly escalating situation by introducing internment, which involved the detention of suspected IRA activists in Long Kesh prison without trial. This course of action proved counterproductive and increased recruitment for the IRA, particularly in the Nationalist/Catholic ghettos of Belfast and Londonderry/Derry.

So called 'peace walls' were erected to separate the warring Loyalist and Republican communities, the most famous being the peace wall separating the Catholic Falls Road from the Protestant Shankill Road in West Belfast. At the same time, lurid murals appeared on the gable ends of houses, extolling the virtues of that particular enclave's paramilitary prowess.

The Peace Process

John Hume was a leading light in Northern Ireland's Civil Rights Movement of the 1960s, '70s and '80s, and later became a key figure in the Peace Process, acting as an intermediary between the British government and Sinn Fein. He was the leader of the Social Democratic and Labour Party (SDLP), which campaigned for a united Ireland.

He was on the Nationalist side of the divide, which was acceptable for Sinn Fein, the political wing of the IRA, while his commitment to non-violence meant he was also respected by Unionists, who felt he was a man they could trust and with whom they could negotiate.

Hume's persistence at trying to find a peaceful solution eventually came to fruition in the form of the 15 December 1993 Joint Declaration of Peace (more commonly known as the Downing Street Declaration), which was issued by John Major, the prime minister of the United Kingdom, and Albert Reynolds, prime minister of the Republic of Ireland, on behalf of the British and Irish governments.

Talks then continued between Hume and Gerry Adams of Sinn Fein, which gave rise to accusations from some Unionists that he was 'supping with the devil', as the IRA continued their campaign of terror unabated. However, these talks were constructive and led to a joint statement on how the violence might be stopped, culminating on 6 April 1994 with the IRA announcing a three-day temporary ceasefire.

Five months later, on 31 August 1994, the IRA announced a permanent cessation of military operations from midnight. Then, on 13 October 1994, a Loyalist paramilitary ceasefire was announced, and a decommissioning of weapons process took place on both sides.

On 1 May 1997 a General Election in the United Kingdom was won by the Labour Party and Tony Blair became the new prime minister. Shortly afterwards, he announced that he valued Northern Ireland's place within the United Kingdom and suggested that the Republic of Ireland should amend articles 2 and 3 of its constitution. The two articles basically stated that the territory of Ireland consisted of the whole island. However, a compromise was reached and the words were amended to say: 'to express an aspiration towards creating a united Ireland by peaceful means and only with the consent of the majority, democratically expressed in both jurisdictions of Ireland'.

On 12 July 1997 the Orange Order, who were now conscious of the new Parades Commission and sensitive to the Peace Process, took the decision to reroute several contentious parades and the twelfth passed off peacefully. Talks continued, and the decommissioning of weapons continued, despite occasional sectarian killings on both sides. This resulted at various times in Sinn Fein and the Ulster Defence Association (UDA) being suspended from the talks, then subsequently being reinstated by Mo Mowlem, Secretary of State for Northern Ireland, after a period of good behavior.

On 25 March 1998 the chairman of the talks, US Senator George Mitchell, accelerated the talks by setting a two-week deadline for an agreement. By 9 April 1998 the talks had gone past the midnight deadline, but the important thing was that both sides were still talking, and progress was being made, so eventually, on 10 April 1998 – Good Friday – at 5.30pm, over seventeen hours after the official deadline, agreement was finally reached, bringing a formal end to the Troubles.

By 2005 both the IRA and the Loyalist paramilitary groups had finally decommissioned all of their weapons and had declared that their respective campaigns were over.

The definitive end of the Troubles finally came in July 2007, following the St Andrew's Agreement of October 2006, which finally allowed the British Army to conclude Operation Banner, the longest-running operation in the history of the British Army.

During more than four decades of guerrilla warfare 3,600 people had been killed, over half of whom were civilians.

Mo Mowlem

Mo Mowlem (1949–2005) was a British Labour politician. She was born in Watford but grew up in Coventry. She became a lecturer in the Political Science Department of the University of Wisconsin, Milwaukee, in 1977 and at Florida State University in Tallahassee from 1977 to 1979, before returning to England to teach at Newcastle University. Mowlem then went into politics and became part of John Smith's Labour party Shadow Cabinet as Secretary of State for National Heritage.

Following the death of John Smith, she played a central role in Tony Blair's leadership campaign, and when he later became prime minister in 1997, she was given the poisoned chalice, otherwise known as the post of Secretary of State for Northern Ireland. Whilst in the role, she played a pivotal part in the signing of the 1998 Good Friday Peace Agreement and in finally bringing peace to the province.

She realised that no progress would be made without compromise. Just as the talks were beginning to break down beyond repair, she stuck her neck out, and, on 29 August 1997, was prepared to accept an IRA ceasefire as genuine, despite hostility from Loyalist parties. The Loyalist parties may well have had a point, but by taking the IRA at their word, multi-party talks were then able to resume on 15 September 1997, rather than break down irretrievably.

On another occasion, she persuaded Ulster Loyalist paramilitary groups to participate in the peace process by making potentially risky unaccompanied trips to visit senior members of these organisations in their prison cells so that she could discuss the issues with them face to face.

As the Labour politician Peter Hain put it in 2005, 'Mo Mowlem was the catalyst that allowed politics to move forward which led to the signing of the Good Friday Agreement in April 1998. She cut through conventions and made difficult decisions that gave momentum to political progress.'

Chapter 18

Current Issues

The Situation in Northern Ireland after the Troubles

Since the Good Friday agreement, the situation in Northern Ireland is far more neighbourly, and the army checkpoints are no more, though the murals expressing the same sectarian views are still present. However, outbreaks of sectarian violence have only occurred sporadically and these are sometimes associated with the marching season. Aspects of the Williamite Wars are still celebrated by the Protestant Orange Order of Northern Ireland, while Catholics also still commemorate the 1916 Uprising.

Parades are an important part of the culture of both communities. Throughout the Troubles, the celebrations of the Easter Rising, the Battle of the Boyne, and the Siege of Londonderry/Derry had the effect of turning Northern Ireland into a powder keg, waiting to explode, as confrontations frequently arose when the traditional routes passed through the opposing sectarian neighbourhoods. However, since the conclusion of the Northern Ireland Peace Process and the establishment of the Parades Commission in 1998, which deals with potentially contentious parade routes, there has been greater dialogue between marchers and residents, and as a result, the parades have generally been more peaceful. Nowadays, violence at parades is very much a rarity. There is nowhere near the same degree of provocation, and the Orange Order now has rules in place stipulating that there must be 'neighbourly' behavior towards Catholics. Nonetheless, the Orange Order marches can include those not affiliated to Orange Lodges and as a result may include those at the more extreme end of the spectrum, such as supporters of Unionist paramilitaries. For many on both sides of the sectarian divide, the old ways are still deeply entrenched.

Jacobitism and Sectarian Tribal Loyalties in the Partisan World of Football

In certain parts of Scotland, the same anniversaries are also celebrated with vigour, particularly in Glasgow and Edinburgh, where sectarianism is also still rife in the tribal partisan world of football. This manifests particularly in the Glasgow derby, which involves Glasgow Celtic (Catholic) and Glasgow Rangers (Protestant); the 'Old Firm' as they are known. The Edinburgh derby is also not for the faint-hearted; it features Hibernian (Catholic) and Heart of Midlothian (Protestant). There are also similar tribal rivalries, although not to the same degree as Rangers v Celtic, in other cities that have historically had an influx of Irish immigration: for example in Liverpool, where Liverpool FC aligns itself with Catholic Irish sentiment and has close ties with Glasgow Celtic; and Dundee, where Dundee United has traditionally represented those with Irish affiliations. Some of these derbies, particularly the Old Firm match, can be lively affairs, not just on the field of play.

On the whole though, despite an undercurrent of sectarian division that still simmers quietly in the background, it seems safe to say that the Jacobite conundrum has now finally been put to bed.

Notes

Chapter 1
1. *englishheritage.org.uk:* A descendant of the original tree is now in situ. There are over 500 pubs in England called the Royal Oak.
2. *Scottish Covenanters Memorials Association:* A plaque now exists in the vicinity of the former prison provided by Greyfriars Kirkyard Trust with the support of the Scottish Covenanter Memorials Association.

Chapter 2
1. *aboutbritain.com:* From the 16th century onwards, Bristol was England's second city after London, due to the prosperity of the port. However, from the Industrial Revolution of the 19th century, the northern English cities grew at a faster rate.
2. The beach is now called Monmouth beach.
3. Walter Besant: *For Faith and Freedom*, 2014: 12. Most of the school children were pupils of Mary Blake and the rest were pupils of Mrs Musgrave, another school mistress in Taunton.
4. *Battle of Sedgemoor Visitor Centre, Westonzoyland, Somerset:* His followers referred to him as King Monmouth, as they couldn't really use his Christian name and call him King James as that was the opposition.
5. *St Mary's Church, Bridgewater:* Godfrey pointed out the Royal encampment to Monmouth from the top of St Mary's Church Tower, Bridgewater. The bell ringing chamber has now been named after Monmouth.
6. Andrew Jackson: *A-Z of Poole*, 2020: The quarters from the hanging, drawing and quartering were sent out to local villages to be displayed prominently in gibbets. These were iron cages used to display the body parts, which were tarred to make them last longer and then left as a grim reminder to cower the local people.
7. *stuarts-online.com:* Many believed the baby was secreted into the bed via a warming pan.

Chapter 3
1. *bbc.co.uk Plantation of Ulster – English and Scottish Planters – 1641 Rebellion:* A feature of the Irish Confederate Wars of 1641–1652, in which Irish Catholics reacted to the plantation of Ireland with English and Scottish settlers and massacred vast numbers of Protestants.

2. *irelandbyways.co.uk:* The besieged could see the ships from the top of St Columb's Cathedral, Londonderry/Derry and sent signals themselves from there, including the crimson flag of distress, which indicated to the ships that the city had still not fallen. The crimson flag forms part of the Protestant commemorative celebrations of the siege.
3. *cotyroneireland.com:* There are memorial tablets to both Colonel Henry Baker and the Captain of the *Mountjoy*, Michael Browning, in St Columb's Cathedral, Londonderry/Derry.
4. *alphahistory.com:* The song, *The sash my father wore* relates to the Siege of Londonderry/Derry, the Battle of the Boyne, the Battle of Aughrim and the Battle of Newtownbutler, which is referred to as Enniskillen.
5. *patrickcomerford.com:* Ireton's Fort and Cromwell's Fort were built during the First Siege of Limerick 1650–1651 during the Cromwellian conquest of Ireland.
6. *Wikipedia.org:* This is the same Hugh McKay, who was William's commander in Scotland in 1689 and who featured at the Battle of Killiecrankie.

Chapter 4
1. *Troopers Den information board – Pass of Killiecrankie:* The spot is now marked for posterity in the Pass of Killiecrankie.
2. *wise-geek.com:* The claymore, like the broadsword, was a double-edged sword. The difference was that the claymore had a basket hilt, which had the advantage of protecting the hand. Some types could also be wielded with two hands.
3. Ref: www.castlesfortsbattles.co.uk
4. *royal.uk:* The succession of the Crown Act (2013) ended the provision by which those who marry Roman Catholics are disqualified from the line of succession. It is still a requirement to be Protestant to succeed to the throne.
5. *Poetryverse.com:* The poem in question, written in 1791 by Robert Burns, is called 'Such a parcel of rogues in a nation'. It has also become the title of a Scottish folk song and is inclined to be sung with reference to Scottish nationalism.
6. *historyandpolicy.org:* One interesting legacy of the Spanish War of Succession and the Treaty of Utrecht that remains is that Britain still retains Gibraltar as a British Overseas Territory.
7. *nationalgeographic.com:* It is believed that George had become aware of Sophia Dorothea and Von Konigsmark's plans to run away together.

Chapter 5
1. *royalmint.com:* Pubs are named the 'White Horse' due to the White Horse of Hanover heraldic symbol and the long-standing tradition of naming pubs as an expression of loyalty to the monarchy.
2. *eileandonancastle.com:* Eilean Donan Castle was a Mackenzie Clan stronghold dating back to 1220.
3. *royalarmouries.com:* The Coehorn mortar was a lightweight mortar designed by the Dutch military engineer Baron Menno van Coehorn.

Chapter 7

1. *undiscoveredscotland:* At this beach, Coileag a'Phironnsa (The Cockleshell Strand of the Prince), a pale-pink sea convolvulys plant blooms and legend says that Bonnie Prince Charlie brought the seeds with him from France. They were first planted inadvertently by him when some seeds fell out of his pocket when he took out his handkerchief.

Chapter 9

1. *theglasgowstory.com:* Jacobite supporters were thin on the ground in Glasgow and the extraction of heavy taxes from the city didn't change that situation one bit.
2. *Scotsman.com:* The notorious, Wolf of Bradenoch was Alexander Stewart (1343–1394). He was the illegitimate fourth son of the future Robert II of Scotland and was made 1st Earl of Buchan in 1382, which gave him the authority of the Scottish Crown in the Highlands. He abused his power and instigated a reign of cruelty and terror. He had up to forty illegitimate children, for which he blamed his wife for being unable to conceive. He tried to end his marriage and was excommunicated by the Bishop of Moray. This caused him to ransack the town of Forres and to destroy Elgin Cathedral in revenge.

Chapter 10

1. Ref: www.britishbattles.com – Cumberland drilled his troops in volley firing and a form of bayonet fighting.

Chapter 12

1. *bbc.co.uk:* The bed the prince slept in has been kept at Moy Hall for posterity, along with a scrap of tartan plaid that he was wearing when he stayed there and was subsequently used to make a canopy for the bed.
2. *rampantscotland.com:* The MacKinnon family tried different variations of the old recipe and it was originally known on the Isle of Skye as 'Dram Buide', the yellow drink, or 'Dram Buideach, the drink that satisfies.
3. *bbc.com:* Bethlem Hospital was a London mental asylum, so notorious that its corrupted name of Bedlam came to be associated with madness.

Chapter 15

1. *en.m.wikipedia.org:* The Glengarry Highland Games in Ontario, Canada, is the largest highland games outside Scotland.

Chapter 16

1. 'Billy Boys' – A Loyalist song from Glasgow which is banned by Glasgow Rangers Football Club due to its overt sectarian nature but is frequently sung by fans anyway. It originates from a 1920's Loyalist Glasgow razor gang led by Billy Fullerton but also refers to King Billy (King William of Orange).

Bibliography

Baxter, Colin, *Scottish Castles – Photography* (Granton-on-Spey: Colin Baxter Photography Ltd, 2007).
Craig, Maggie, *Damn Rebel Bitches: The Women of the 45* (Edinburgh: Mainstream, 1997).
Cullingford, Cecil, *A History of Dorset* (Bognor Regis: Phillimore, 1984).
Draper, Jo, *Dorchester Past* (Bognor Regis: Phillimore, 2001).
Draper, Jo, *Dorset: The Complete Guide* (Wimborne: Dovecote Press 1988).
Else, David, *Lonely Planet: Britain* (London: Lonely Planet Publications Pty Ltd 2003).
Flude, Kevin, *Divorced Beheaded Died* (London: Michael O Mara Books, 2015).
Hadaway, Bridget and Sue Jacquemier (eds), *R.J. Unstead. Struggle for Power* (1977).
Hilliam, David, *The Little Book Of Dorset* (Stroud: The History Press 2010).
Jackson, Andrew, *Poole Pubs* (Stroud: Amberley Publishing, 2019)
Jackson, Andrew, *A-Z of Poole* (Stroud: Amberley Publishing, 2020).
Jenner, Lorna, *The Monmouth Rebellion and the Battle of Sedgemoor 1685* (Somerset County Council Heritage Service, 2007).
Kamm, Antony, *The Jacobites* (National Museums Scotland, 2020).
Love, Dane. *Jacobite Stories* (EU: Neil Wilson Publishing, 2019).
McHardy, Stuart *The White Cockade: Historical Tales of the Jacobites* (Edinburgh: Birlinn, 2020).
McNabb, Andy *Seven Troop* (London: Random House, 2008).
Page, M, *The Battle of Sedgemoor, Westonzoyland, Somerset* (FR Hist Soc.).
Potts, Joanna, *Phillips Encyclopedia* (London: Octopus Publishing, 2004).
Ramsay, Alex, *Collins Touring Guide Scotland* (London: Harper Collins, 1996).
Sorenson, Phillip, *Stitched up for the Cup* (London: Austin MaCauley Publishers, 2021)
Tabraham, Chris, *Culloden 1746: Fight for the Throne* (Broxburn: Scottish Guides, Lomond, 2017).
Tincey, John, *Sedgemoor 1685 Marlborough's First Victory* (Barnsley: Pen and Sword, 2005).
Whaley, Peta, *West Country History: Dorset* (Bristol: Intellect Books, 1977).
Williamson, David, *The Kings and Queens of England* (London: National Portrait Gallery Publications, 2000).
Stonehouse, Anne, *50 Walks in Dorset* (Basingstoke: AA, 2009).

The History of the Kings and Queens of England and Scotland (Wigston: Armadillo Books, 2007).
Heritage of Britain (London: The Reader's Digest Association Ltd, 1985).
Illustrated Guide to Britain's Coast (London: Drive Publications Ltd, 1987).
Illustrated Guide to Britain (London: Drive Publications Ltd, 1971).

Additional Information from:
Alice Lisle Pub, Rockford, Near Ringwood, Hampshire.
Botany Bay Inne, Winterborne Zelston, Dorset.
Bridgewater Museum.
Glencoe Visitor Centre.
Glenfinnan Visitor Centre.
Inverness City Heritage Trust leaflet.
Monmouth Ash Pub, Verwood, Dorset.
National Trust for Scotland, Culloden Battlefield and Visitor Centre.
Pass of Killiecrankie – Troopers Den Information Board.
Scottish Covenanters Memorial Association.
Sedgemoor Inn, Westonzoyland, Somerset.
Sherborne Castle Visitor Information and Map.
Somerset Museum.
St Mary the Virgin Church, Westonzoyland.
Two Men in a Trench, BBC.
Walking through History, C4.
Wimborne Minster.
Worlds End Pub, Almer, Dorset.

Websites
www.aberchaldestate.co.uk
www.aboutbritain.com
www.adventuresinhistoryland
www.alphahistory.com
apprenticeboysofderry.org
www.artsandculture.google.com
www.askaboutireland.ie
www.battlefieldanomalies.com
www.battlefieldsofbritain.co.uk
www.battlefieldwordpress.com
www.battleofprestonpans1745.org
www.bbc.co.uk
www.biography.com
www.biography.yourdictionary.com
www.boynevalleytours.com
www.brittainexpress.com
www.britanica.com

www.britroyals.com
www.britishbattles.com
www.britishheritage.com
www.britishmuseum.org
cainulster.ac.uk
carmishaelwatsonblogspot.com.
www.cotyroneireland.com
www.cranntarascot.com
www.cullodenbattlefield.wordpress.com
www.culturenorthernireland.org
www.derryguidedtours.com
www.dib.ie
www.digital.nls.uk
www.discoverglencoe.scot.com
www.discoverireland.ie
www.eileandonancastle.com
www.englishmonarchs.co.uk
www.electricscotland/The Story of Leith
www.encyclopedia.com
www.encyclopediavirginia.org
www.englishheritage.co.uk
www.englishmonarchs.co.uk
www.everything2.com
www.enniskillencastle.co.uk
www.falkirkherald.co.uk
www.findmypast.com
www.forces.net.com
www.Fromthe42ie-delivered
www.futurelearn
www.generalhistory.com
www.helion.co.uk
www.heritage.nf.ca
www.highlandtitles.com
www.historiamag
www.historicengland.org.uk
www.historic-uk.com
www.historyand policy.org
www.historyextra.com
www.historyhit.com
www.historyireland.com
www.historynet.com
www.historyofmassachusetts.org
www.historyofparliamentonline.org
www.historyofwar.org

www.historytoday.com
www.hvp.org.uk
www.infoplease.com
www.irelandbyways.co.uk
www.irelandseye.com
www.jacobites.net
www.keepmilitarymuseum.org
www.kinglaoghaire
www.legislation.gov.uk
www.nam.ac.uk
www.nationalarchives.gov.uk
www.nationalgeographic.com
www.navalandmilitarypress.com/Life of Lieut General Hugh McKay of Scourie
www.newhistorian.com
www.newworldencyclopedia.org
www.northerntimes.co.uk
www.nottingham.ac.uk
www.nts.uk
www.oldappin.com
www.outlanderspasttimes.com
www.oxfordreference.com
www.palgrave.com
www.parliament.uk
www.peacepalacelibrary.com
www.poetryverse.com
portal.historicenvironment.scot
www.qub.ac.uk
www.rampantscotland.com
www.rctuk
www.rdgmuseum.org.uk
www.researchgate.net
www.reviewhistory.ac.uk
www.royalacademy.org
www.royalarmouries.com
www.royalhampshireregiment.org
www.royal-irish.com
www.royalmile.com
www.royalmint.com
www.royal.uk
www.rte.ie
www.scottishhistory.com
www.scottishplacesinfo.com
www.scotslanguage.com

www.scotsman.com
www.spanishsuccession.nl
www.stuartsonline.com
www.tartansauthority.com
www.theconversation.com
www.theglasgowstory.com
www.theiririshhistory.com
www.thejournal.ie
www.thenationalscot.com
www.thersclan.wordpress.com
www.scotsman.com
www.thesiegemuseum.org
www.thesonsofscotland.co.uk
www.thestuartsociety.org
www.thoughtco.com
www.timeanddate.com
www.undiscoveredscotland.co.uk
www.unofficialroyalty.com
www.vanityfair.com
www.visitmons.co.uk
www.visitscotland.com
www.warfarehistorynetwork.com
www.warhistoryonline.com
www.westhighland museum.org
www.westmorlandgazette.co.uk
www.wise-geek.com
www.wordpress.com/Bonnie Dundee 1689
www.youirish.com
en. m wikipedia.org